What Is a Canadian?

What Is a Canadian?

Forty-Three Thought-Provoking Responses

EDITED BY

IRVIN STUDIN

Dear Lawier,
Enjoy the read!
Best wishes,

⟦A DOUGLAS GIBSON BOOK⟧

100

McCLELLAND & STEWART

Library and Archives Canada Cataloguing in Publication

What is a Canadian? : forty-three thought-provoking responses /
edited by Irvin Studin.

"Douglas Gibson Books."
ISBN-10: 0-7710-8321-1
ISBN-13: 978-0-7710-8321-1

1. National characteristics, Canadian.
2. Canada – Civilization – 21st century.   I. Studin, Irvin

FC97.W48 2006   306'.0971   C2006-901893-6

We acknowledge the financial support of the Government of Canada
through the Book Publishing Industry Development Program and that
of the Government of Ontario through the Ontario Media Development
Corporation's Ontario Book Initiative. We further acknowledge the support
of the Canada Council for the Arts and the Ontario Arts Council for our
publishing program.

Typeset in Minion by M&S, Toronto
Printed and bound in Canada

This book is printed on acid-free paper that is 100% recycled,
ancient-forest friendly (100% post-consumer recycled).

A Douglas Gibson Book

McClelland & Stewart Ltd.
75 Sherbourne Street
Toronto, Ontario
M5A 2P9
www.mcclelland.com

1 2 3 4 5   10 09 08 07 06

For Papa and Mama

CONTENTS

PREFACE

What is a Canadian?

The question is bluntly put.

A Canadian is . . . undertaking to answer this question, at the dawn of the twenty-first century, so that he may better appreciate the essence of his fellow Canadians. And while this same Canadian fancies himself a Canadian patriot – tribally speaking – the bald, unvarnished answers he is seeking in this work speak more to the practical curiosity of a concerned citizen than to an eagerness to exalt Canadian identity. In short, the goal here is analytical. The context may be patriotic, but not prejudicially so. Indeed, this Canadian is convinced that a frank assessment of the exact meaning of *the Canadian* is not only long overdue in the Canadian discourse, but is a critical underpinning for any intelligent debate on the future of our increasingly complex national project.

I was inspired to commission these short essays after reading the magnificent collection of fifty essays assembled in 1958 by David Ben-Gurion, first prime minister of Israel. Each of those essays responded to the question "What is a Jew?"[1] Ben-Gurion had asked the question of fifty Jewish "sages" – great thinkers within Israel and the Jewish diaspora – in order to inform Israeli policy on mixed marriages (that is, whether the offspring of a marriage between a Jewish man and a non-Jewish woman could legitimately be deemed Jewish). The Ben-Gurion essays included a who's who of the global Jewish intelligentsia, such as the brilliant Oxford philosopher Isaiah Berlin, the great American jurist Felix Frankfurter, and the Lubavitcher Rebbe Menahem Mendel Schneersohn. The whole exercise was much in keeping with the long-standing tendency of the Jewish nation to ask questions about who they are in order to arrive at a more solid spiritual grounding, and to position themselves for excellence in practical affairs.

As a child of détente Jews from the former Soviet Union, I read the Ben-Gurion essays with relish. As a staunch Canadian, however, I found that the book immediately raised the question of why such a clear and honest question could not be asked about *the Canadian*, with leading Canadian thinkers challenged to answer it. After all, it is often the seemingly obvious that is most difficult to explain or justify. And that, very simply, is the genesis of the short essays in this collection, contributed by the forty-two Canadian sages who have answered my question, What is a Canadian? (I suggest a forty-third answer – my own – in the afterword to this book.) Each sage was invited to submit a response of between fifteen hundred and two thousand words that answered the question directly and non-prescriptively ("what *is*" and not "what *should be*," as is the Canadian tendency), beginning with the words *A Canadian is* . . .

I am not shy about defending the legitimacy of the Canadian sages I have included in this collection. They are without exception distinguished Canadian thinkers and achievers from all walks of life – politics, the civil service, academia, literature, journalism, business, the arts – from both official language groups, and from all regions of the country, as well as from the Canadian diaspora. They include Canadians *de souche*, Aboriginals, immigrants and self-styled "exiles." Nonetheless, I am certain that the list will be vulnerable to the very Canadian critique of *representativeness* – regional, linguistic, professional, sexual, ideological-political, religious and ethnic – and for any inadequacies in this respect I alone bear the responsibility. I would only qualify this acceptance of fault with the telling words of the late journalist Bruce Hutchison: "Seeking the Canadian whole, I concluded that it defied logical analysis and lacked any outward symmetry."[2] In my case, seeking *the Canadian* I did not know which Canadian to ask! But I did know, more or less, who could deliver an interesting opinion.

Because most of the thinkers in this collection wrote to me between 2003 and 2005, certain recent events in the world and in Canada (such as the January 2006 federal election) are not factored into any of the responses. I also regret that I did not get this project off the ground several years earlier, which might have allowed me to extract answers from such recently departed Canadian sages as Fernand Dumont, John Kenneth Galbraith, Jane Jacobs, Pierre Berton, Mordecai Richler, Irving Layton (my favourite poet), Carol Shields, Pierre Elliott Trudeau, Robert Stanfield and Dalton Camp. Sadly, Claude Ryan, former editor of *Le Devoir* and *éminence grise* to the late Quebec premier Robert Bourassa, had enthusiastically agreed to participate in this project shortly before passing away. A number of still-living prominent intellectuals, on sober reflection, determined that they had nothing to say on the subject, at least for this book.

It is also worth noting that I had considerable difficulty in convincing francophone Quebec intellectuals to participate in the project, notwithstanding my assurances from the outset that I had no interest whatsoever in censoring the content of their replies. Most avowed separatists automatically and wrongly took the question (*Qu'est-ce qu'un Canadien?*) to be necessarily celebratory in nature, and thus declined to participate. And whether federalist, separatist or agnostic – most francophone Québécois being at least moderately nationalist – most appeared extremely anxious about the way that their particular take on the question would be received in French Canada. This consternation lost me numerous good writers. I am especially grateful, therefore, for the courage of those who did put pen to paper. For the record, also, I note my anxiety in respect of the diffidence – a sign of the times – of too many Quebec thinkers to opine openly on what seems to me so fundamental a question.

If anything, I have tried, through this collection, to poke at the conventional wisdom surrounding the perpetual Canadian identity debate with a degree of edge and frankness that might challenge received or official ideas. Whether I have been successful will be a matter for readers – Canadians and non-Canadians alike – to determine, but I hope to have achieved this goal by not discriminating (at all) among the various views offered by the contributors on the basis of some prior criterion of acceptability. As a consequence, a number of the contributors revealed themselves to be far less proud, or more conditional, Canadians than I; and many offered definitions or understandings of *the Canadian* with which

I could not agree. I have nevertheless been happy to include their responses in this collection.

I should confess, moreover, that in assembling this volume, I have often asked myself whether the question itself – What is a Canadian? – is not too parochial a concern for anyone who, like me, is not solely exercised by Canadian affairs, but is an avid observer and student of the world, and is at once deeply troubled and thoroughly captivated by what appears to be a world on fire. War in Iraq, jihadist terrorism, nuclear proliferation, genocide in Sudan, mass poverty and disease in sub-Saharan Africa, Sino-American rivalry, growing Russo-Western suspicion – and I am asking What is a Canadian? In this angst, however, I am comforted by the hunch that even the presumptive *citoyen du monde* longs for a *patrie*: a fixed or stable reference point from which he can understand himself and his fellow citizens. Having said this, I stress that I do not intend for this book to be interpreted by some Canadians as a call for increased examination of the national self *at the expense of* international affairs – the old "take care of business at home before looking abroad" argument. Nothing could be further from the truth. I merely propose that what Thomas Franck in his response calls the "summons to self-definition" is very much a natural and healthy proclivity for societies, and for reflective individuals, both parochial and cosmopolitan. And better that the appraisal be blunt.

Irvin Studin
April 2006
Canberra, Australia

Notes

[1] Eliezer Ben-Rafaël, *Qu'est-ce qu'être Juif* (Paris: Éditions Ballard), 2001. See also Dr. Ronen Reichman, "Wer ist Jude?" *Frankfurter Allgemeine Zeitung*, March 11, 2005, p. 8.

[2] Bruce Hutchison, *The Unfinished Country: To Canada with Love and Some Misgivings* (Vancouver/Toronto: Douglas & McIntyre, 1985), p. 12.

THE RESPONSES

ALLAN FOTHERINGHAM

---

1. **A CANADIAN IS** . . . someone who crosses the road to get to the middle.

2. A Canadian is a person who tolerates a "head of state" who lives across a large ocean in a large palace in a foreign country.

3. A Canadian is a person who inhabits a country of only 32 million persons and routinely has a government with over thirty cabinet ministers. The Excited States of America, with 290 million bodies, gets by with sixteen cabinet ministers. And Tony Blair, with some six hundred members of the House of Commons in Westminster, gets by with twenty-two cabinet ministers.

4. Canada is a nation that has been ruled for thirty-six of the last thirty-eight years by prime ministers from Quebec (all lawyers) and is still fearful of Quebec separatists.

5. Canada is undoubtedly the only country on Earth where the finance minister of nine years learned that he had been fired – on his car radio.

6. Canada is the only nation, surely, that sent to the Athens 2004 Olympic Games 266 athletes – and almost as many officials.

7. Saskatchewan, my home province, is famous for having funny names for its small towns. There is Elbow. And Eyebrow. And also, down near the Alberta border, Climax, home of Bryan Trottier, who was the

long-time captain of the New York Islanders. The town has a news-paper. It is called the *Weekly Climax*.

8. Canada is the nation where the Quebec problem goes back to 1759. In most military battles in history, there was a clear winner and a clear loser. The Battle of Waterloo. The Battle of Trafalgar. The Battle of Gettysburg. When Wolfe beat Montcalm on the Plains of Abraham in 1759, the French thought it was a *tie*!

9. Henry Steele Commager, the distinguished American historian, wrote that "never in the history of colonial wars has the victor treated the vanquished so generously."

10. The Brits, as we know, left the French with protection for their language, their religion and their Civil Code in the law.

11. The result is the current Montreal joke: Guy walks into a pharmacy and asks for some condoms. "Certainly," says the druggist. "They come in sixes, nines and twelves." The puzzled customer says, "What's that mean?"

    "Well," explains the druggist, "the sixes are for my newspaper columnist customers. You know, Monday, Tuesday, Wednesday, Thursday, Friday, Saturday."

    "And the nines?"

    "That's for my francophone customers. You know, Monday, Tuesday, Wednesday, Thursday, Friday, Friday, Saturday, Saturday, Sunday."

    "And the twelves?"

    "My anglophone customers. January, February, March . . ."

12. Frank Scott, the Montreal professor and poet who was one of the authors of the founding constitution of the Cooperative Commonwealth Federation (forerunner of today's NDP), wrote that "Canadian politics, in the Maritimes, is a religion. In Quebec, a passion. In Ontario, a business. On the Prairies, a cause. In British Columbia:

entertainment." He told us that in the last century. It still applies in this new century.

13. The other day, I signalled to a cab at the taxi-rank at the Four Seasons Hotel in Toronto – the best-known hotel in Canada's largest city, after the Royal York. I gave the driver my address, some ten minutes away, off of Yonge Street (which, according to the *Guinness Book of World Records*, is the longest street in the world, stretching nearly two thousand kilometres into the bush of northern Ontario). He seemed to have no idea where Yonge Street is. Somewhat puzzled, I instructed him to go left here, turn at the light, turn here, turn there. Bemused by his obvious ignorance of the city, I said, "How long have you been driving taxi?" There was silence. Thinking that he might be hard of hearing – he appeared about fiftyish – I shouted, "How long have you been driving taxi?" There was a short silence. He replied, "Yesterday." That is Canada in the twenty-first century. He was from Iran.

14. Frank Scott, again: He wrote that "Mackenzie King never does anything by halves that he can do by quarters." This seems to be the philosophy of our current prime minister, Stephen Harper, who "united the right" and brought the Conservatives to power, but does not seem to want to talk to reporters, let alone voters.

15. Canada is Rompin' Ronnie Hawkins, who came to Ontario from Arkansas, the home of Bill Clinton, during the Fifties when rock and roll was about to become America's greatest export to Canadian teenagers. Rompin' Ronnie was such a success, taking his band to every small town in the province, that he eventually went bankrupt. He explained: "I made ten million dollars. I spent nine million of it on wild women and song. The rest of it I wasted."

16. Canada, we must realize, at the end of the Second World War was a "middle power" in the world. Lester Pearson had won the Nobel Peace Prize for his role in solving the Suez Canal crisis. Then the United Nations was invented. Canadians never realized that Indonesia – which

they couldn't find on a map – had the fourth largest population on Earth. Or that Nigeria – where? – had twice the population of Canada. Ottawa no longer has the clout on the East River in New York, where countries we cannot even spell have the same vote that we have. Canadians, in the twenty-first century, are still puzzled as to what happened.

17. Prime Minister John Diefenbaker, who did not like John Kennedy – and vice-versa – once claimed that after a visit of the White House gang to Ottawa he had found a note under a table that indicated that JFK had scribbled to his staff that Dief was "a sonofabitch." Informed of this, JFK told a Washington journalist that he never thought that the PM was an SOB. "I just thought," said the president, "that he was a prick."

18. At the height of the Cuban missile crisis, Bobby Kennedy said, "In an emergency, Canada will give you all aid short of help."

19. Our cleaning lady in Toronto is twenty-six. She is from Bolivia. Her father died when she was eight. She had to leave school and work to help support the family. She was married at sixteen and brought by her husband to Canada. She could not speak English. She became pregnant. Her husband did not want the responsibility of raising a child. When he became argumentative and abusive, she told him to leave. She has raised her child, now nine, on her own, relying on government assistance, cleaning houses, telemarketing and working in the food court at Sunnybrook Hospital. Many times she was near starving – never telling us that she could not afford lunch while working for us. She has had stomach problems due to stress. She now has, with my wife's help, an apprentice job in a hairdressing salon. This is Canada in the twenty-first century.

20. Canada is such a dysfunctional country that Prince Edward Island has four seats in the House of Commons in Ottawa for some 138,514 people. Which works out as one MP for every 34,628 people. Quebec has 75 seats for 7,410,504 people. Or an MP for every 98,806 people.

Until recently, Alberta had 26 MPs for 3,064,249 people – or one MP for every 117,855 bodies. And British Columbia, with a population of 4,095,934, had 34 seats or one MP for every 120,468 suckers. And we wonder about western alienation?

21. Canada is a country where former defence minister John McCallum, in a press release, did not know the difference between Vichy – seat of the occupying Nazi government in France – and Vimy Ridge, where Canada became a nation in its valiant role in the First World War. And former Prime Minister Paul Martin twice in a speech spoke of the brave Canadian soldiers who stormed the beaches of Norway – moving them a long way from Normandy in northern France.

22. This scribbler has worked on Fleet Street in London and worked in Washington for five years covering Ronnie Reagan and the senior Bush. I could make a good living there. I have travelled the world, through eighty-nine countries, reported from the Soviet Union and China, visited Africa six times, seen every one but four of the fifty American states. But I live and work in Canada, because I know it is the best country in the world.

Toronto, Ontario
Copyright © 2006 by Allan Fotheringham

Allan Fotheringham

"Canada's most consistently controversial newspaper columnist ... a tangier critic of complacency has rarely appeared in a Canadian newspaper." – Time *magazine*

Saskatchewan-born Allan Fotheringham joined the Vancouver Sun *as a sports reporter in 1954 and became a columnist in 1968, eventually travelling to more than eighty countries. He was inducted into the Canadian News Hall of Fame in 1999. Fotheringham has published several books and wrote a regular column for* Maclean's *magazine from 1975 to 2002.*

THOMAS HOMER-DIXON

A CANADIAN IS . . . almost always unsure of what it means to be Canadian. Maybe this is a strength. Maybe it is evidence of our tolerance and pluralism and of our enlightened postmodernness. Let a thousand identities bloom! Or maybe it just reveals our hollow core – a vacuity at the centre of our soul. Outside of Quebec, at least, we do not really know who we are or what we represent – other than that we have made ourselves remarkably comfortable in a cold land, and that we are good at hockey.

A country with a clear identity and self-understanding would find it easier to develop a consensus around its *projet de société*. To the extent that Canadians do not have a clear identity, it hampers our larger social task of deciding what kind of society we want, and then getting on with building it.

Still, we have created an extraordinary country, one that regularly ranks among the very best in terms of quality of life. People from around the world strive to come here to enjoy our economic opportunity, social tolerance and political freedoms. Canadians today are among the most fortunate human beings to have ever lived. But sometimes it seems to have happened almost by accident – as if we have created this remarkable country more by luck and happenstance than by consensus and design.

Like so many Canadians, I am proud of my country at the same time that I am exasperated by it. Too often we seem to be less than we could be. Second-best or even third-best is good enough. We have one of the most highly educated populations in the world, yet a bare handful of Nobel Prize winners. We have a population almost twice the size of Australia's, yet Australians win four times as many Olympic medals. Our fiction writers are renowned around the world, but astonishingly few Canadian non-fiction writers or public intellectuals are known beyond our borders. Margaret MacMillan, Jane Jacobs, and Naomi Klein come to mind, but that is about it (Michael Ignatieff and David Frum made their reputations outside of Canada). In terms of our numbers, we are about as big as California, but we have not mustered one-tenth, and probably not one-hundredth, of California's influence or achievement. California is a mighty engine of creativity, ideas, culture and research. Why isn't Canada?

In foreign affairs, tiny Norway (population 4.5 million) works to build peace from the Middle East to Sri Lanka, and honours a great peacemaker annually with the Nobel Peace Prize. And what is Canada doing on the world stage? We are bleating about lumber tariffs, whining about BSE-induced restrictions on our beef exports. We rebuffed the United States' ballistic missile defence system, but only with the requisite hand-wringing about the possible American reaction. Our military is pathetically equipped for modern conflict. Despite having the world's second-largest land mass and its twelfth-largest GDP (out of over two hundred countries), despite possessing staggering natural resources, and despite a favourable geopolitical and economic location adjacent to America's heartland and bordering on two of the world's great oceans, Canada is not a noted leader in a single domain of global affairs or international public policy. Why not?

Our greatest failing of all is our unwillingness to face the reality of our second-rate performance in so many areas, and to do something about it. We are too comfortable being average, even mediocre. We are too happy in our complacency, and too sure in our self-righteousness. We wrap ourselves in a national superiority complex, especially when we talk about the United States, but it is really just a cover for our insecurity, and it is not at all justified.

Almost every one of us is responsible for this lack vision, leadership and, to be frank, courage. In a thousand and one ways, we subtly disparage anyone who is daring or takes risks. We bicker incessantly, over health care policy, for example, and we delight in finding victims everywhere, both within and outside our borders. We detest our politicians and pillory them as utter lowlifes, but we are not willing to enter politics ourselves. We love to see the mighty fall: indeed, *Schadenfreude* – which means a malicious satisfaction in the misfortune of the once great (like Conrad Black) – should truly be a Canadian word.

Canada's culture of complacency threatens our survival as an independent society. We drift along without properly addressing our challenges, whether it is the never-ending menace of Quebec separation or our vulnerability to the vagaries of the American economy. Sometimes we do not even see the gravest threats to our survival. Here, for example, is a terrifying but far too plausible scenario: a terrorist group infiltrates the United States through Canada, and launches a radiological or nuclear attack against a major American city, like New York or Washington. Tens of thousands of people are killed, and the United States reacts by demanding unfettered access to all Canadian territory for its military, intelligence and internal security forces. As America establishes a continental security perimeter, Canadian sovereignty ceases to exist – in fact, if not in law.

We should be having a vigorous national discussion about this very real danger, and we should be working together, urgently and across the country, to lower the chances of an attack being routed through our country. Instead, we are looking at our navels.

We can do far better than this. Let us dramatically raise the standard of public discourse about issues of critical national importance. (We can start by expressing our outrage when our self-appointed national newspaper wastes newsprint by plastering across its front page the headline "Boatpeople Eat Human Flesh.") Let us identify a few areas of intellectual, scientific, athletic and cultural achievement where Canada can be a world leader, and then make it so. Let us establish a presence on the international stage by focusing our foreign policy resources on one or two issues of critical concern to humanity. (A number of years ago, Canada succeeded with this approach by promoting an international treaty banning landmines.) Let us stop whining about our politicians, and instead each invest our personal talents and resources in the political action that will make this country what it should be.

If we do these things, then maybe someday we will know ourselves well enough and we will be confident enough in our talents, culture, and achievements to say: "A Canadian is, simply, a Canadian."

Fergus, Ontario
Copyright © 2006 by Thomas Homer-Dixon

Thomas Homer-Dixon

Thomas Homer-Dixon is the director of the Trudeau Centre for Peace and Conflict Studies at the University of Toronto, and associate professor in the department of political science at the University of Toronto.

He was born in Victoria, British Columbia, and received his BA in political science from Carleton University in 1980 and his PhD from MIT in international relations and defence and arms control policy in 1989. He then moved to the University of Toronto to lead several research projects studying the links between environmental stress and violence in developing countries. Recently, his research has focused on threats to global security in the twenty-first century, and on how societies adapt to complex economic, ecological and technological change. His books include The Ingenuity Gap, *which won the 2001 Governor General's Award for Non-Fiction, and* Environment, Scarcity, and Violence. *In 2006 he published* The Upside of Down: Catastrophe, Creativity and the Renewal of Civilization.

ROCH CARRIER

UN CANADIEN EST ... un citoyen de ce pays où l'on se demande souvent: qu'est-ce qu'un Canadien? À cette question, aussitôt, l'hiver, la bise, la neige, la glace tempêtent dans mon esprit. Le climat rugueux n'est-il pas le premier facteur définissant la nature d'un Canadien? Ces éléments climatologiques n'ont-ils pas été transmutés à l'état de dieux de notre mythologie? Le hockey, notre sport national, a dompté l'hiver, domestiqué la glace; dans les joueurs se sont incarnés, pour notre société urbanisée, les qualités barbares des pionniers, défricheurs et bûcherons. Admirant leurs exploits, dans le confort de son fauteuil préféré, un Canadien se souvient vaguement qu'il est issu d'une «race de violents, de forts, de hasardeux», comme dit le poète Alfred Desrochers. Il a de temps à autre cette vague intuition que l'âme de ses ancêtres vient hanter son univers à température contrôlée.

(Avouerai-je que je prépare ces notes dans un ranch au Mexique, jurant à mes hôtes que leur soleil mexicain ne me donne pas un bonheur aussi sublime que le matin glacial d'un jour de février, quand le thermomètre est à 30 degrés au-dessous de zéro. Je sais bien que ce matin-là, je reprocherai aux dieux de ne m'avoir pas fait naître au Mexique. N'est-ce pas là un comportement canadien?)

Son pays est si vaste que, généralement, un Canadien ne le connaît pas, semblable à ce propriétaire si riche qu'il ne distingue plus ce qui lui appartient et ce qui ne lui appartient pas. Parfois, il se demande: a-t-il besoin de tout cela? Ne serait-il pas plus rentable de se défaire de tel ou tel secteur? À la fin, il décide, que, puisqu'il l'a hérité, il fera fructifier son patrimoine, se réservant le droit inaliénable de se plaindre des complications inutiles que ce pays impose à son activité. Il regrette de ne pouvoir se servir

12

dans la Constitution comme il pige dans les tablettes du magasin *Home Depot*. Quelqu'un ose-t-il utiliser la même stratégie? Alors, il s'insurge, pour, à la fin retrouver son sens commun fondamental.

Un Canadien est convaincu que la réalité dans laquelle il vit est complexe, mais qu'il peut la comprendre: elle ne l'étouffe ni le submerge, il peut la juger, et surtout agir sur elle. La preuve lui a été faite que son action peut améliorer la situation, résoudre un problème. Sauf s'il évolue dans l'industrie de la procrastination, un Canadien ne se complaît pas dans l'insolubilité des problèmes; il aime les solutions. En général, un problème pour lui n'est qu'un pont vers sa solution.

Souvent il blâme les autres pour ses difficultés, mais il le fait pour le principe: il sait que, dans ce cas, il n'est pas sincère. Parfois le jeu politique l'invite et l'incite à transférer à d'autres sa responsabilité. Cependant, parmi les difficultés de sa vie quotidienne, il ne s'en décharge pas, persuadé que ses défis ne seront relevés que par ses efforts personnels et, probablement, par un accord avec des partenaires. Un Canadien est champion du compromis: non pas celui qui immobilise, mais celui qui crée.

Essentiellement, au fond de ce grand compromis qu'est la Confédération, on peut percevoir le dialogue de deux grands philosophes, l'un français, l'autre anglais. Montesquieu, d'une part, suggère que la liberté de l'individu ne peut exister que dans une communauté réduite dont les membres se reconnaissent; un grand pays, avec ses différences régionales, ne peut susciter que conflits. Seule une autorité de fer peut y maintenir l'ordre. Donc un grand pays ne favorise pas la liberté de l'individu. Au contraire! affirme Hume. Un pays vaste, avec sa diversité géographique, économique, ethnique et les contraintes de la distance exige un raffinement du pouvoir qui doit se nuancer, à cause de la nécessité de le distribuer en plusieurs niveaux de responsabilité. Si un Canadien n'a pas nécessairement lu Montesquieu ni Hume, il n'en est pas moins ballotté entre leurs visions divergentes; l'option Montesquieu lui sourit mais il choisit généralement celle de Hume. Foncièrement, il souhaiterait une fusion de ces deux pensées; il ne serait totalement heureux que si ces deux philosophies antinomiques étaient appliquées simultanément et harmonieusement à la conduite des affaires. Malgré ses contradictions, il songe parfois que si les humains se décident, un jour, à imposer le respect de l'individu, la liberté et la paix dans le monde, ils devront inventer une sorte de confédération planétaire qui ne serait pas très différente de celle que les Canadiens installent et perfectionnent eux-mêmes.

Pour ma part, je suis Canadien-français, comme on disait à l'époque où, jeune étudiant, je découvrais mon identité et mes différences. Je suis fait de l'histoire de mes ancêtres, des gens simples, venus au Canada il y a 350 ans, fuyant leur vie de servitude en France. J'ai été modelé par leur misère, leur aspiration à la liberté, leur détermination, leur endurance et leur espérance. Je comprends et accepte que beaucoup de Canadiens ne se reconnaissent pas dans mon histoire; la leur est différente, plus jeune ou moins roturière. Je respecte la leur et la mienne. Et comme pour eux, c'est pour moi un devoir et un honneur de la propager et de la perpétuer.

Je célèbre ce grand pays où ma culture française, minoritaire sur son territoire, luttant comme il faut lutter quand on veut survivre, a pu croître, s'affirmer, s'épanouir avec originalité, force et une jeunesse vivifiante ... Il y a trois siècles, mes ancêtres, français à l'origine, étaient déjà fiers de s'appeler Canadiens. À cette époque, ils revendiquaient le territoire qui s'étendait de la baie d'Hudson jusqu'à la Louisiane, des glaciers jusqu'aux marécages, comme on a dit. Malgré les efforts, les batailles et le sang versé, ils ont échoué; leur rêve n'a pas été réalisé. Aujourd'hui, moi, leur fils, je suis persuadé de ne pas les trahir en faisant mien le rêve canadien de partager un territoire immense et de vivre dans une société juste, diverse, tolérante, fraternelle et pacifique, où les multiples différences ne sont pas considérées comme des problèmes, mais, plutôt, comme des richesses.

Être Canadien, c'est n'avoir pas tout à fait oublié d'où l'on vient en décidant où l'on va. Adolescent, quand je m'assoyais à la table familiale pour les célébrations des fêtes, nous étions tous Canadiens-français, tous blancs, tous catholiques romains; tous appuyaient le même parti; nous avions tous lu le même journal et écouté la même radio. Aujourd'hui, autour de la table, notre famille agrandie a des racines québécoise, ontarienne, anglaise, polonaise, coréenne, israélienne, française, péruvienne, écossaise, italienne, danoise, mexicaine, chilienne, américaine. Ainsi, à travers tout le pays, dans d'autres familles, s'écrit le plus récent chapitre de l'histoire du Canada. La définition du mot Canadien sera enrichie d'une nuance nouvelle et essentielle.

Dans la sécurité de ce Canada illimité, nous demeurons modestes. Conscients de notre passé, nous vivons dans le présent. Un Canadien s'efforce de choisir la paix plutôt que la pollution, l'entraide plutôt que l'égoïsme, le partage plutôt que la cupidité, la confiance plutôt que la suspicion, le pardon plutôt que le châtiment, l'espoir plutôt que la désespérance, l'acceptation plutôt que le rejet, le questionnement plutôt que la certitude, le dialogue plutôt que la prédication. Certains peuples se définissent par rapport à d'importants documents législatifs; je tiens plutôt à définir le caractère canadien à partir des qualités de son coeur. Celles qu'il a . . . Celles qu'il souhaiterait avoir . . .

Quand on demande à un Canadien de définir sa personnalité nationale, il commence, presque immanquablement par les mots: «D'abord, nous ne sommes pas Américains . . .» Lors d'un voyage dans un pays dictatorial, il y avait dans notre groupe un observateur américain qui ne devait absolument pas se faire identifier. S'ingéniant à répéter certaines locutions canadiennes, il s'entraînait à marcher comme un Canadien (évidemment nous avons une manière absolument caractéristique de mettre un pied devant l'autre). Participant à ces réunions internationales, j'ai appris qu'un Canadien a l'exceptionnel pouvoir, et l'exceptionnel privilège, de discuter amicalement avec tous les participants, qui sont parfois ennemis, de recevoir leurs confidences, sans qu'aucun ne se sente trahi ou joué, sans perdre la confiance de l'un ou de l'autre.

Un Canadien ressent à tout moment une pointe de culpabilité de n'avoir pas vraiment mérité toutes ces faveurs dont il jouit et auxquelles tant d'individus ne peuvent même rêver. Sachant que la majorité des peuples ont été modelés par les guerres, les révolutions, un Canadien est peiné que la vie ne soit pas plus juste envers tant d'hommes et de femmes. Il n'est pas sans éprouver parfois un certain malaise de vivre au milieu de tant de bien-être, tant de liberté, tant de possibilités, tant de paix; de ces bienfaits, dont il n'a jamais payé le prix généralement exorbitant, il jouit autant qu'il le peut mais jamais il n'oserait proclamer: «Dieu est de mon côté». Ce qu'il possède lui vient de son labeur et d'une chance exceptionnelle. Sincèrement il regrette qu'elle n'ait pas accompli le même miracle pour tous. À cause de ce sentiment, il y a, au fond de son coeur, un désir d'aider ceux à qui la méchanceté, les traditions, la politique, les religions ou les catastrophes ont imposé une vie misérable. Un Canadien ne comprend pas ceux qui s'efforcent d'augmenter le malheur des gens, quels que soient leurs motifs.

Être Canadien, c'est donc savoir que tant d'avantages peuvent être gagnés, non par la force violente, mais plutôt par la force paisible des efforts quotidiens. Héritiers, nous ressentons un certain malaise de n'avoir pas mérité notre richesse; nous reconnaissons ne pas penser assez souvent à la fragilité de cet héritage. Cette conscience nous oblige à une certaine prudence, à une certaine mesure, à une certaine gentillesse qui évite l'affrontement, à une certaine politesse dans nos comportements, qu'ils soient nationaux ou internationaux. Nous bougeons avec la prudence de celui qui transporte un objet cassant. Les cowboys politiques ou les martyrs explosifs font la manchette des médias globaux; les Canadiens, au moins, ne gâtent pas leur vie ni celles des autres.

Revenu au Canada, alors que l'automne flamboie dans les feuilles des arbres, je me promenais, hier, et je me suis approché, parce que je suis curieux, d'un chantier de construction où l'un de ces entrepreneurs massacrait un autre couvent pour le convertir en «prestigieux immeuble résidentiel avec appartements haut-de-gamme», ne conservant que les murs de pierre, la coquille du couvent. L'on creusait le sou-sol pour «maximiser l'espace de vie». Penchant la tête dans une fenêtre béante de la chapelle, j'ai aperçu dans un coin un baril rempli de crânes, d'os, de tibias déterrés par la pelle mécanique. Ces personnes étaient-elles canadiennes? Probablement. Cependant nous ne pouvons avoir qu'une certitude: elles étaient des personnes. Les Canadiens n'ayant pas encore donné naissance à un Shakespeare qui épiloguerait sur le thème des os retrouvés, je me bornerai à proposer que la meilleure définition du terme «Canadien» devrait être similaire à celle de «personne humaine».

Baja Californie, Mexique
Copyright © 2006 by Roch Carrier

ROCH CARRIER

A CANADIAN IS . . . a citizen of this country where people often ask themselves, "What is a Canadian?" Right away, this question brings winter and the north wind howling into my mind, along with snow and ice. For isn't it true that our harsh climate is the main factor in defining the nature of a Canadian? Haven't these climatic elements achieved the status of gods in our mythology? Hockey, our national sport, has tamed winter, domesticating our ice; our urban society likes to see in our modern hockey players the fierce qualities of pioneers clearing the bush with pick and shovel, or of lumberjacks. Admiring their exploits from the comfort of his favourite armchair, a Canadian vaguely remembers that he comes from "a race of violent, strong and risk-taking men," as the poet Alfred Desrochers put it. From time to time he even has the vague feeling that the spirit of his ancestors comes to haunt his temperature-controlled universe.

(Here I must confess that I am writing this on a ranch in Mexico, assuring my hosts that their Mexican sun doesn't bring me the same sublime happiness as a fine icy morning in February at home, when the thermometer stands at thirty degrees below zero. I know very well in my heart of hearts that on such a morning I will reproach the gods for not allowing me to be born in Mexico. Isn't that a Canadian reaction?)

His land is so vast that, generally speaking, a Canadian is not familiar with it. His situation is a bit like a man so rich that he doesn't bother distinguishing between what he owns and what he does not. Sometimes he may ask himself: "Do I really need all this? Wouldn't it be more profitable to sell off such and such a part?" In the end, he decides that since he has inherited it he really should do what he can to increase his inheritance, all the while retaining the inalienable right to complain loud and long about the useless complications this country imposes on him as he tries to make a living. He regrets not being able to pick and choose what he likes from the Constitution the way he can from the shelves of Home Depot. Would anyone really dare to try these tactics? In the end, after a spell as a rebel, he regains his basic common sense.

A Canadian is convinced that the reality in which he lives is complex but that he can understand it; it doesn't baffle him or overwhelm him. He is able to weigh it up, and above all to affect it by his actions. Experience has shown him that he has the ability to improve things, to resolve problems. Unless he becomes enmeshed in the procrastination industry, a Canadian takes no pleasure in the apparent insolubility of problems: he likes solutions. A problem for him is, in general, just a bridge toward a solution.

Often he blames others for his difficulties, but he does it as a matter of principle, just to keep his hand in; he knows very well that he doesn't really mean it. Sometimes the political game invites and incites him to transfer his responsibility to others. But among all the difficulties of daily life he tends not to offload such responsibilities, in the belief that his problems will be fixed only through his own efforts and, probably, by working things out with the others involved. A Canadian is a champion at compromise; not the type that holds things up, but creative compromise that moves things along.

Essentially, at the heart of the grand compromise that makes up Confederation, we can see the dialogue of two great schools of philosophy, one French, the other English. On the one hand, we have Montesquieu, who suggests that freedom for the individual can only exist in a small, restricted community where everyone knows one another: a large country, with its regional differences, is bound to provoke conflicts, to the extent that order can only be maintained by a central authority with an iron hand. As an inevitable result, a large country will have a system that is unfriendly to individual freedom.

Not at all! says Hume. A huge country, with its geographic, economic and ethnic differences and with the constraints forced on it by distance, positively requires sophistication and nuance in its exercise of power. In fact, that central power has to be carefully restrained, because of the need to distribute it among several levels of government.

Even if the typical Canadian has not necessarily read Montesquieu or Hume, he still finds himself bounced between their two very different views; he likes the Montesquieu option, but he usually chooses Hume's. Basically, he would like a mixture of these two theories; he would only be totally satisfied if these two opposite and irreconcilable philosophies were applied to our public life simultaneously and harmoniously. In spite of his contradictions, he sometimes thinks that if the human race some day decided to impose respect for the individual, freedom, and peace on the entire world, it would have to invent a sort of planetary confederation that would not be very different from the one that Canadians already have in place, and are working to improve.

As for me, I'm French Canadian, as we used to say in the days when I was a young student discovering my identity and the things that made me different from others. I am the result of the story of my ancestors, simple people who came to Canada 350 years ago, fleeing a life of servitude in France. I have been shaped by their misery, their aspiration to be free, their determination, their endurance, and their hope. I know and accept that many Canadians won't see themselves in my history; their own is different, perhaps younger, or less ancient. I respect both their story and my own. And like them, I find it both a duty and an honour to spread my family's history, and to keep it going.

I celebrate this great country where my French culture – despite holding a minority position in the land, and having to struggle as you must when you're fighting for your life – has been able to grow, to assert itself, and to spread with originality, force and invigorating youthfulness . . . Three centuries ago, my ancestors, originally French, were already proud to call themselves Canadians. In those days, they claimed the territory that stretched from Hudson Bay to Louisiana, from the glaciers to the swamps, as the saying went. Despite heroic efforts, many battles and much blood spilled, they failed. They never achieved their dream. Today I, their son, am determined not to let them down, and so I have adopted the Canadian dream of sharing a huge territory and of living in a society that is just, diverse, tolerant, caring and peaceful, where our many differences are not seen as problems, but as rich advantages for us all.

To be a Canadian is to remember where you've come from as you decide where you're going. When I was a teenager, when I sat at our dinner table to celebrate special family occasions, we were all French Canadian, all white, all Roman Catholic. All of us supported the same political party, and we had all read the same newspaper and listened to the same radio programs. Today, around our table, our expanded family has roots in Quebec, Ontario, England, Poland, Korea, Israel, France, Peru, Scotland, Italy, Denmark, Mexico, Chile and America. In just the same way, right across the country in countless other families, the most recent chapter in the history of Canada is writing itself for all to see. The definition of the word *Canadian* will be enriched by a meaning that is both new and essential.

Secure in this Canada without boundaries, we have stayed modest. Although aware of our past, we live in the present. A Canadian does his best to choose peace over pollution, assistance to others over selfishness, sharing over greed, trust over suspicion, forgiveness over punishment, hope over despair, acceptance over rejection, questioning over certainty, dialogue over preaching. Some nations define themselves in reference to important legislation; I prefer to define the Canadian character from the qualities of its heart. Those which it has – and those it would like to have.

When you ask a Canadian to define his national personality he almost invariably begins with the words: "First of all, we're not Americans." Once I was travelling in a country ruled by a dictator. Our group included an American observer who felt it was very important not to be identified as such. Besides working hard to learn a few distinctively Canadian turns of phrase and pronunciations, he also practised walking like a Canadian (it seems that we have an absolutely characteristic way of putting one foot in front of the other). By taking part in these international meetings, I learned that a Canadian has the exceptional power – and the exceptional privilege – of having friendly discussions with all of the participants, who are sometimes at daggers drawn, and of learning their secrets, without anyone feeling betrayed or tricked, and without our losing the trust of one side or the other.

A Canadian is always bound to feel a little guilty about not really deserving all of the advantages he enjoys, which so many people can't even dream about. Knowing that most nations have been shaped by wars or revolutions, a Canadian is saddened by the fact that life treats so many men and women unfairly. Sometimes he is bound to feel uncomfortable about living in the midst of so much good fortune, so much freedom, so many possibilities and so much peace. He enjoys these benefits, for which he has not had to pay the usual exorbitant price, as much as he can, but he would never dare to announce "God is on my side!" What he has comes to him thanks to his own efforts, along with exceptionally good luck. He sincerely regrets that luck can't perform the same miracle for everyone. Thanks to this feeling, deep down he has the desire to help those whose lives have been made miserable by wickedness, cruel traditions, politics, religion or natural disasters. A Canadian simply does not understand those who work to increase people's unhappiness, no matter what their motives may be.

To be Canadian, then, is to know that so many improvements can be made, not by violence but rather by the quiet power of daily effort. As people who have inherited so much, we feel slightly uncomfortable about not deserving our wealth. We're aware that we don't think often enough about just how fragile that heritage is. This awareness obliges us to be careful, and to show a degree of caution, along with a sort of supple courtesy that avoids confrontation, a polite way of behaving both at home and abroad. We move with the caution of someone carrying something fragile. Political cowboys and suicide bombers may hit the headlines across the world; Canadians, at the very least, don't ruin their lives or the lives of others.

When I returned to Canada, the flames of autumn lighting up the leaves, I went for a walk, just yesterday. Because I'm inquisitive by nature, I walked up to a hut on a building site where a developer was gutting an old convent in order to turn it into "a prestige residential building with upscale apartments," keeping only the stone walls, the merest shell of the old convent. They were digging away under the basement to "maximize the living space." Sticking my head through one of the gaping windows of the chapel, I noticed in the corner a barrel full of skulls, shinbones and other bones dug up by the mechanical shovel.

Were these people Canadians? Probably. We can be certain of one thing: they were people. Since Canadians have not yet produced a Shakespeare who can make a fine speech on the theme ("Alas, poor Yorick") of dug-up bones, I'll restrict myself to suggesting that the best definition of the term *Canadian* might be very similar to that of *human being.*

Baja California, Mexico
Translation copyright © 2006 by Douglas M. Gibson

Roch Carrier

When Roch Carrier grew up in Sainte-Justine-de-Dorchester, Quebec, it was a village with no library. Today, the library that stands there is named for him, one of Canada's most celebrated authors. Until recently, he was also Canada's National Librarian, a post he held for five years, establishing himself as one of the country's most vocal advocates for literacy. Before becoming Canada's National Librarian, he was principal of the Collège Militaire Royal, head of the Canada Council for the Arts, and a member of numerous boards.

Carrier is a prolific writer. He has penned countless novels, short stories, plays, film and television scripts, essays, travel books and poems. He has won the Stephen Leacock Medal for Humour, along with numerous other prizes and honours. An excerpt from one of his most loved stories, The Hockey Sweater, *is reprinted on the back of Canada's five-dollar bill.*

Canadians can enjoy two very different recent books by Carrier. The Flying Canoe/La Chasse-Galerie *has been published in both English and French for young readers. His latest adult novel,* Les moines dans la tour, *is a reflection on the events of September 11, 2001.*

JAKE MacDONALD

A CANADIAN IS ... in some cases, someone who wishes this eternal, narcissistic, self-pleasuring celebration of our national identity would get to the money shot so we can feel safe, at last, from the necessity of keeping a shoe handy to throw at the radio when some CBC panellist chuckles and quips, "How very Canadian of you!"

Do these people actually possess functioning brains? Racial stereotyping has fallen from fashion, but we still tolerate and even encourage absurd generalizations about nations of people – not their current governments, which obviously take on the biases of their leaders, but the people themselves. Even our so-called intellectuals, people paid to appear on the radio or write newspaper columns, don't seem to feel much hesitation at summing up an entire nation with a few simple-minded clichés. The French are "sophisticated"; Americans are "rude and opinionated" (unlike, say, *Globe and Mail* columnists); and Canadians are "deferential to authority" and "humble about their own accomplishments." These stereotypes have been flogged so relentlessly that they've acquired a credibility, especially among the people who invented them. But ordinary Canadians understand this is utter nonsense. No one can sum up the "national character" of 33 million individuals.

Even if it were possible to make pat generalizations about a collectivity that includes people as diverse as Inuit, Alberta oilmen, Sikh cab drivers from Winnipeg, radical feminists, ornery pulp cutters from northern Ontario, REAL Women, and organizers of the Toronto Gay Pride parade, most of the current popular generalizations about Canadians are malarkey. We Canadians are supposed to be altruistic folks, particularly when compared to our hard-nosed neighbours to the south. But

Americans give much more to charity than Canadians. We're supposed to be defined in some ways by our openness to other cultures, but according to recent surveys Americans score higher on issues of multiculturalism than Canadians. The Yanks are aggressive and combative, according to Canadian mythology, while we're diplomatic and easygoing. But their national sport is the pastoral, grassy ritual of baseball, while we prefer mayhem on ice. Our health care system is often described as the best in the world, but a number of reputable international groups have consistently placed Canada near the bottom of the list. We're supposedly a society of nature buffs, the sort of hearty, self-deprecating folks who, according to the late Pierre Berton, "know how to make love in a canoe." But most Canadians now live in cities. They get their fish from the supermarket, their birch firewood from the convenience store, and their respect for nature, let's face it, falls a long way down the list from their respect for money.

The city of Victoria, for example, pumps hundreds of thousands of tonnes of raw human waste into the ocean. Why? Because Victoria's nature-loving taxpayers have deemed it too expensive to build a treatment system. It's the same story, with slightly different program notes, across the country. Hampered by environmental laws in their own countries, European farmers are now moving to the Canadian prairies, where slack laws and cheap land enable them to set up huge hog factories that contaminate local streams and fill the air for miles around with a stink that would blister paint. Our Great Lakes might more accurately be called our Great Sewers. In recent years, according to the Canadian Wildlife Service, over ten thousand loons have died of botulism poisoning on Lake Erie. And Lake Ontario water is perfectly safe, as long as you don't let it come in contact with your skin.

If we were a nation of nature-lovers, we would show some evidence of it. We would surely demand that corporate and individual violators be held accountable. The deliberate extermination of the northern cod, for example, should have resulted in national fury, and judicial investigations at least equal to the "Adscam" sponsorship inquiry. After all, the media are supposed to cover the news. Crooked politics in Quebec is not news. The near-extermination of a species upon which our nation was built is news. The cod collapse should have resulted in cabinet ministers getting frog-marched out of their offices in handcuffs. Instead, the news media framed it as an "unemployment" story. Cod fishermen, it seemed, were out of work. What a shame. If it had happened in the 1880s, our TV broadcasters presumably would have dispatched pretty reporters in gumboots to interview the legions of angry, blood-soaked and out-of-work buffalo hunters. And the federal government, to prove that it felt their pain, would presumably have offered subsidies so that the poor yokels could retool their killing machinery for other species.

Perhaps the most groundless stereotype is that Canadians are modest. I once met a shopkeeper in Budapest who said, "You're a Canadian? Where's your flag? I've never met a Canadian who couldn't wait to tell you where he comes from." A recent study by the Pew Center for Global Research discovered that 94% of Canadians believe their country is beloved by other nations, while only 26% of Americans operate under that delusion. If the surveyors had probed deeper, they might have found that foreigners have not so much a positive impression of Canada as no impression at all. I once asked a Japanese businessman what images and values came to mind when he thought of Canada. "Many lakes!" he exulted. "Large fish!" In the interests of drawing more tourists, the Canadian government is hard at work trying to revamp the nation's international image. But there has been a backlash from people who actually work in the tourism industry. The fact is that most foreigners think of Canada as a wilderness of mountains and moose, clean, pure, and absent of concrete principles or personality.

Canada once held a respected place on the world stage. We were once the fourth largest military power in the world, a qualification that enabled us to sit at the adults' table and exert a real influence on world affairs. Today we let the Americans provide our security, while reserving the right to lecture them about how they do the job. Canadian writers and performing artists, with an admirable dedication to art and risk, have earned their own stripes in the capitals of the world. But that's their accomplishment, not ours. Canadians, at this point in history, are claiming laurels they don't deserve. They may have once been a "humble people," but that's surely no longer the case. Today, Canadians are suffering from high self-esteem.

The price of pride is complacency. As long as Canadians persist in regularly holding these national group hugs, congratulating themselves on what a wonderful society they live in, they'll be less motivated to address the many serious problems that litter the national landscape. The fact is that our tests are back from the doctor's office, and the results don't look good. International borders are dissolving, and many of the institutions that once bound us together as a nation have been scrapped. Multinational corporations are taking over the world. Our most cherished notions of what defines us as Canadians seem to be erroneous.

Marriage counsellors and therapists have an old rule of thumb: "Most patients need either a slap on the back or a kick in the butt." Canadians have been slapped on the back often enough.

Winnipeg, Manitoba
Copyright © 2006 by Jake MacDonald

Jake MacDonald

Winnipegger Jake MacDonald has written eight books, including a recently published story collection titled With the Boys. *His memoir,* Houseboat Chronicles, *won three book awards, including the Pearson Writers' Trust Non-Fiction Prize. He writes for a living, and divides his time among Winnipeg, Toronto, and a floating cedar cottage in Minaki, Ontario.*

GEORGE ELLIOTT CLARKE

A CANADIAN IS . . . according to literary critic Northrop Frye, "an American who rejects the [American] Revolution." Frye's definition, dating back fifty years plus, is still, I wager, sage. In the twenty-first century, one sees that, despite the continued (and increased) popularity of American entertainment in Canada and the commercial integration (collusion) of our two nations since 1988, Canadians still define themselves as un-American: *not* (as) "God-fearing," *not* (as) homophobic, *not* (as) jingoistic, and *not* (as) anti-government as their neighbours. From the vantage point of our nearly invisible – but Mounted Police-symbolized – monarchy, one ruled by offshore royalty, Canadians look askance at the excesses of "republicanism." A Canadian is someone who subscribes to a hierarchically organized democracy, where language, race, religion, region and ethnicity determine, peacefully but effectively, one's ultimate class position and access to organs of persuasion: media, government and educational institutions. (No wonder that Tory *philosophe*, Thomas Chandler Haliburton – English Canada's greatest writer of the nineteenth century – imagined a society based on aristocracy, but semi-socialist, involving a ruling class titled the "People's nobility.") Despite the lip service paid to multiculturalism, *and* the actual blending of peoples and cultures in the major metropoles of the nation, the poor remain Aboriginal and the powerless remain "people of colour." Our (monarchical) parliamentary democracy exalts Anglo-Saxon and Gallic Canadians and Christianity (in Protestant and Catholic guises), with all other ethnicities and faiths forced to struggle and strive ferociously for their measure of equality. Pierre Elliott Trudeau's vision that Canada could become a "Just Society" remains unrealized. Our kingdom, though

20% "visible minority" (note the exquisitely polite racialism of that official phrase), still chooses to see itself as "white," perhaps to offset the "white-black" duality (complicated by Hispanics) of the United States. It's our "Great White North" versus their "Great Republic": Nordic, Caucasian "civility" versus a loud-mouthed, mongrel rabble. At least, that's how our cartoon self-concept reads.

Given our collective predilection for hierarchy, for elitism, for High Tea as opposed to Long Island Iced Tea, our arts and culture are unusual, strange, bizarre, eccentric, exciting, nasty, and macabre. A Canadian is a creator who fuses classicism and Gothicism, French champagne and Russian vodka, cheese and fries, poppies and corpses. We prefer our prime ministers in buckskins, not top hats, and we expect our philosophers to wear plaid jackets, not tweed ones. Our bush pilots are permitted to practise cannibalism, so long as this for-emergency-use-only meal is prefaced by the saying of a pious grace. Our Euro-classical architecture is Gothic, because brown-black-grey autumnal shadows and wintry greys-blacks-whites determine much of our landscape's palette. Our legislatures and hotels inhabit the same types of brooding piles, for they are both citadels of stashed booze, private vice, cryptic plots. (Remember, in his only Canadian film, *I Confess*, Hitchcock's dark, opening shot of the Château Frontenac – a malevolent palace of secrets, overlooking a sombrely glittering St. Lawrence River.) Sasquatch governs the woods; the Windigo patrols the barrens; mad trappers (with potted marijuana plants) roam the wilds. We mount animals on our coins: the Royal Canadian Mint is an exercise in taxidermy as opposed to hero worship. It is not surprising that two of our most celebrated film directors – David Cronenberg and Atom Egoyan – are known for themes of horror chills and technological coldness. (My critic friend, the Haligonian John Fraser, advises, "Whenever you see a man being kicked when he's down, you're watching a Canadian film.") Our cruelty is gratuitous. When our journalists scrum members of Parliament in the foyer of the House of Commons, the pile-up of microphones and cameras resembles a slo-mo assassination attempt – as if the conspirators intent on stabbing Caesar had been photographed at the exact instant before the daggers plunged. On the highways of our biggest cities – Toronto and Montreal (with Ottawa as an addendum)

– we drive like homicidal maniacs, happy to kill each other with our cars, if not with handguns. (Cronenberg's *Crash* is set, rightly, in suburban Toronto.) It's no accident that our greatest works of public sculpture are monuments to the war-slain. Don't English Canada's most celebrated poems treat murder (Robert W. Service's "The Shooting of Sam McGee"), euthanasia (Earle Birney's "David"), and trench slaughter (John McCrae's "In Flanders Fields")? Our greatest tragic hero was our very own version of Joan of Arc, another warrior-visionary: Louis Riel. Naturally, we hanged Riel, according him a wonderfully medieval punishment: perfect. We like realism at its most ugly.

A Canadian is a being who revels in puns, irony, metaphors, nuance and contradiction, and so enjoys advertising that teases the intelligence. Suspicious of hucksterism and boosterism, a Canadian rejects exclamation points in favour of question marks. If an American ad promises its product is "Number One," the Canadian ad will hint that its equivalent product is not second-rate. Normally, though, the Canadian ad will ask its audience to *think through* a statement – to ascertain the superiority of one brand over another. Canadian colours may be less bold, less brash, less vivid than American ones (we like pastels, not brilliants), but they are deployed with finickiness, so as to be subtly eye-catching. We are wary of spice, of noise, of splash, of sizzle, of hoopla, of razzle-dazzle. We prefer landscapes to nudes. We admonish our poets to write obtuse, abstruse, abstract, archly intellectual lyrics, believing that, somehow, such verse approximates the tastes of the Queen or of Oxford/Cambridge/Harvard/Yale. Among American poets, we loathe Whitman, but love Eliot. Our jazz must be sanitized, so it is Dixieland or *bossa nova*, European and nasal, never African or funky. Our most cherished image of a singer is a pallid gent or maiden strumming an acoustic guitar and whining "blues" – best if countrified or "Celtic" – that describe intellectual *angst*. Our filmmakers must be *auteurs* who craft high-art films that mainly critics choose to see – and then criticize for not being sufficiently avant-garde. Any English-Canadian film that makes money is 1) high-end animation; 2) *cinéma vérité* documentary; 3) (political) satire; or 4) stupid, boorish "comedy" ([don't] see *Porky's*). We are afraid to trust our own (dramatic) stories. We exalt skiers and skaters, not boxers.

A Canadian demands that political parties be clear in their interests. Thus, the major parties are titled "Liberal," "Conservative," "Bloc Québécois," "New Democrat" and "Green." Most of these party names identify definite ideologies – liberal, conservative, (Quebec) nationalist, and environmentalist. The only party whose title does not denote an ideology – New Democrat (which really means "democratic socialist") – is also one whose wishy-washy identity corrodes its electoral potential, especially at the federal level. Despite these pinpoint labels and ideological inclinations, party members may propose opposite views. Conservatives who believe in state intervention and wealth redistribution are dubbed "Red Tories"; Liberals who like tax cuts and free trade are known as "economic liberals" (or traitors); the Bloc Québécois is, on paper, leftist, or to quote Mao Zedong, "left in form but right in essence"; the New Democrats are "tax-and-spend" progressives; the Green Party has formed no government yet, but is actually *haut-bourgeois* Tory. The potent ideological fluctuation within parties means that, traditionally, leaders must exercise extraordinary party discipline to ensure that members vote with unanimity in legislatures, even though raucous debates occur in caucus and in policy conventions.

A Canadian likes debate, even if he or she will opt, in the end, for compromise. The culture is awash with open-line phone-in shows (where cranks may vent their spleen and spew their idiocy for fifteen seconds of infamy), but also with more sedate conversation, in classrooms and at dinner tables. Thanks to the publicly funded Canadian Broadcasting Corporation, Canadians are permitted a high level of more-or-less bias-free, "objective" news and commentary that the corporation-dominated (and thus propagandized) American public envy. The tradition of public discussion and dissent, furthered by a modicum of public control over broadcasting, means that the Canadian people may respond to matters of grave public policy, as opposed to media circuses around sensational ephemera. A Canadian partakes in a café culture of dialogue and ideas that may, at its best, alter government(s) for the better.

A Canadian is a citizen of the world, but is unsure of whether "the Canadian people" (an odd, Trudeauvian phrase) truly exist – or should continue to exist. He or she wants to win a lottery and own a cabin or cottage on a lake, or a river, or an ocean. He or she considers himself or herself to be a decent human being, a responsible citizen. All the crimes for which humanity is collectively guilty were committed, a Canadian believes, by other people in other places. It is we, not the Americans, who proclaim our *innocence*, proudly, to the world. And the world credits our plaintive bellows because it does not care to know the truth. A Canadian is someone who always lives in the best of all possible worlds. We think that Nature's perfections are our very own. Terrorists need not label us "Little Satan" and threaten us with bomb blasts: we terrorize ourselves whenever we fear that we might be inferior to the United States.

Toronto, Ontario
Copyright © 2006 by George Elliott Clarke

George Elliott Clarke

George Elliott Clarke was born in Windsor, Nova Scotia, in 1960, a seventh-generation Canadian of African-American and Mi'kmaq Amerindian heritage. He earned a PhD in English from Queen's University and is the E.J. Pratt Professor of Canadian Literature at the University of Toronto, a prize-winning poet and a Trudeau Fellow. His latest book is the acclaimed novel George & Rue. *In 2001, he won the Governor General's Award for English Poetry for* Execution Poems.

MARGARET MacMILLAN

A CANADIAN IS . . . someone who makes statements sound like questions. A Canadian is someone who prefers to start with a *what* and end with a question mark. So I will start not with bold assertions about "a Canadian is . . ." but with the more tentative "What is a Canadian?" – a question that has been asked in this country for as long as I can remember. Are we the Scandinavians of North America or are we really closet Americans? Are we a nation founded by two peoples or three? Do we live happily together or is Confederation doomed to come apart? There are many questions and many answers.

So all I can do is give my own. A word of warning: a middle-aged woman, living in the middle of Canada, born to a father whose ancestors came here from Scotland in the nineteenth century and a Welsh mother who was trapped here by the Second World War may not ask the same questions or give the same answers as a francophone from Quebec or a Mennonite from Manitoba or a recent arrival from Asia. But that is part of being Canadian – that we are many peoples with many different stories.

For me, part of what makes a Canadian is our land. Yes, most of us live in cities, but in our imaginations we inhabit great spaces. In Toronto, I know that, just to the north, there is the rolling southern Ontario farmland and, beyond that, the woods and lakes of the Shield and, further north still, Hudson Bay and the Arctic islands. Our skies seem to me to be spacious in a way that the ones over Europe are not. To my eye, European sunsets are charming and cozy; ours are huge and bold. European clouds carry the moisture of lands that have been settled for centuries. Ours roll in from the west, bringing water from the vastness of the prairies and the Great Lakes.

Our climate is ferocious. Our storms are sudden and violent. The summers roast us and the winters plunge us into the cold. In one day we can go from fanning ourselves to shivering. Our springs slip by almost unnoticed. Trees that were bare suddenly burst into leaf. Grass turns green over night. Our autumn is at once our most beautiful and our most melancholy season. The golden larches in the Rockies, or the red maples in Ontario, remind us that summer has gone and winter is closing in. Living in such seasons, a Canadian alternates between pessimism and optimism. We always know that nature can and will throw something unexpected at us, that we must expect the worst – but that summer will come again.

Every Canadian ought to drive across this country at least once in a lifetime. From my hometown, Toronto, it will take you a long day to drive to Quebec City and another to the Maritimes and the Atlantic. If you head west, it will take another two days to get out of Ontario. Go around the north shore of Lake Superior and you will see hills and bays that could be in the south of France – except that there are few towns and few tourists to break the wilderness. You will go through mile after mile of forest and then, in the space of a few minutes' driving, will notice that the trees and rocks disappear. Now you are in the prairies, not dull or flat, but rolling out like the sea, where you can see the curve of the planet itself. And then what you think are clouds will reveal themselves as the snow-tipped mountains of the ranges that lie between the rest of Canada and the Pacific. How can such a country not be in our imaginations? And how can we not feel insignificant beside it?

Perhaps that is why Canadians so often seem to lack self-confidence. We are surprised when other countries value us more highly than we do ourselves. We are pleased that international bodies such as the United Nations rate Canada one of the best places to live in the world – but we do not really believe it. If you read our newspapers, you would think that our health care system is hopeless, our city streets as dangerous as those in Kabul, our different levels of government locked in unending combat. When our swimmers fail to win medals, any medals at all, at the Olympic Games, we carry on as though we were a failure as a nation.

Canadians are world-class at least at grumbling. We complain about our weather. Even on a gorgeous summer day we tell each other to remember that we will soon be paying for it. We complain endlessly about ourselves. We relish gloomy statistics. Yet at the same time we tell ourselves that we are glad not to be Americans. We flock to movies which show the United States as filled with violent, obese teenagers. We fret about American imperialism even while we watch American television avidly. But when September 11 happened, Canadians reacted instantly, without hesitation, to care for the American planes and their passengers that had to land here.

We are proud when Canadians do well, and we like it when they are recognized abroad. We are also a bit suspicious. It may not be true, but certainly could be, that one Canadian woman greeted the news that a prime minister had won the Nobel Peace Prize with the exclamation: "That Lester Pearson – who does he think he is?" We keep an eye on successful Canadians because we suspect that they are likely to get too big for their boots.

That attitude can be maddening, but it is also healthy. Canadians like pricking the balloons of the self-important. We are generally polite, but we are not excessively deferential. We poke fun at our leaders but we also laugh at ourselves. The Canadian sense of humour is gently satirical rather than savage; clever rather than crude. No wonder we produce so many great comedians.

Our history and our land have helped to make us. I once thought Canadian history dull because it did not have the great stories of other nations. I am now deeply grateful for that. Our history has its own dramas: the encounters, for example, between so many different peoples, starting with the First Nations, and on through the French, the English, and, more recently, the waves of immigrants from every corner of the earth. The extraordinary travels of the early traders and explorers. But we have not had a civil war like the British or the Americans, nor a revolution like the French or the Russians. We have never been successfully invaded.

We moved slowly and gently toward independence from the British Empire. We have no single moment of independence – no Boston Tea Party, no storming of the Bastille. For that we should be thankful, but too often it means that we do not know or value our own past and the society it produced. To be Canadian is, too often, to take Canada for granted and not to recognize what a success it is in a world where so many peoples are at odds with each other. For the most part we have lived peaceably with each other.

It is our great achievement, one of which we scarcely seem aware, that we have a society and institutions strong enough and resilient enough to absorb peoples of many cultures. Our governments take credit for multiculturalism, but it is really something done by ordinary people, by the Canadians who eat each other's national foods, listen to each other's music, and become friends with each other. I like the announcements in the papers when a man with a Sikh name marries a woman with a Filipino one, or a baby is born to a couple with a Chinese name and a Scottish one. That is multiculturalism.

We do not always appreciate Canada. We also have myths about ourselves: Canada as a peacekeeping nation, for example. We have been peacekeepers, but we have also been fighters. (Sometimes, of course, you can't get peace without fighting for it.) Canadians fought in four major wars in the twentieth century, from the Boer to the Korean. They fought well. Canadian soldiers had a reputation for being bold, ferocious and cunning. And they were cheeky to their officers. Perhaps we forget our record in war because we are not a militaristic society. Our soldiers are citizens, not a warrior caste.

Another myth is that we are nice. Indeed *nice* is a very Canadian word. We are nice. People like Saddam Hussein are not nice. The weather is nice or it is not. Yet this nice people play the fastest, most violent game in the world. Hockey demands speed, power and skill. It takes courage to play, to crash into the boards and have your cuts stitched up and come back on the ice. At its best, it is beautiful to watch. Like Canadians in every generation, I grumble that it is not what it was. I grew up on *Hockey Night in Canada*. I remember the commentary of Foster Hewitt, and Juliette singing at the end of each game. I am nostalgic for the days when there were six teams and almost all the players were Canadian.

Canadians watch hockey on television, but they also play themselves. Whether it is midnight or four in the morning, the rinks across the country are busy. Boys play it and, increasingly, girls play it. Grey-haired men play it, their old hockey sweaters a bit tighter every year. Canadians love hockey; no, they adore it. So much so that they tolerate young boys being taken from their families into an indentured servitude as minor league players. Scandal after scandal, wicked coach after wicked coach, do not shake a system that is a national disgrace. Canadians would have put an end to it long ago if it happened in any other sphere but hockey.

We like to think of ourselves as a compassionate society. We are and we are not. Many Canadians quietly raise foster children, volunteer for charities, go on walks to raise money for good causes. Yet we try to ignore the dismal state of many Aboriginal Canadians. We allow the mentally ill to sleep out on our streets. We worry about the horrors out there in the world (and many Canadians try to do something about them), but as a country our foreign aid is pathetic.

I am a Canadian, so let me admit that I too can be at once smug and worried. I sometimes make the mistake of thinking that what is luck in being born here is the result of moral superiority. I enjoy seeing the pompous slip on banana peels. I do not trust ideologies or religions that claim to explain everything in the world. I like to think that I am tolerant and fair-minded, even when I frequently am not. And, although I would find it hard to admit publicly, I am secretly very proud of this country.

Toronto, Ontario
Copyright © 2006 by Margaret MacMillan

Margaret MacMillan

Margaret MacMillan is provost of Trinity College and a professor of history at the University of Toronto. In 2007, she will take on the position of warden of St. Antony's College at the University of Oxford. She is the author of the multiple award-winning Paris 1919: Six Months that Changed the World. *Her most recent book is* Parties Long Estranged: Canadian-Australian Relations, *co-edited with Francine McKenzie. Margaret MacMillan was appointed an Officer of the Order of Canada in 2006.*

THOMAS FRANCK

A CANADIAN IS ... humanity's best answer to the most complex puzzle of the twenty-first century: how to accommodate, within a functioning persona, the multiple identities layered on each person in an era in which responsibility to the global must coherently contend with loyalties to the national and the local, the ethnic and the religious.

When I was growing up in Vancouver, in the 1940s, despite the fact that we had just emerged from a desperate struggle against Germany and Japan, one Mrs. John T. McCay, a very ordinary housewife and mother, annually organized the extraordinary Vancouver Folksong and Dance Festival. For three nights – if I remember correctly – it filled the Vancouver Auditorium with thousands of delighted kids and their parents to watch ecstatic folk dancers and musicians, drawn from the disparate ethnic communities of our town, as they joined in celebration of both their varied heritages and their unifying Canadianism. Unlike in the modern St. Patrick's Day and Columbus Day parades up New York's Fifth Avenue, these people were not just taking individual pride in what they had been, but celebrating together the diversity of what, in a new place, they were becoming. This was a festival of convergence, based neither on apartheid nor melting pot. It seemed – and still seems today – to offer a very modern third way, a Canadian way, in a world riven by petty nationalisms and racisms.

For almost twenty years after settling down to a fulfilling academic career in the United States, I resisted taking out American citizenship because I so valued what seemed to me the post-nationalist maturity of Canadians. Indeed, "the thistle, shamrock and rose" really did, or so it seemed to me, "entwine the maple leaf forever." So I regretted the substitution of a lonesome maple leaf for the old "red duster" with its Union Jack, fleur-de-lys, harp and other allusions to our unique unity-through-diversity. But I still celebrated Canada's continued exemplary role at the United Nations, with Lester Pearson more or less inventing "peacekeeping" and with Canada among the first to provide the people to staff that new way to avert war. Compared with America, Canada seemed to have a viable vision of how persons should relate harmoniously to their diverse communities, nations and the world.

After a time, I felt it my responsibility to play a citizen's role in the politics of the place where I had chosen to live and so, after much prevarication, I took out my new citizenship. Imagine my delight, very shortly thereafter, when, having lunch with then prime minister Pierre Trudeau, he informed me that Parliament had just passed a law that permitted dual nationality. So, it seemed, I was still a Canadian after all. Some years later, the United States also adopted the principle of dual nationality. Today, scores of nations have accepted the notion that, within one's identity, more than one national affiliation can coexist.

It cannot but be readily apparent that our age is not one marked only by internationalism, powerful as that impetus may be. From the Balkans to Bukavu in the Congo, the aura of old yet vigorous, and sometimes murderous, localism or tribalism vies with newer strains and constraints of globalization. Again, it is from Canada that there seems to emanate the message that these all-too-human tendencies, however loaded in potential for deadly conflict, can be managed by creative compromise and accommodation. As long as Alberta and Quebec can do it, why not Bosnia and the Republika Srpska?

There is no greater challenge to a society's creativity than the summons to self-definition. In many places, self-definition consists primarily of defining – usually in negative stereotype – the other that one is not. If humanity is to have a future, it will be because we have found a different, better way of defining ourselves, our identities. Such a definition will begin by recognizing that each of us is many things; that we are an amalgam of layered affiliations and loyalties. Canada's multilingualism is an unfinished but imaginative approach to an important aspect of that task. It compares well, for example, to American efforts to teach English as a second language to children of immigrants or, for that matter, to the well-established multilingualism of Switzerland, where all four languages (Romansch, French, German and Italian) are equal but each is dominant in a separate region and few persons speak more than one. Canada has embarked, however haltingly, on a different path. The Cecil Rhodes primary school, where I received an excellent education and learned to sing what, for me, were essentially impenetrable Scottish folk songs, has become a French immersion school.

The accommodation of layered identity and construction of unity through multiplicity is also evident in Canada's pursuit of group rights, in contrast to America's exclusive preference for the rights of individuals. This is evident in legislative and constitutional approaches to the rights of women, First Nations and gays, where the emphasis has been on diversity and self-constituting, rather than on majoritarian conformity.

In many societies, conformity is enforced as the inevitable price of social cohesion and interpersonal responsibility. Only if my neighbours, palpably, are people like me, it is said, would I be willing to support them in overcoming adversity. But Canada's net of social services is a powerful refutation of that argument for conformity. Canadians are expected to be a lot less like each other than, say, their neighbours to the south, yet they have demonstrated a greater forbearance and willingness to be responsible for one another than is possible in the context of the class- and region-driven social policies of the United States.

It is not the purpose of these few lines to show that Canada is far superior to other nations. It is not. The Canadian does not innovate the way the American does, he does not cook or dress as well as the Frenchman, or have the inculcated French sense of beauty or Chinese penchant for decorum. The Canadian literary tradition has some way to go before it equals that of England or Ireland. But Canadians have a sense of mutual accommodation that, despite the periodic outbreaks of Quebec nationalism and British Columbian isolation, quite simply has to be the way of the future. For, if it is not, there will be no future for humanity. It is the spirit in which I was reared, which shaped my career as an international lawyer, and for which, as a citizen of the world and also of two of its great democracies, I am proud and grateful.

Thomas M. Franck

Vancouver-born Thomas M. Franck is Murray and Ida Becker Professor Emeritus at the New York University School of Law. He is the author of numerous books and articles on international and comparative law, and teaches in both fields. Franck is past president of the American Society of International Law and former editor-in-chief of the American Journal of International Law. *He has acted as legal advisor or counsel to many governments and as a judge ad hoc and as an advocate before the International Court of Justice, where he recently represented Bosnia in a suit brought against Yugoslavia under the Genocide Convention.*

ROSEMARIE KUPTANA

A CANADIAN IS . . . a person with origins in other parts of the global village. A Canadian is an English- or French-speaking person whose rights are enshrined in the Canadian *Constitution Act, 1982*. This Constitution finds its roots in Great Britain – roots that date back to the time when England was a world power, and Canada one of its many Commonwealth satellites. Today, Inuit and other Aboriginal peoples are recognized in section 35 of the Canadian *Constitution Act, 1982*. Our history with the more dominant society has not been an easy relationship, and between us there is much unfinished business.

I am a Canadian by virtue of geography and history. First, however, I am an Inuk (person), and I belong to the Inuit Nation. Inuit live in four nation-states: Canada, Denmark (Greenland), the United States of America and Russia. We number approximately 150,000 worldwide. Canadian Inuit were neither conquered nor defeated by war; instead we opted to participate in a so-called democratic society and in the Canadian tax structure, and to welcome and accommodate those who took over our lands, resources and way of life without our knowledge or consent.

I was born in an igloo in 1954, while my parents were out seal-hunting. Tiktalik, my grandmother, the clan's midwife, assisted in my birthing process. This act entitled her, along with my parents, evidently, to assist in moulding and shaping my character.

In 1957, my parents settled into Sachs Harbour, situated in the Western High Arctic. The Royal Canadian Mounted Police and the Ministry of Transport, then agents of the Canadian government, were parachuted into Inuit territory to assert sovereignty over the Arctic islands, which were considered to be vacant of human occupation during the Cold War.

41

When I was seven or eight years of age, I was forced to attend residential school in Inuvik, Northwest Territories. Although I received a good education, the experience of separation from my family, and the assimilationist policy of the government of the day, had a deeply negative impact upon me. This is a piece of my own history that I have come to embrace through a lot of hard work and forgiveness for those that had "good intentions."

In the 1960s, my identity as an Inuk was not recognized; my culture, my language, my history and my name held no value for the powerful white guardians. I was beaten and belittled simply because of the colour of my skin and my mother tongue. This was around the same time that one of Canada's icons, Joseph Idlout, and his hunting party were imprinted on the Canadian two-dollar bill. It is suspected that Idlout later committed suicide after a night of heavy drinking. Like me, he was caught between two worlds. This was at a time when Inuit were objectified. We lived on the margins of Canadian white society, not allowed to fraternize with the powerful white people who came to our lands to take care of us and imposed their values and traditions, language and laws upon us.

I remember my mother and her sisters being forced to sew winter clothing for the RCMP officers – work that they performed for free. The Inuit men were prohibited from hunting some animals and birds "out of season" or without a licence, despite the fact that our ancestors had been doing so for thousands of years. Our practices of hunting, trapping and fishing were based on our scientific (traditional) knowledge. By the time the season opened for Inuit and other Canadians, the snow geese, for instance, were long gone. I remember the hunger and the pain in my father's eyes as the geese he killed "out of season" were taken away. We were excluded from participating in the democratic processes that other Canadians enjoyed as fundamental human rights. We were not allowed to vote until 1960. We were not permitted to consume alcohol. As Inuit, we lived in a police state under apartheid rule, not fully understanding the underpinnings of the new rules, but fully understanding the consequences if we were caught disobeying.

Inuit – and Canada, for that matter – have come a long way since then. In the span of fifty years, I have come from being born in an igloo, to living a nomadic lifestyle, to creating satellite television for Inuit and other Aboriginal peoples and politicking in the halls of power in Canada and abroad. My purpose is to tell the story of the climate change occurring in our homelands, and to continue the struggle for the recognition and entrenchment of the inherent rights of Aboriginal self-government and self-determination in Canadian law and in the international covenants to which Canada is a signatory. I was on the Canadian team that negotiated changes to the *Migratory Birds Convention, 1916* in 1995 to harmonize the convention with the land claims agreements that are recognized and protected in the Canadian Constitution.

Apparently liberal pluralism works to some extent in Canada. When I was the chief negotiator for the Inuit during the constitutional discussions that culminated in the Charlottetown Accord, Inuit and other Aboriginal peoples were invited to the discussions "which applied only to them." I asked the question: "What part of the Canadian Constitution does *not* apply to Inuit?" Inuit and other Aboriginal peoples participated as equals in the discussions because we were and are Canadians. In fact, as Inuit, we felt so strongly Canadian that when Quebec began its arguments for separation, Quebec Inuit opted to stay within Canada.

How we got to the table was interesting. The Meech Lake Accord was rejected as a result of the feather-waving antics of Manitoba MLA Elijah Harper. The Oka Crisis fuelled the unrest and raised the profile of Indigenous peoples in Canada. (It is unfortunate that the rights of Indigenous peoples in Canada are never taken on their own merit, but are ever intertwined with Canada's identity crisis.) Furthermore, English Canada tended to pit peoples against one another, as was the case in the Quebec-Aboriginal debate, which hindered the climate of negotiations. It is high time that Inuit and other Indigenous peoples' issues were addressed on their own as a piece of Canada's unfinished constitutional business.

There was a defining moment in nation-building in 1992 when Canada's top political and Aboriginal leaders came to an agreement on the recognition of the inherent right of Aboriginals to govern themselves and to establish their governing structures as the country's third order of government. Canada can never go back on its word: no more broken promises and treaties! That is old history, with roots in the nineteenth century. The Inuit position is that the inherent right of self-government is an aspect of the international right of self-determination. This recognition is dependent upon many factors, including the political will of Canada and other nations, as well as upon the ability of the Inuit political leadership.

I am personally disappointed when I see the current Inuit leadership often left out of the power-brokering discussions on fundamental issues that determine our collective future, such as health care. At the territorial level, I am even more disappointed when I see that Inuit who have chosen to live outside their traditional territory have fewer rights than the multicultural community; that Inuit cannot access education funds; and that there remain some huge flaws needing remedy in the Nunavut land claims. As Inuit, we have been stating that the conventional wisdom of social, political and economic policies often does not work for us. That is why it is necessary to shape and implement Inuit-specific programs. There is not one Aboriginal people in Canada, just as there is not one Asian, African or White people in the world: there are many Aboriginal peoples and, as Inuit, we are distinct from First Nations and Métis. We are Inuit *and* we are Canadians.

Inuit are symbols of Canada. However, the Canadian Arctic is everything that Canada is not. Canada is a party to world power; many Canadians are affluent, with a wealth that is the envy of the world. The United Nations has named Canada as one of the best countries in which to live. The Canadian Arctic, on the other hand, has some very harsh realities. Many Inuit, young and old, are caught between two worlds, and our progress is compromised by lack of education, high unemployment, poverty, high criminality – mostly associated with alcohol and substance abuse – lack of housing and a suicide rate that is five times the national average. Add to these banes the fact that everything – airfare, housing, energy – is extremely expensive in the Canadian Arctic, and the cumulative toll on human development becomes plain. We still experience illnesses that have been eradicated in industrialized countries. And yes, the common Inuk still experiences external as well as internal racism and intolerance. But in Canada, the political arena allows for public discourse and dissent (except in Inuit territory) – after all, we live in a democratic society.

One Canadian need not be identical to the next. As Canadian Inuit, we are a unique people with a unique history, and can play a unique role in nation-building. This is where Canada can stand alone and lead in the human rights arena – through the distinctiveness of the governance of its many ethnic enclaves.

Even with all the barriers that many Inuit and I have experienced, I am still proud to be a Canadian – all the more so when I land back on Canadian soil after travelling in other countries where standards of fundamental human rights and basic living conditions are unacceptable in this day and age. For instance, 2004 marked the twentieth anniversary of the Ethiopian famine. I remember the gripping and haunting pictures of the faces of starvation brought back to Canadian homes by CBC foreign correspondent Brian Stewart. It was in 1989 that I had an opportunity to visit Eritrea. There I saw people fighting for the basic necessities of life – food, clothing and shelter. Yet there was a magnificence of soul and spirit among the people. There were fighting to govern themselves, building underground factories and laboratories. The Eritreans told me that it was the women who helped to win the war, having joined their men on the front lines once the sanitary napkin factories were established and they no longer needed to sit in their huts during their menstrual periods. I identified with the Eritrean people: they were a people at war, and yet they possessed a sense of peace I've not experienced in modern North America. They had a generosity of spirit and they knew what they wanted.

Canada is not a little sister to the United States or the European Union. Canada is a country where I feel safe in voicing my opinion with little fear of reprisal. It is a country – even with all its flaws of governance – into which I am lucky to have been born. Canada, I believe, is the best country to live in, and I am proud to be a Canadian Inuk.

Sachs Harbour, Northwest Territories, and Ottawa, Ontario
Copyright © 2006 by Rosemarie Kuptana

Rosemarie Kuptana

Rosemarie Kuptana is an Inuvialuk from Sachs Harbour, Northwest Territories. She is an internationally recognized advocate for Inuit rights and culture, and an avid environmentalist. In 1979, she started her career with the CBC as a broadcaster, hosting programs dedicated to the cultural, political and social issues of the Western Arctic. She has served as president of the Inuit Broadcasting Corporation, the Inuit Tapirisat of Canada and the Inuit Circumpolar Conference. Kuptana has received many honours and awards for her work and holds honorary doctorates from Trent and York universities.

GÉRALD-A. BEAUDOIN

UN CANADIEN EST . . . celui qui est né au Canada et qui l'habite; c'est quelqu'un dont les ancêtres sont venus et sont restés, pour employer les mots de Louis Hémon. Mes ancêtres sont arrivés au XVIIe siècle. Je suis de la dixième génération.

Un Canadien, c'est celui qui a choisi le Canada et qui est venu s'y établir. Quelqu'un qui venait de France, du Royaume-Uni, de l'Europe et des autres continents. Un Canadien, c'est un Amérindien dont les ancêtres nomades sont venus il y a dix mille ans, voire même vingt mille ans. Le Canada doit ses fils et ses filles aux immigrants.

Jacques Cartier vint à Gaspé en 1534 et y planta une croix au nom du Roi de France. Notre premier Gouverneur fut Samuel de Champlain, qui s'arrêta à Port Royal en 1604 et qui fonda Québec en 1608. Il a laissé une trace indélébile au Canada.

La Nouvelle-France était, pour un certain temps, une grande colonie du centre, de Gaspé à Bâton-Rouge, sur le Golfe du Mexique. La Vérendrye se rendit tout près des Montagnes Rocheuses.

Le sort des armes chambarda l'Amérique de Nord au XVIIIe siècle. Les Acadiens furent chassés de leurs terres en 1755. C'était la déportation! Suivit la bataille des Plaines d'Abraham à Québec en 1759. La France céda la Nouvelle-France aux Britanniques. La Louisiane espagnole devint la Louisiane française. Napoléon en 1803 vendit la grande Louisiane, soit presqu'un tiers du territoire américain, aux Américains; Thomas Jefferson était alors Président des États-Unis; il avait rédigé en 1776 la Déclaration d'indépendance avec l'appui d'un comité.

La France avait épousé la cause des rebelles américains avec Lafayette et Rochambeau. Des Américains vinrent à Montréal pour convaincre nos ancêtres de joindre les Américains. Le Premier ministre Lord North qui perdait les États-Unis voulut garder nos ancêtres «canadiens» en 1774 par *l'Acte de Québec*. Cette loi britannique adoptée par le Parlement de Westminster rétablissait au Québec les lois civiles françaises et accordait aux catholiques sur les bords du Saint-Laurent plus de droits que les catholiques en avaient, à l'époque, au Royaume-Uni. Il s'agissait d'un coup de maître de la part du Premier ministre Lord North. Nos ancêtres restèrent dans le Royaume britannique.

Ainsi naquait au Canada, alors colonie britannique, un État bi-juridique qui avec le temps devint très impressionnant. Une forme de bilinguisme s'établit aussi de façon indirecte.

Le Haut-Canada, en 1791, devint une province séparée du Québec (Bas-Canada) et instaura chez lui le système de common law.

Le Canada hérita, en 1791, du système parlementaire britannique. D'autres provinces virent le jour; des loyalistes Américains s'établirent dans l'est et le centre du Canada.

Une Rébellion eut lieu en 1837 au Québec et en Ontario et fut maîtrisée. *L'Acte d'Union* de 1840 fit du Québec et de l'Ontario (le Haut- et le Bas-Canada) une seule province à la suite du Rapport Durham. En 1848, la province du Canada obtint le gouvernement responsable, un an après la Nouvelle-Écosse. C'est à Lafontaine et Baldwin que l'on doit le gouvernement responsable pour lequel s'était battu Louis-Joseph Papineau.

George-Étienne Cartier, le leader du Québec, et John A. Macdonald, le leader de l'Ontario, se rendirent à Charlottetown en 1864, à l'Île-du-Prince-Édouard. Après trois constituantes, à Charlottetown et à Québec en 1864, et à Londres en 1866 les Canadiens adoptèrent le fédéralisme qui fut enchâssé dans le *British North America Act* (maintenant la *Loi constitutionnelle de 1867*), notre constitution.

John A. Macdonald aurait préféré un État unitaire, mais Cartier obtient le fédéralisme avec l'appui des provinces maritimes.

Le fédéralisme sur papier était centralisé en 1867. Le comité judiciaire du Conseil privé, par son interprétation, en fit un fédéralisme mieux équilibré. Onze mois avant la Confédération, le Québec avait adopté un Code civil qui s'inspirait du Code Napoléon de 1804, mais qui fut adapté aux besoins du Québec.

Ce Code civil influença le Comité judiciaire du Conseil privé. Les autres provinces ont adopté la common law.

Le fédéralisme canadien est l'un des plus anciens à l'ère moderne. Le premier fut celui des Américains en 1787, suivi de la Suisse en 1848 et du Canada en 1867. Il fut suivi par l'Australie en 1901 et par beaucoup d'autres. On compte 25 États fédéraux maintenant au monde.

Pour bien comprendre l'histoire du Canada, il faut connaître l'histoire de France, du Royaume-Uni et des États-Unis. Ces trois pays font partie de notre histoire.

Le Québec a joué un rôle fondamental dans l'histoire du Canada, par son système à lui de droit civil, par la langue française, la religion catholique, la culture. J'y suis moi-même très attaché. Nos dix provinces ont les mêmes pouvoirs législatifs. Cependant, le Québec est une société distincte depuis 1774. Un État unitaire était impossible au Canada. Le sénateur Eugene Forsey disait: "Quebec is not, has never been, and will never be a province like the others; it is the Citadel of French Canada."/«Québec n'est pas, n'a jamais été et ne sera jamais une province comme les autres, c'est la Citadelle du Canada français».

Le Canada est une grande démocratie. Il a procédé par étapes comme d'autres démocraties. En 1982, il a enchâssé dans sa Constitution la Charte canadienne des droits et libertés, qui fait l'envie de beaucoup d'autres pays. Le droit de vote est devenu universel. L'égalité devant la loi, l'égalité des hommes et des femmes, la présomption d'innocence, le droit à la vie privée, la liberté de religion, de conscience, de presse, d'association, etc., sont inscrits dans notre loi fondamentale.

Les États fédéraux ont en commun un partage de pouvoirs, des compétences entre le centre et les régions (États, provinces, Länder, cantons) et ce au sein des trois grandes branches de l'État: l'exécutif, le législatif et le judiciaire.

Cependant, il y a des institutions différentes dans ces fédérations qui sont imposées par l'histoire; il y a des variations d'un fédéralisme à l'autre.

Le Canada est l'une des plus anciennes fédérations, on l'a dit. Il lui est arrivé de connaître des périodes difficiles. Jusqu'ici, il a su s'adapter à un équilibre entre la centralisation et la décentralisation. Il ne faut pas craindre d'innover. Il faut avoir de l'imagination créatrice. J'ai passé ma vie à m'intéresser au fédéralisme et aux chartes des droits. J'ai vécu de bien beaux moments.

Le contrôle de la constitutionnalité des lois au Canada est rigoureux. Une loi sur le bilinguisme adoptée en 1890 fut déclarée inconstitutionnelle en 1979 et en 1985, soit près d'un siècle plus tard. On peut citer plusieurs autres arrêts.

La Cour suprême compte neuf juges, comme la Cour suprême des États-Unis.

Le Canada est un pays du nouveau monde. Il n'a pas été un empire. Il s'est affranchi des deux grands États: la France et l'Angleterre, qui lui ont donné des structures, des lois, des institutions et tout le reste. Nous sommes arrivés à l'indépendance par étapes. Aux cours des deux grandes guerres mondiales, le Canada donna son appui à ces deux grands pays. Il envoya des soldats outre-mer.

Avant la venue des Français et des Britanniques, vivaient au Canada depuis des millénaires les nations amérindiennes. En 1867, nous n'avions pas saisi toute l'ampleur et toute la reconnaissance que nous devions leur donner. On a prévu dans la Constitution que l'ordre fédéral du gouvernement avait compétence sur les Indiens. En 1982, lors du rapatriement de la Constitution, on a reconnu dans la Constitution le rôle unique qu'ils ont joué dans notre histoire. On a donc enchâssé dans la Constitution leurs droits et leurs coutumes. Il s'agit de droits collectifs. On leur a reconnu alors tous les droits qui sont les leurs.

Au chapitre des droits et libertés, nous avons adopté en 1867 la même protection que celle qui existait au Royaume-Uni. On s'était interrogé sur la Charte des droits. Thomas Jefferson aux États-Unis était un partisan de la Charte des droits. Il était à Paris lorsque la Constitution américaine fut écrite en 1787 à Philadelphie. Il écrivait à son ami James Madison, alors âgé de 36 ans, et qui était secrétaire de la Constituante, que la Constitution était remarquable mais qu'elle avait un défaut: elle ne comprenait pas une Charte des droits. Madison, qu'on considérait déjà comme le «Père de la Constitution», fit passer les dix premiers amendements à la Constitution; ils constituèrent un Bill of Rights. L'école Jeffersonnienne était née.

Pierre Trudeau et son ami Frank Scott de McGill ont toujours été des adeptes d'une Charte des droits dans la Constitution. Je suis moi-même de cette école. Enfin, en 1982, Pierre Trudeau eut la chance de sa vie: il enchâssa une Charte dans la Constitution.

Bilingue, bi-juridique, indépendant depuis le Statut de Westminster de 1931, le Canada a pris place sur la scène internationale. À la fin de la deuxième guerre mondiale, il fut considéré comme une puissance moyenne très en vue. Il fait maintenant partie du G7 et du G8 et il lui arrive de faire partie du Conseil de Sécurité des Nation Unies.

Le Canada a deux caisses de résonance dans le monde, le Commonwealth et la Francophonie, où il joue un rôle important. Le Canada est devenu multiculturel et pluraliste.

Le Canada, c'est le pays des espaces immenses. C'est un territoire très étendu, le second après la Russie. C'est le pays où la nature est belle, riche. Il regorge de beautés naturelles: les forêts, les lacs, les rivières et les fleuves qui ne finissent pas! La chance lui sourit au moment où le monde a besoin d'eau. Il a les plus nombreuses réserves d'eau douce de la terre. La nature nous a choyés.

Le Canada, c'est le pays qui a inscrit dans sa Constitution les droits collectifs des Amérindiens qui étaient venus bien avant nous sur le sol de l'Amérique de Nord. En 1982, on a reconnu le rôle unique qu'ils ont joué dans notre histoire.

Le Canada, c'est le pays où la Constitution est suprême; le pays où le contrôle de la constitutionnalité des lois est rigoureux. Il y a séparation de l'Église et de l'État. C'est fondamental. Le Canada, c'est le pays du bi-juridisme et du bilinguisme.

Nous avons de bons rapports avec notre voisin du sud: la plus grande puissance au monde; mais nous savons nous affirmer.

Le Canada, enfin, c'est mon pays et je l'aime!

Gatineau, Québec
Copyright © 2006 by Gérald-A. Beaudoin

GÉRALD-A. BEAUDOIN

A CANADIAN IS . . . someone who was born in Canada and lives here – or someone whose ancestors came here and stayed, as Louis Hémon once said. My own family arrived in the seventeenth century. I am a tenth-generation Canadian.

A Canadian is also someone who chose to come to Canada to live. Some came from France, from Britain, from Europe, and from the other continents.

A Canadian is also an Aboriginal, one of our First Peoples, whose nomadic ancestors came here up to twenty thousand years ago. Canada owes all of its sons and daughters to immigrants.

Jacques Cartier came to Gaspé in 1534 and planted a cross there in the name of the king of France. Our first governor was Samuel de Champlain, who landed at Port Royal in the Annapolis Basin in 1604 and founded Quebec in 1608. He left a lasting imprint on our country.

There was a time when New France lay at the heart of a huge colony that stretched from Gaspé to Baton Rouge on the Gulf of Mexico. In the West, La Vérendrye got very close to the Rocky Mountains.

War tore North America apart in the eighteenth century. The Acadians were driven out of their land in 1755, in the infamous deportation. Then came the battle on the Plains of Abraham in 1759, after which France handed over New France to the British. Spanish Louisiana became French Louisiana. In 1803, Napoleon sold Louisiana – making up roughly one third of the United States – to America. As for Thomas Jefferson, the American president of the day, he was the man who, with the help of a committee, had written the Declaration of Independence in 1776.

France had supported the American rebels with forces led by Lafayette and Rochambeau. American spokesmen came to Montreal to persuade our ancestors to join the American side. But the British prime minister, Lord North (who has gone down in history as losing America), was determined to keep our ancestors "Canadian," by means of the 1774 *Quebec Act*. This law, adopted in Westminster by the British Parliament, re-established French civil laws in Quebec, and even gave Catholics on the banks of the St. Lawrence River more rights than Catholics in Britain enjoyed at the time. It was a master-stroke by the British prime minister; our ancestors remained part of the British realm.

Thus was born in Canada – at the time a British colony – a state with two sets of laws which, with the passage of years, became a very impressive one. A form of bilingualism also came into being, albeit in an unplanned way.

In 1791, Upper Canada became a province separate from Lower Canada (Quebec) and established a system of common law. In that same year, Canada inherited the British parliamentary system. Other provinces were set up as Loyalist Americans established themselves in the East as well as the centre of the country.

A rebellion broke out in 1837 in Quebec and in Ontario. It was put down. In 1840, in the wake of the Durham Report, the *Act of Union* joined Quebec and Ontario (Upper and Lower Canada) together. In 1848, the province of Canada achieved the system of responsible government, one year after Nova Scotia. We owe this system, for which Louis-Joseph Papineau fought, to Lafontaine and Baldwin.

George-Étienne Cartier, the leader of Quebec, and John A. Macdonald, Ontario's leader, met in 1864 at Charlottetown, PEI. After three rounds of meetings, at Charlottetown and Quebec in 1864 and London in 1866, Canadians adopted the federal system that was enshrined in the *British North America Act* (now the *Constitution Act, 1867*), which is our Constitution.

John A. Macdonald would have preferred a unitary state, but Cartier gained a federal system with the support of the Maritime provinces.

Federalism on paper was centralized in 1867. The Judicial Committee of the Privy Council, through its interpretation, made it an even better balanced form of federalism. Eleven months before Confederation,

Quebec had adopted a Civil Code, inspired by the Napoleonic Code of 1804, but adapted to Quebec's needs. The Civil Code greatly influenced the Privy Council Judicial Committee. The other provinces had adopted the Common Law.

The Canadian Confederation is one of the oldest in the modern era. The very first one was that of the United States, in 1787, followed by Switzerland in 1848, with Canada appearing on the scene in 1867, followed by Australia in 1901, and many others, so that there are now twenty-five federations in the world today.

To fully understand Canada's history, it is necessary to know the history of France, the United Kingdom and the United States of America. These three countries all play a part in our history.

Quebec has played a fundamental role in Canadian history, through its unique civil law system, its French language, its Catholic religion, and its culture. I am very attached to it. Our ten provinces have the same legislative powers. Quebec, however, has been a distinct society since 1774. A single unitary state was not a possibility for Canada. As Senator Eugene Forsey said: "Quebec is not, has never been, and will never be a province like the others; it is the Citadel of French Canada."

Canada is a great democracy. It has developed, step by step, like other democracies. In 1982, it enshrined in its Constitution the Canadian Charter of Rights and Freedoms, which is the envy of many other countries. Universal suffrage has been established, along with equality before the law, the equality of men and women, the presumption of innocence, the right to privacy, freedom of religion, the freedom of the press, the freedom of association and so on – all are written into our fundamental law.

Federal states all share their powers and responsibilities between the centre and the regions (whether they are called states, provinces, länder or cantons), and all have at their heart the three branches of the state: the executive, the legislative and the judicial. There are, however, different institutions to be found in the federal systems, imposed by history.

Canada, as we have seen, is one of the oldest federations. It has gone through difficult periods. Up to this point it has always managed to find a balance between centralization and decentralization. There is no need to shrink from innovation. All we need is a creative imagination. I have spent my life immersed in questions of federalism and the Charter of Rights. It has been a life filled with many good moments.

In Canada, we have rigorous oversight of the constitutionality of our laws. A law on bilingualism dating from 1890 was declared unconstitutional in 1979 and again in 1985, almost a century later. There are several other such examples.

Our Supreme Court has nine judges, like the Supreme Court in the United States.

Canada is a country of the New World. It was never an empire. Its future shape was stamped by two great states, France and Britain, which gave it structures, laws, institutions and all the rest. We achieved our independence in stages. During the two world wars Canada lent its support to these two nations, sending its soldiers abroad.

Before the French and the British settlers came, Native peoples lived here for thousands of years. In 1867, we did not fully understand all of the recognition and the respect that we should properly have awarded them. The Constitution gave the federal government responsibility for Canada's Indians. In 1982, when the Constitution was repatriated, the unique role that they have played in our history was formally recognized in the Constitution, where their rights and customs are enshrined. It was a matter of collective rights, and all of theirs were fully recognized.

On the subject of rights and freedoms, in 1867 we adopted the same protections as those of the United Kingdom. People wondered about the Bill of Rights, of which Thomas Jefferson, the American politician, was a strong supporter. He was in Paris when the American Constitution was written in Philadelphia in 1787. He wrote from there to his friend James Madison, then thirty-six years of age and the secretary of the Constitutional Committee, that the Constitution was remarkable, but had one fault: it did not include a Bill of Rights. Madison, already considered to be "the Father of the Constitution," saw to it that the first ten amendments were duly passed; they constituted a Bill of Rights. The Jeffersonian School was born.

Pierre Trudeau and his friend Frank Scott of McGill had long been strong supporters of having a Charter of Rights in the Canadian Constitution. I myself am of the same school of thought. At last, in 1982, Pierre

Trudeau had the chance of his life; he added a Charter of Rights and Freedoms to our Constitution.

Bilingual, with two legal systems, independent since the Statute of Westminster in 1931, Canada has taken its place on the international scene. At the end of the Second World War Canada was regarded as a very prominent middle power. Now it belongs to the G7 and G8, and has been a member of the Security Council of the United Nations.

Canada has two other great podiums in the world, the Commonwealth and the Francophonie, and plays an important role in both. Canada has become multicultural and diverse.

Canada is a land of immense spaces, a land so extensive that it is second only to Russia in size. It is a land full of natural beauties – forests, lakes, streams and rivers that go on for ever. Fortune will smile on us when the world runs short of water, since Canada has the globe's greatest reserves of fresh water. Nature has spoiled us.

Canada, I repeat, is the country that wrote into its Constitution the collective rights of the Native peoples who came to North America long before we did. In 1982, we recognized the unique role they have played in our history.

Canada is the country where the Constitution is supreme: the country where the constitutionality of our laws is rigorously supervised. There is separation of church and state, which is fundamental. Canada is the country of two legal systems and two languages.

We have good relations with our neighbour to the south, the most powerful nation on earth. Yet we know how to stand up for ourselves.

Finally, Canada is my country, and I love it!

Gatineau, Quebec
Translation copyright © 2006 by Douglas M. Gibson

Gérald-A. Beaudoin

Gérald-A. Beaudoin is a leading specialist in constitutional law, having written numerous legal articles and treatises. A former professor of law at the University of Ottawa, he was appointed to the Senate in 1988 and retired in 2004. Born in Montreal in 1929, he holds an honorary doctorate of law from Louvain-la-Neuve in Belgium and is an Officer of the Order of Canada and the French Legion of Honour. He has received the Walter S. Tarnopolsky Medal for human rights and the Ramon John Hnatyshyn Prize for the advancement of the law. He is a member of the Royal Society of Canada and the Quebec Academy of Letters.

PETER W. HOGG

A CANADIAN IS . . . a person who receives justice through law.

Perhaps the leading characteristic of Canada's Constitution is the "rule of law," an idea that is not written down in the Constitution of Canada (although it is mentioned in the preamble to the Charter of Rights). It is a vague term – indeed one that some intellectuals have described as meaningless rhetoric, or even as a smokescreen to conceal a system of oppression. But it does have meaning. It describes a society with a culture of obedience to law. This means that we have a system of reasonably just laws that are generally obeyed. When they are disobeyed, they are enforced, and enforcement extends to the rich and powerful no less than to the poor and powerless. Corruption is absent or highly unusual.

An essential part of the rule of law is that law must bind governments as well as private organizations, and public officials as well as private individuals. In the famous Roncarelli case in 1959, Premier Duplessis of Quebec was ordered by the courts to pay damages to a restaurateur whose liquor licence had been cancelled by the premier. The premier had cancelled the licence as part of a campaign of harassment of Jehovah's Witnesses, of whom Mr. Roncarelli was a prominent member. (He had irritated the premier by often standing bail for fellow Witnesses after their frequent arrests by the Quebec police.) Although there was a statutory power to cancel liquor licences, the Supreme Court of Canada held that the power could only be exercised for reasons related to the sale of liquor. Premier Duplessis had abused his power by exercising it for an improper purpose. Under Quebec's Civil Code, this was a civil wrong (delict or tort), for which damages were payable, and the Court ordered the premier to pay damages.

In the 1950s, the Jehovah's Witnesses were very unpopular in Quebec for their intemperate and provocative attacks on the Roman Catholic Church. Premier Duplessis' campaign against them was undoubtedly supported by most of the people. But the Supreme Court did not allow him to act outside of his legal powers, and the Court granted a remedy when he did so. Part of the rule of law is the presence of an independent legal profession that will defend unpopular individuals and take up unpopular causes. And another part of the rule of law is an independent judiciary that will decide cases according to law, without fear or favour, even if one of the parties is a powerful government official. An independent legal profession and independent judiciary are needed to make the rule of law a reality. And, every year, there are hundreds of cases in which individuals seek judicial review of the decisions of officials and tribunals. It never occurs to a Canadian that, just because something has been decreed by a government official or tribunal, it must stand, even if it is contrary to law. The assumption is that government will be held to the law.

The rule of law is an important protection for civil liberties, as the Roncarelli case demonstrates. An independent legal profession and judiciary will ensure that government actions conform to the laws of the land. But what do you do if the laws themselves are unjust? The laws of Nazi Germany or apartheid South Africa were unjust, and even if they were impartially applied, the results would often be unjust. Even in Canada, we have had laws that were based on racial prejudice. The internment of the Japanese Canadians during the Second World War is one example of an unjust action that proceeded in compliance with the law. As well, laws that discriminated against Chinese Canadians were common at the end of the nineteenth century. We have also come to understand that many laws in the modern era discriminated against women or against gay and lesbian Canadians. The best protection against these kinds of laws is a functioning democracy, supported by freedom of speech and an opposition party in the Parliament and legislatures. In a democracy of the quality that we enjoy in Canada, the unjust law will be rare. But, of course, a sense of emergency or fear or widely held prejudices can still cause a majority in our legislative bodies to enact oppressive legislation.

The principal remedy for unjust laws is the political process. Politicians have to be persuaded to change the laws in the Parliament of Canada or the legislatures of the provinces. Until 1982, this was the only remedy. The rule of law was powerless to change the law itself. Only the legislative bodies could do that. In 1982, under the leadership of Prime Minister Trudeau, Canada adopted the Charter of Rights and Freedoms as part of the Constitution of Canada. The Charter guarantees a set of human rights, including freedom of expression, freedom of religion, freedom of assembly and association, due process for criminal defendants, equality and language rights. The Charter applies to Parliament and the legislatures, as well as to government officials, including police officers, and it overrides ordinary statute law. This means that any law that offends any of the guarantees of the Charter can be challenged in court, and, if the court holds that it does offend the Charter, the court will strike down the law.

As a remedy for unjust laws, a charter of rights can only work in a society governed by the rule of law, because individuals have to believe that their rights will be vindicated by the courts, lawyers have to be willing to bring cases against government, judges have to be prepared to decide cases against government, and governments have to be willing to obey decisions that they dislike. This certainly works in Canada, where close to a hundred laws have been struck down since 1982 under the Charter of Rights. This does not take account of the striking down, in many more cases, of the actions of police officers and other government officials that were held to violate the Charter.

So far, I have spoken of the rule of law as a protection of civil liberties. That is important. What is also important is the role of the rule of law in creating a prosperous country. Canadians live in a country with a small population and a severe climate, and yet they enjoy one of the highest standards of living in the world. When we speak of poverty in Canada, we have to remember that nearly everyone in Canada lives in a home that is heated in winter, with clean running water, electricity, and appliances such as stoves, refrigerators, televisions and telephones. In many of the countries of the world, such a standard of living is imaginable only for the very rich.

There is a close correlation between prosperity and the rule of law. Those countries with levels of prosperity similar to Canada's tend to respect the rule of law in much the same way that Canada does. It used to be common for this correlation to cause commentators to say that the rule of law was fine for wealthy countries, but was a luxury that poor countries could not afford. A body of scholarship, known by the general title of law and economics, has shown that this view is mistaken. The correct proposition is as follows: A country cannot *become* prosperous without the rule of law.

It is not hard to see why this is so. Property cannot be developed unless property rights are protected. Large-scale commercial activity cannot take place unless long-term contracts are enforced. Banking, insurance and the rest of the infrastructure of commercial life are all based on the protection of property and the enforcement of contracts. Even agricultural activity that goes beyond subsistence requires the borrowing of money and the purchase of manufactured equipment. Without the rule of law, there is no security for property or contract, and commerce cannot flourish, except at the level of the bazaar or with the cooperation of gangsters. Honest people will not invest in a country where the investment is not protected by law.

My point is that the impact of the rule of law goes far beyond holding government to the law and protecting civil liberties. The rule of law makes economic development possible. Capital can be safely accumulated; property can be developed; energy can be produced and transported; railways, roads and airports can be built; businesses can be organized, and goods can be manufactured and distributed over wide areas.

Without the rule of law, the collection of taxes is very difficult. Indeed, income tax, which relies so heavily on self-assessment, is not a useful source of revenue in countries where there is no culture of obedience to law. With the rule of law, a variety of taxes can be collected, and with those taxes, courts, hospitals, schools, universities and libraries can be established, society can be regulated, and the social safety net can be financed. We take these things for granted, but they are not taken for granted, and are not possible, in many of the countries of the world.

I was born and raised in New Zealand, and came to Canada in 1970, initially on a one-year sojourn as a visiting professor at the Osgoode Hall Law School. The visit became permanent, citizenship followed, and I (and my family) became very happy Canadians. New Zealand and Canada share many attributes, and both always rank highly on lists of the best places in the world to live. Much of Canada's Constitution is very different from that of New Zealand, but the similarities are telling. One of those is the rule of law.

I opened this essay by saying that a Canadian is a person who receives justice through law. The rule of law is an unseen and mostly unacknowledged presence in our lives. And yet it profoundly affects our daily lives through its contribution to personal liberty and prosperity. It is one of the many blessings of being Canadian.

Toronto, Ontario
Copyright © 2006 by Peter W. Hogg

Peter W. Hogg

Peter W. Hogg, CC, QC, LSM, FRSC, is scholar in residence at the law firm of Blake, Cassels & Graydon LLP. He is professor emeritus and former dean of the Osgoode Hall Law School of York University. He is the author of the classic Constitutional Law of Canada *and of* Liability of the Crown *(with Patrick J. Monahan), as well as other books and articles. He has appeared as counsel in constitutional cases, including in the landmark government reference to the Supreme Court on same-sex marriage.*

GEORGE BOWERING

A CANADIAN IS . . . a person who will probably be dumbstruck if you ask him the question "What is a Canadian?"

And we will not be mistaken if we take that to be a good thing. It means that our country could use a sign overhead at all airports, border crossings and ports of entry: UNDER CONSTRUCTION. It means that we cannot yet brainwash our schoolchildren and television watchers that this is the country God picked to be the best, or the country that history had in mind, or the country that invented everything important.

We invented basketball, the potato-peeler and the Jolly Jumper. That is enough to make a Canadian happy, but not enough to crow about. Canadians do not crow about Canada. Our young people put little Canadian flags on their backpacks, but not to boast. It is more that they want to show that they are not something else. For the same reason, lots of young people who are not Canadians put little Canadian flags on their backpacks. That does not make us mad; we just smile and say, "What a good idea!"

If a young person from another country asks, "What is a Canadian?" the reply might be, "I don't know. It's a beer, isn't it?"

Here is another good thing: if you ask a Canadian what a Canadian is, and she does not have a good answer, she is not filled with anxiety. There is no punishment for not knowing the answer. In some countries, you can go to jail for not knowing the right answer. In the United States – as they say – of America, I'll bet that most people will tell you what an "American" is, but many people will not be able to locate the USA on a map of the world.

I do not imagine that I am a typical Canadian, but I might be viewed as a symbolic Canadian. One of my grandfathers was English and the other was USAmerican, from the Ozarks, of all places. I grew up naturally speaking our Canadian English, saying *wrench* rather than *spanner*, spelling it alumin*um* rather than alumin*ium*, and trave*ll*er rather than trave*l*er. One of my grandmothers was a Mennonite from Oregon, and the other was a German-Canadian girl from an Ontario town so small that all that now remains is the building she went to school in.

What is a Canadian? A policeman once told me that I was not. Just before three policemen beat me up in the basement of the Vancouver "public safety building" one night in the early Sixties, another policeman with a form to fill out asked me my nationality. I said, "Canadian." He said there was no such thing unless you were an "Indian." I guess that he wanted to know my great-grandfather's nationality. According to your logic, then, I told him, I must be an Indian. That's when they beat me up. Apparently if you were an Indian, policemen beat you up. Who knew?

He wanted me to say "English," I guess. Maybe there was a rule against writing down a colour, so they needed code words. But I was not going to say "English." I had been struggling against the English all my life, even though where I grew up in the South Okanagan Valley, my grandfather and my girlfriend and her parents were all English. The Southern Okanagan Valley had a lot of English immigrants in it, because land grants were made to veterans of the First World War, as long as they were "British subjects" – a phrase I loathed. I lived just fourteen miles north of the International Boundary that lay invisible across the valley, separating our Okan*a*gan from their Okan*o*gan.

So I was three thousand miles from Ontario and Quebec, where all the Canadian stuff came from, and fourteen miles from the USA, land of my dreams. The USAmericans are among the most expert people in brainwashing their children and childlike adults, and many of the techniques by which they do so are available to curious boys just barely inside that country to the north, whatever it is. I listened to US radio stations, watched US movies, read US comic books and sports magazines, and listened to US music. I could hardly wait to grow up and become an

"American" citizen. If I were an "American" citizen, I reasoned, I would be able to redeem my Popsicle wrappers for great prizes. I would be able to travel the world and have foreigners admire me and my country.

The alternative was English stuff. The English were the colonizers. They had all the good jobs around my hometown. In the late eighteenth century, they had stupidly worn red coats and fought against the valiant freedom-seekers they were suppressing. Their automobiles were dicky little things that looked as if they belonged in the Thirties. They spoke in an accent whose purpose seemed to be to put you in your place.

At the movies you had to sing "God Save the King (or Queen)." They left the lights on to make sure you were standing still. Any Canadian magazines that made their way into the Southern Okanagan Valley (*Star Weekly, New Liberty*) had someone from the British royal family on the cover, usually the young princesses of the day, Elizabeth and Margaret. A couple weeks before I graduated from high school, the new British queen had her coronation. Time for me to head for college in the States. But then my English girlfriend went to normal school in Victoria. I followed her, enlisting as an artsman at Victoria College, gnashing my teeth at the irony in the name.

Well, I was not successful at college, so I went to work for the provincial (oh, how I resented the fact that my province was called "British") government in the topographical survey up north. But I was not successful at that, either, so I joined the Royal (gnash gnash) Canadian Air Force (the RCAF), and got shipped to Quebec for basic training, Ontario for trades training, and Manitoba for my regular posting, from which I went to Alberta for temporary duty. In the RCAF we had a lot of contact with other NATO air forces, including the USAF. We always felt superior to these latter, calling them Semis, pronounced "Semeyes," and noticing that while it took five Canadians to service an F-86, it took twelve Semeyes to handle the same job. It was while I was in the air force in mosquito country south of Lake Manitoba that I began to be a Canadian.

For a young man from the far southern interior of British Columbia, being a Canadian was a matter of choice. Okay, I said more and more, I will not choose to become a Yank; I will choose to be a Canadian. I will now spell flavours with a *u*, even if there are not as many available to me as there would be in California.

Three of my grandparents chose to be Canadians, I remembered. And the fourth had relatives in Buffalo, New York, I think, so she made that choice, too. Even my grandfather, who was born in England, was scheduled to be a preacher in Idaho, but obliged his church's request that he go to Alberta, instead. I do not know whether my parents chose to be Canadians; I know that my father's older brother Llew got married to a USAmerican girl in Seattle, but he eventually came home. I decided that I would follow a family tradition and choose Canada. Maybe, I began to think – I was becoming an artist-academic, and such people are paid to perform slick-sounding theories – maybe all Canadians make that choice.

I don't really think that. I have met a lot of pickup-driving guys in sideburns who actually believe that ice hockey is preferable to baseball. On the negative side, I know a writer who was going to move across the line until he developed a medical condition that would be terrifically expensive down there where medicine is a business. But while I still do not particularly like having Queen Elizabeth's profile on my coins, I also believe that "the land of the free" is a slogan that is no more historical than "the home of the Whopper."

So I know for sure that I am a Canadian. Now, if I could figure out what I am, I might have a step up to figuring out what a Canadian is.

I said that we do not tell our children that God picked Canada to be the best country in the world. But in recent years it has become a habit for Canadian newspapers to look around for surveys that rank Canada as the best country in the world to live in. If the Yanks can sing or say "God Bless America," then maybe we can be taught to sing "The UN Recommends Canada." I, for one, do not particularly want to live in a country that considers itself the best in the world. I want us to look around and see what needs fixing. We do not want to be smug; smugness is the benign form of a mental disease that results in nationalism, the delusion that other places were the failures on the path to your own perfection.

I like the fact that a Canadian, asked what a Canadian is, will likely say, "Let me get back to you on that." That is why you should not be surprised to hear someone say: "I have looked all over, and I can't find a Canadian."

Here's your obvious reply: "That's okay. Give me a Blue."

Vancouver, British Columbia, and Port Colborne, Ontario
Copyright © 2006 by George Bowering

George Bowering

George Bowering was born and brought up in the Okanagan Valley, British Columbia. There was no ice, so he never became a hockey player, but he did manage some baseball and basketball. He spent a lot of years as a professor, and more as a writer of fiction, non-fiction and poetry. In 2002, he became Canada's first Parliamentary Poet Laureate. While holding that post, he was shanghaied into the Order of Canada and the Order of British Columbia. His most recent book is Changing on the Fly.

CHRISTIAN DUFOUR

UN CANADIEN EST ... au départ un *Canayen*, un *Habitant* de la vallée du Saint-Laurent qui parle français. Rappelons qu'il ne fut que cela pendant la majorité de l'histoire du pays, presque deux cent ans: de la fin du XVII siècle à la fin du XIXème siècle, les seuls à s'appeler eux-mêmes et à être appelés par les autres des «Canadiens» furent les ancêtres des Québécois francophones d'aujourd'hui. Il n'y a pas si longtemps, ma vieille locataire de Limoilou parlait encore des Canadiens anglophones comme des «Anglais», et des francophones québécois comme des «Canadiens». À l'étranger comme au Canada même, y compris au Québec, on oublie de plus en plus cette incontournable réalité que, sur le plan de la construction de l'identité canadienne, les Québécois franco-phones sont les premiers Canadiens. Par rapport à l'identité canadienne, l'identité québécoise est pourtant fondamentale, toute sauf postérieure ou périphérique, comme l'Écosse l'est par rapport à la Grande-Bretagne ou la Slovaquie par rapport à l'ancienne Tchécoslovaquie.

Oublions un instant la réécriture de l'histoire par la rectitude politique à la mode. Sur le plan identitaire, il n'y a pas trois ou même deux peuples fondateurs au Canada: il n'y en a qu'un, formé des ancêtres directs des francophones québécois d'aujourd'hui, les seuls qui se considèrent Canadiens depuis un siècle lorsqu'arrivent les Britanniques en 1763. Ils cohabitent alors avec les premiers occupants du territoire, les Amér-indiens, à qui il ne viendrait jamais l'idée de s'appeler Canadiens, car le processus de «canadianisation» de leur identité ne commencera qu'au milieu du XXème siècle: au début des années 90, la crise d'Oka con-stituera un épisode important de ce processus. Aux «Anciens Canadiens» se joindront après 1763 des Britanniques qui mettront, eux, un peu plus d'un siècle à se sentir *Canadian* – à la fin du XIXème siècle, à l'époque de Sir Wilfrid Laurier. Sans évidemment compter tous ces nouveaux Canadiens issus de l'immigration, qui ne sont ni autochtones ni d'origine française ou britannique.

Laurier, le premier Canadien français à devenir premier ministre du Canada, exhortera les Canadiens anglais de son époque à se sentir moins membres de l'Empire britannique et davantage Canadiens, comme leurs compatriotes de langue française l'étaient déjà un long moment. Cent ans plus tard, un nombre substantiel de Québécois voudraient faire du Québec un État souverain, alors que la majorité des francophones ne se sentent plus à l'aise dans le Canada d'aujourd'hui. Que s'est-il donc passé pour que les plus canadiens d'entre tous en soient venus à une telle attitude négative à l'égard d'un pays qui fait objectivement l'envie de l'univers? Il est impossible de le comprendre si l'on se limite à la seule vision canadienne-anglaise des choses, sans tenir compte du fait qu'il existe aussi un autre point de vue ancré dans l'histoire du Canada, la vision du pays spécifique aux Canadiens de langue française.

Sous ses allures canadienne-française depuis 1840 et québécoise depuis 1960, l'identité des francophones québécois demeure l'identité canadienne de base, historiquement parlant: les Québécois, y compris les souverainistes, sont les Canadiens les plus enracinés. Si l'on oublie ce facteur, ce déchirant deuil à faire de l'identité canadienne qu'ils ont mise au monde, il est impossible de comprendre la difficulté des francophones québécois à décrocher contre toute logique d'un Canada où ils sont de plus en plus marginalisés. Leur premier choix serait un Canada où le Québec bénéficierait d'un statut tenant compte du fait qu'il abrite la seule société moderne non anglophone au nord du Rio Grande.

Mais trêve de considérations théoriques et politiques! Au-delà de ces vieilles histoires et de la sempiternelle question de la place du Québec au sein du Canada, où est-ce que je me situe personnellement en ce qui a trait à l'appartenance canadienne? Le fait d'avoir accepté d'écrire un texte sur ce thème de «Qu'est qu'un Canadien?» m'a amené à m'interroger à nouveau à ce sujet, ce que je n'avais pas fait depuis l'échec de l'Accord du lac Meech il y a quinze ans. Cela m'a rappelé que, lors de la conclusion de cet accord, pour la première fois de ma vie adulte, je m'étais senti Canadien sur le plan émotif: c'est pourquoi j'avais accepté que la traduction anglaise du «Défi québécois» soit sous-titrée «A Canadian Challenge». La rédaction de ce texte me rappelle également mon enfance au Saguenay-Lac-Saint-Jean, l'une des régions les plus françaises du Québec, colonisée au XIXème siècle en réaction à l'exode des Canadiens français aux États-Unis. À l'époque, mon frère cadet, aujourd'hui décédé, avait l'habitude de dire: «Quand j'ai appris, vers cinq ou six ans, qu'il y avait des gens qui ne parlaient pas français, j'ai été étonné. Plus tard, quand j'ai réalisé qu'il y avait plus d'Anglais que de Français au Canada, cela m'a bouleversé».

Mais je continue à tourner autour du pot. En fait, je suis un peu mal à l'aise parce que je sais bien que ce texte sera avant tout lu par des gens qui, au-delà de différences souvent majeures, partagent en commun le fait de se sentir tous fièrement Canadiens. Comment leur dire la vérité tout en restant poli? Comment ne pas blesser inutilement des Canadiens qui je connais un peu, qui j'aime bien et qui je respecte beaucoup? Me reviennent les souvenirs de ces mois passés dans la langueur de Victoria, la douceur d'un automne s'étirant jusqu'en janvier, la gentillesse de tous ces gens dont je me demande encore parfois, aujourd'hui, après toutes ces années, ce qu'ils ont bien pu devenir. Connie Niblock, Rod Dobell et tous les autres. Comment faire un bon thé. De l'autre côté de l'eau, la vue des monts Olympiques dans l'État de Washington.

Mais il faut dire la vérité – ma vérité – ne prétendant en cette matière représenter personne d'autre que moi-même. Après y avoir repensé, je réalise donc que, même si le Canada est incontestablement l'un des pays les plus tolérants, les plus civilisés et les plus privilégiés qui soit, même si je suis rationnellement conscient que mon identité est quelque part canadienne, ne serait-ce que sur le plan historique, je réalise donc qu'en 2005 mon attachement émotif pour le Canada est nul. Inexistant. *Nothing*. Repensant aux gens de Victoria, mettons «à peu près» nul.

Pour moi, le Canada est devenu le pays des autres: celui des anglophones, bien sûr, mais aussi des autochtones, des Acadiens, des gens de l'Ouest, des immigrants asiatiques de Vancouver, des Torontois, des fonctionnaires fédéraux, des gens de Terre-Neuve. Et d'autres encore. Mais le Canada pour moi, ce n'est pas le pays de cette majorité francophone, de cette modernité québécoise auquel se rattache le coeur de mon identité et de tout mon être. Si je ne souhaite aucun mal au Canada, il me faut avouer que sa disparition me toucherait cent fois moins que la perte de ce Québec-là. C'est triste, ce n'est pas (encore) dramatique mais, dans la chaleureuse compagnie de millions de compatriotes québécois, je me sens exilé en mon propre pays. Étranger. Aliéné. Endormi, sinon mort, à cette identité qui fut celle de mes ancêtres. Un peu comme si le mythique Canadien errant du XIXème siècle était revenu dans un Canada qui ne le reconnaissait plus.

Pourquoi cette indifférence à l'égard d'un pays béni des dieux et qui fait l'envie de tous? Je me rappelle ce moment où j'ai eu le goût d'y croire et de jouer le jeu, de m'identifier comme Canadien. L'accord du Lac Meech m'était apparue inespéré, presque trop beau pour être vrai, la suite des choses devant démontrer qu'il était de fait trop beau pour être vrai. Je crois que mon indifférence à l'égard du Canada vient de son refus – que je sens quelque part profond – de la modernité de mon identité québécoise, alors que mon attachement au pays ne saurait passer que par cette identité-là. Je n'ai pas d'intérêt pour une identité canadienne qui nie le coeur de ce que je suis.

Voilà! Je sais qu'il ne faut pas rester accroché au passé. Que dire de plus sinon qu'avant que je ne décroche du Canada pour m'immerger dans d'autres mondes, j'ai vu les débuts de ce nouveau nationalisme canadien bien-pensant, intolérant à l'égard de la modernité québécoise, une idéologie répugnante et sans avenir parce que bâtie sur la négation du coeur québécois du Canada. Si j'ai salué l'apparition du fédéralisme asymétrique dans l'accord fédéral-provincial sur la santé à l'automne 2004, l'espoir d'une véritable réconciliation historique Québec-Canada ne m'habite plus vraiment. En ce domaine, je suis devenu vieux.

Je souhaite «Bonne chance» aux Canadiens et aux Québécois des générations futures. Trouveront-ils, eux, le moyen de faire en sorte qu'un fier Québécois ne soit pas incompatible avec un fier Canadien, comme c'est malheureusement le cas aujourd'hui? J'espère aussi que tout cela ne finira pas mal, comme je le crains. La rédaction de ce texte m'a rappelé la tristesse, le chagrin et le gâchis de la relation Canada-Québec, que j'avais réussie ces dernières années à oublier dans la richesse du Québec et du monde. L'univers est si grand dans nos têtes et dans nos vies. Montréal, Québec, les Laurentides, le Saguenay, Charlevoix . . . Les USA, la France, l'Europe, l'Asie, le Maghreb.

Je ne vais plus au Canada anglais, mais je repense parfois à Victoria.

Montréal, Québec
Copyright © 2006 by Christian Dufour

CHRISTIAN DUFOUR

A CANADIAN IS ... at the outset a *Québécois*, a *habitant* who lives in the St. Lawrence Valley and speaks French. It is worth recalling that the name meant that, and only that, during most of the country's history; for nearly two hundred years, from the end of the seventeenth century to the end of the nineteenth, the only people who called themselves *Canadiens* and were called that by others were the ancestors of today's French-speaking Québécois. Not so long ago, my old tenant in Limoilou still spoke of Canadian anglophones as "English" and francophone Quebeckers as "Canadiens." Abroad and at home in Canada, including in Quebec, people more and more tend to forget the unavoidable reality that, in the blueprint for constructing the Canadian identity, Quebec francophones are the very first Canadians. Nevertheless, in relation to the Canadian identity, the Quebec identity is anything but subsequent or peripheral, as Scotland is to Great Britain or Slovakia is to the former Czechoslovakia; rather, it is fundamental and central.

Let's forget for a moment the rewritten history that political correctness has given us. In identity terms, Canada does not have three or even two founding peoples – only one, made up of the direct ancestors of today's Québécois, those people of old who were unique in regarding themselves as Canadians a century before the British arrived in 1763. In those days they lived alongside the first inhabitants of the land, the Aboriginals, who never thought of calling themselves "Canadians." The process of their "Canadianization" only began in the middle of the twentieth century: indeed, the Oka Crisis played a large part in this in the early 1990s.

The "Old Canadians" were joined after 1763 by British arrivals who then took more than a century to feel that they had become Canadian, something they achieved at the end of the nineteenth century, in Sir Wilfrid Laurier's day. And obviously, this does not include all of the new Canadians brought here by immigration, who are not Aboriginal or French or English.

Laurier, the first French-Canadian to become prime minister, urged the anglophones of his day to feel less like members of the British Empire and more Canadian, as their French-speaking compatriots had become long before. Now, a hundred years later, a substantial number of Québécois want to make Quebec into a independent state, since the majority of francophones no longer feel comfortable in modern Canada. What has happened to make these people – the most "Canadian" of all – feel so negatively about a country that is objectively looked at with envy around the world? It is impossible to understand this development if you take an exclusively English-Canadian view of the matter, without taking into account the fact that there is another point of view that is anchored in Canada's history, a vision of the country that is specific to French-speaking Canadians.

As "French Canadians" since 1840 and "Québécois" since 1960, these people provided the bedrock of Canadian identity, historically speaking: the Québécois, including the sovereigntists among them, are the Canadians with the deepest roots. If you forget this factor – the heart-rending loss of the Canadian identity that they brought into the world – it is impossible to understand the difficulty that Québécois have in unhooking themselves, against all logic, from a Canada in which they are increasingly marginalized. Their first choice, their preferred choice, would be a Canada where Quebec benefits from a formal legal recognition that it shelters the only non-English-speaking modern society north of the Rio Grande.

But that's enough theoretical and political stuff! Beyond these old stories and the never-ending question of Quebec's place in Canada, where do I stand personally on this business of belonging to Canada? The fact that I have agreed to write an essay on the subject "What Is a Canadian?" has led me to start asking myself questions about this subject once again – something I have not done ever since the failure of the Meech Lake Accord, a full fifteen years ago. This has reminded me that at the time the accord was put together, for the first time in my adult life, I felt fully, emotionally Canadian. That was why I had agreed that the English translation of "Le défi québécois" should be subtitled "A Canadian Challenge." Writing this text also reminds me of my childhood in Saguenay-Lac-Saint-Jean, one of the most exclusively French areas of Quebec, colonized in the nineteenth century as a counterbalance to the exodus of French Canadians to the United States. At the time, my younger brother, now deceased, used to say: "When I learned, at the age of five or six, that there were people who could not speak French, I was surprised. Later, when I realized that there were more English speakers than French speakers in Canada, that really stunned me."

But I am still skirting around the issue. To tell the truth, I am a little uncomfortable because I realize that this essay will be read primarily by people who, although holding many different opinions, have in common the fact that they are all proud to be Canadians. How can I tell them the truth and still be polite? How can I avoid giving pain for no good reason to Canadians whom I know a little, like quite well, and respect a lot?

Back come the memories of the months spent in sweet Victoria, the softness of its fall weather stretching into January, and the kindness of all these people about whom I still wonder, after all these years, "Whatever happened to . . .?" To Connie Niblock, Rod Dobell and all of the others. I remember that they taught me the right way to make tea. And I remember, across the water, the view of the Olympic Mountains in Washington State.

But I have to tell the truth – my own truth, as I see it – not pretending to represent anyone but myself when I do so. Having thought about it over and over, I realize that even if Canada is indisputably one of the most tolerant, civilized and privileged countries in the world, and even if I am aware, on a rational level, that my own identity is partly Canadian, even if only in historical terms, I now realize that, in 2006, my emotional attachment to Canada is zero. Well, now I think of those people in Victoria, let me settle for "almost zero."

For me, Canada has become the land of others; the land of English speakers, certainly, but also of Aboriginals, Acadians, Westerners, Asian immigrants in Vancouver, of Torontonians, of federal bureaucrats, of

Newfoundlanders. And still others. But for me Canada is not the land of this francophone majority, this modern Quebec to which the heart of my identity and all of my soul is so firmly linked. If I wish Canada no harm, I have to admit that its disappearance would affect me a hundred times less than the loss of this Quebec. It is sad, it is not tragic (yet), but in the warm company of millions of fellow Québécois, I feel exiled in my own land. A foreigner. Alienated. Numbed, if not dead, to this identity that belonged to my ancestors. A little as if the mythical *Canadien errant* of the nineteenth century had returned to a Canada that no longer recognized him.

Why do I feel this indifference toward a country blessed by the gods and envied by all? I remember the moment when I really wanted to believe in it, and to play the game of identifying myself as a Canadian. The Meech Lake Accord seemed to me beyond anything I had hoped for, almost too good to be true – and as things turned out, it was indeed too good to be true. I believe that my indifference to Canada comes from its rejection – which I think comes from something very deep – of the modernity of my Québécois identity, when all the while my attachment to Canada runs directly through that identity. I have no interest in a Canadian identity that denies the very heart of what I am.

There! I know that we do not have to stay yoked to the past. That sums it up, except that before leaving Canada to immerse myself in other worlds, I saw the rise of this new Canadian nationalism, intolerant of modern Quebec, an ideology that seems repugnant and without any future because it is apparently based on denying that Quebec lies at the heart of Canada. Even if I hailed the appearance of asymmetrical federalism in the federal-provincial agreement on health that was reached in the fall of 2004, today I no longer hold any hope of a real historic reconciliation between Quebec and Canada. When it comes to that whole area, I have become old and disillusioned.

I say "good luck" to the Canadians and the Québécois of future generations. Will they find a way of making it possible for a proud Québécois to be at the same time a proud Canadian, something that is unfortunately not the case today? I also hope that this will not end badly, as I fear. Writing these words has reminded me of the sadness, the grief and the simple messiness that marks the relationship between Canada and Quebec – which I have managed to forget these last few years, thanks to the richness of Quebec and the wider world. The universe is so huge in our imaginations and in our lives – Montreal, Quebec, the Laurentians, the Saguenay, Charlevoix, the USA, France, Europe, Asia, the Maghreb...

I no longer visit English Canada, but I sometimes think about Victoria.

Montreal, Quebec
Translation copyright © 2006 by Douglas M. Gibson

Christian Dufour

Christian Dufour was born in 1949 in Chicoutimi and trained as a lawyer. He now conducts research and teaches at the École nationale d'administration publique in Montreal. He is a much sought-after speaker and analyst on the themes of Canadian federalism, Quebec–Canada relations, identity issues and major government reforms.

Christian Dufour is the author of a new book titled Le défi français – Regards croisés sur la France et le Québec. *He has also contributed to several edited works and is the author of many articles in academic journals and newspapers.*

PAUL HEINBECKER

A CANADIAN IS ... a promissory note, a bearer of hope in troubled times, a bet that diversity will work, that people can get along and that peace is possible. A Canadian is a global citizen, wired to a wider reality, at ease in a world that is itself increasingly at home in Canada – transforming our national character and changing our physical complexion, and giving us an interest literally and figuratively in every corner of the planet. A Canadian is a work in progress, at once cosmopolitan and provincial, competitive and complacent, compassionate and crying poor, a history amnesiac, a citizen of tomorrowland.

Living in the long shadow of the only superpower, Canadians seem esteem-challenged vis-à-vis their alpha neighbours, only too conscious of limits, of what cannot be afforded, of having little choice, disposed sometimes to going along to get along, and given other times to disagreeing awkwardly. Perhaps inevitably, given the circumstances of our birth, and with geography being what it is, we tend to define ourselves in contradistinction to Americans: as North American but not American, quiet where they are loud, polite where they are aggressive, suspicious of their motives but nonetheless admiring of their culture and respectful of their qualities (if too often satisfied with only tenths of their performance), and given to cataloguing our reassuring differences. Why else would we regard our social programs as self-defining, as some sort of distinctive feature of who we are? If the Americans gave themselves universal health care, would that make them Canadians? If we had more comprehensive social programs, would that make us Swedish?

Internationally, we regard ourselves as peacekeepers, the leading practitioners of a Canadian invention for which Prime Minister Lester Bowles

Pearson was awarded the Nobel Peace Prize; we have even built a monument to ourselves in the nation's capital. To the world's poor, we imagine ourselves to be generous, setting a standard for altruistic assistance, striving for the development assistance norm of 0.7% of gross national product that Mr. Pearson commended to the world a generation ago. We consider ourselves to be environmentalists, indeed to be world leaders in protecting the environment. All in all, some of us like to think we punch above our weight.

A Canadian needs a wake-up call. As a nation, we have been in retreat from international responsibility for a generation. On military deployments abroad, we have fielded troops that are as competent and courageous as any on earth, but we have diminished their numbers to the point that they cannot practise what we preach about protecting the innocent. We have allowed ourselves to slide dramatically far down the list of contributors to UN missions, below countries with a small fraction of our population and wealth. Even allowing for NATO deployments, we do not crack the top ten in international military contributions to peace and security. On development assistance, we rank closer to the bottom of donor generosity than to the top. On the environment, we relinquished our international leadership a decade ago.

It does not have to be that way. There is no reason why we cannot choose to speak up and, more importantly, to stand up for what we believe in. Our wallet is not the problem; never in our history have we been richer or better able to afford an effective, responsible, targeted foreign policy. Nor is competence the problem. We were one of the very few countries, for example, that could have led an effort to find a compromise in the UN on Iraq. The proof of that assertion is that we were the only country that did. In worlds as disparate as Angola, Kabul, Bosnia, Broadway, Nashville and Hollywood North, Canadians have made a difference. Few countries can match us at foreign policy innovation, perhaps because we think about policy more than we conduct it. Ideas "R" Us; implementation is sometimes someone else.

Having lived abroad and represented Canada for much of my adult life, I have seen ourselves as others see us, to paraphrase Robbie Burns. Our neighbours the Americans, on those occasions when they do look northward, see us mostly benignly, if obscurely, through the distorting lenses of their powerful myths. To the sons and daughters of the American Revolution, Canadians are artifacts of an earlier time – an American-like people inexplicably and a little obtusely still tied to the English Crown. A Canadian is a cousin – a polite, self-effacing version of their more adversarial, patriotic selves, who rarely attracts their attention, except as the dispatcher of winter cold fronts. To Americans (the inventors of base-ball), Canadians (the inventors of ice hockey) are boring! Because we can speak fluent American, the success of countless Canadians in the United States goes largely unnoticed. Like aliens in a B-movie, Canadians move among Americans undetected!

In Washington, Canadians are assumed to share American values, and presumed to hold the same world view, albeit given to occasional, puzzling manifestations of independence of mind, generally regarded as in error. Canadian endorsement of an increasingly aggressive American foreign policy is simply expected, the supposed quid for the American quo of protection from whomever the Americans currently consider their enemy. In Washington, the Canadian embassy is located at the corner of Interdependence Avenue and Indifference Street, little more welcome than most other foreigners to the closed circuit of American policy making. Intergovernmental disagreements and bilateral disputes are assumed to be the consequence of a regrettable Canadian confusion of inferior information, moral unclarity, faulty analysis and dubious motives. As depicted in the American media, a Canadian is a little too liberal, overly welcoming of the world's huddled masses, insufficiently aware of the world's clear and present dangers, a keeper of a porous border, even a harbourer of terrorists, but still a welcome supplier of energy and pharmaceutical drugs, as well as a dealer in less legal sub-stances, and a surprisingly witty observer of America itself.

To the wider world, which sees Canada in more distant perspective and less stark detail, Canadians are the fortunate citizens of a young nation and a mature democracy, one of the world's oldest states. We out-number the populations of 155 other countries (out of 191 UN member states), our much derided military spending ranks us fifteenth worldwide, our economy is in the top twelve, and our quality of life is enjoyed by only a small handful of countries. The world sees us as the nice Americans, with the openness characteristic of our continent, and the egalitarianism inherent in our New World culture, but without the pervasive presence in their lives and latent menace that American power sometimes entails. The world, also, sees us as regrettably turning inward, less willing than we once were to put our shoulder to the world's wheel, at a time when the need is great and we have never been richer. Still, the world really does respect us for our successful, prosperous, bilingual, multiethnic, law-abiding, cultivated and often compassionate society, one that values diversity and that integrates immigrants into national life and purpose as well or better than anyone else. We are regarded as a country that tries (and mostly succeeds) to respect human rights and to protect minorities, albeit one that ought to do better by its Aboriginal population. Canadians are seen to enjoy an enviable quality of life and a very high standard of living. We are recognized for a culture that generates remarkable excellence in the arts, especially literature, and science, albeit not in Olympic athletics – ice hockey excepted. We are respected as the country with the sad but proud distinction of having been awarded more posthumous UN military service medals than any other.

As Canadian ambassador to the United Nations, I was invariably given a willing hearing, whether the issue was seeking a principled compromise on Iraq, helping at the birth of the nascent International Criminal Court or proposing innovations in the way the UN does business. When Canadian representatives abroad speak, they are listened to, first and foremost, because of who Canadians are. As much by virtue of our values, of what we stand for, as by what we do in the world, we are heard.

It was always an honour to represent a country so well regarded by others. With all of our foibles and failings, and undoubtedly there are both, there is no other country that I would have been as proud to serve. Ultimately, a Canadian is a happy citizen to be.

Ottawa, Ontario
Copyright © 2006 by Paul Heinbecker

Paul Heinbecker

Paul Heinbecker is the inaugural director of the Laurier Centre for Global Relations, Governance and Policy and senior research fellow at the Centre for International Governance Innovation, both in Waterloo, Ontario. In the course of a lengthy career with the Canadian Department of Foreign Affairs, he served in seven posts abroad, including New York and Washington, and attended ten G8 summit meetings. In 2000, Paul Heinbecker was appointed Canada's ambassador and permanent representative to the United Nations, where he was a leading advocate of the International Criminal Court. He was also the leading proponent of a Security Council compromise on Iraq that would have given UN weapons inspectors time to complete their work.

MARY ELLEN TURPEL-LAFOND

A CANADIAN IS . . . fascinated by how people survive in what can seem a harsh and unforgiving environment. The pre-urban world marks our psyche, and many continue to live away from the metropolis, connected closely to the land. A Canadian looks to the past to understand how the relationship between people and land has been sustained through time. Beginnings take them to the First Peoples – the "Aboriginal peoples" – the First Nations, Inuit and Métis peoples. A Canadian wants to know how the First Peoples lived here before, and later with, the settlers.

Canadians have a palimpsest of this mythic foundation of Canada. The First Peoples believe that every object in the natural world has a spirit and is a living being. It is not merely animate or inanimate. It lives. The enormous granite outcroppings of the Canadian Shield have a spirit and voice that the First Peoples celebrate and respect. The same holds for the infamous blasted pine of poet F.R. Scott. Where others might see emptiness, a barren landscape, or hardscrabble terrain, First Peoples see the richness of creation, and many others celebrate that vision.

Great Canadian artists of both indigenous and European ancestry have connected with this sentiment and portray the landscape as other than barren and alienating, finding it richly detailed in a way that is not simply reflective of another location (such as a European homeland). Paul Kane, Emily Carr, the Group of Seven, and Woodland artists like Norval Morriseau and Daphne Odjig depict the landscape, sky and natural world as full of colour, nuance and connection. Reflect on the treasured paintings of Norval Morriseau. A single creature like a bear is transformed into a brilliant array of colours with tentacles of spirits connecting outward to all of creation. Each being is connected to the world of spirits, the world of the quotidian, and the world of the future. The abundance of the land-scape is continually celebrated, and our interaction with it is always con-nected to shifting relations.

A Canadian is someone shaped by the landscape and capable of seeing it as abundant. The First Peoples have helped us gain this appreciation. The practice of observing the natural world and living close to the land gives insight into the cycles of life; the ancient and modern medicine wheel reminds us of these cycles of the seasons and their parallels with our own stages of life: infancy, childhood, maturity and old age. The wheel turns and generations come and go.

Canadians look skyward. The elegant, endangered sandhill cranes make their journey north, then return south, stopping in open Saskatchewan fields to sample the summer harvest. The First Peoples believe that birds are the messengers of the spirit world, and parts of birds, like the eagle whistle, are among the most sacred objects carried in the medicine bundles of the Elders, as they have been for centuries. The creatures of the North, such as the bears, muskoxen, and caribou, all have a spirit that is connected to us in the belief system of the First Peoples. Even the smaller creatures of the boreal forest, living in the shade of the black spruce, poplar and birch trees, are considered our relations, reminding us to make gentle footprints on the mossy forest floor.

The first languages of Canada, with their verb-centred structures, are a testament to listening to the natural world. The sound of the flapping wings of the prairie chicken has a name in Plains Cree, a language that is always discerning movement and action. The ceremony and dance of the First Peoples is most perfectly executed when dancers convincingly mimic in regalia and movement the phenomenon in the natural world they seek to portray. Yet the colours are contemporary and remind us that a culture changes its outward expressions but retains its connections. As anyone who has enjoyed a powwow on a summer evening can recall, we watch the grass dancer sway to the drum as he connects to the spirit of the windswept tall prairie grass. The Earth is celebrated for its abundance and cycles of transformation.

The First Peoples have the *Weesageechak*, or trickster character, to remind us that if we assert ourselves too aggressively at the apex of creation, we can be comically and/or tragically struck down. From these trickster stories, the First Peoples learn to listen, to be limited in our ego strivings, and to quest for a connected place with all of creation. Getting along with others different from ourselves is essential to our success in these stories, as it is in our national politics.

To be a Canadian is to know this history and culture. There is a social and political tradition stemming from it that allows us to reach out to people from all parts of the world as they come to Canada. The spirit of sharing exemplified by the First Peoples infuses our identity. It is our bedrock. Some say the First Peoples shared to a fault, but perhaps it is more a criticism of how enthusiastically some newcomers took advantage of the generosity. History is not without injustice, but it is quintessentially Canadian to acknowledge, study, remember and respond to injustice. We must continually come to terms, discuss our differences, and that process is hardwired from our experience of the landscape.

We can reflect on the gift of the canoe, the York boat, and the indigenous knowledge of the land, waters and natural medicines to remember that sharing has been a core value for Canada. There is something in this tradition that forges our identity as people who believe in taking care of others, in respecting differences while learning from each other, and reaching out a hand of friendship.

Canada is both a place and a state of mind, continually recreated through this alchemy of values and tradition shaped by the land. Sometimes labelled as tolerance, diversity, or even a full-blown "Northern sensibility," it is not something to be taken for granted or assumed. It is not an abstract ideology exported around the world, but the works of helpful and modest people connected to the land, who will try to do their best to assist others in need, either by welcoming them to these shores or by going abroad to make a contribution to the world, just as the First Peoples did in the beginning. It beckons us to look skyward at the sandhill crane, and to remember that the great Canadian Shield will outlive us all – a reality that the palimpsest encodes through our modesty.

Muskeg Lake Cree Nation, Saskatchewan
Copyright © 2006 by Mary Ellen Turpel-Lafond

Mary Ellen Turpel-Lafond

Honourable Judge Mary Ellen Turpel-Lafond has been a Saskatchewan Provincial Court judge since 1998. Prior to this, she practised law in Nova Scotia and Saskatchewan, and was a tenured professor of law at the Dalhousie University Faculty of Law. She has published widely in law and public affairs. Judge Turpel-Lafond taught at several universities in Canada and the United States. She holds a BA (Carleton University), LLB (Osgoode Hall Law School), LLM (Cambridge University) and a doctorate of law (Harvard Law School). She has been named twice (1993, 1999) by Time magazine as a member of the new generation of leaders for Canada.

Judge Turpel-Lafond is a member of the Muskeg Lake First Nation in Saskatchewan and the mother of four young children.

JOHN C. CROSBIE

A CANADIAN IS ... one of the most fortunate and favoured persons on our Planet Earth.

Canadians, of course, often do not appreciate the advantages we have. We suffer from intense regional jealousies and rivalries, with five distinct regions across our vast continent, all competing in an ever-evolving federal system of parliamentary government.

We are blessed with having two founding peoples, the English and the French, from two strong world nations that settled in Canada over five hundred years ago. This has caused us to be sensitive to the rights, needs and views of minorities, and to accept the need for compromise in the working out of our political system. Today this means working with our Aboriginal peoples, and with people who have arrived in our country from around the world since the Second World War – people who have helped build a most vibrant multicultural society.

Canadians will only continue as fortunate and favoured people if we earn our fortune and favour through enterprise, hard work and fiscal restraint, so that we can rebuild the influence we had in the world community following the Second World War. This influence was earned by the military capability we developed and the effort and resources we devoted to aiding peoples less fortunate than ourselves, as well as through the effort and the resources we devoted to vigorously pursuing our foreign policy wherever peace was threatened and crises arose.

In our domestic affairs, the inability of our leaders to devise an effective and affordable, efficient and productive health system is a serious threat to our continuing as a fortunate and favoured people. A system whose basic workings are dictated by feelings of envy and jealousy, where sensible reforms to create efficiency in the system are frowned upon and deliberately obscured, does not encourage optimism that we will any time soon improve our living and health standards.

We must, if we are to remain a fortunate and favoured people, return to a constructive and responsible role for Canada in the world; to constructive, rational and effective approaches in domestic policy, not only in health, but in education, immigration and security; to a vigorous, thoughtful and substantive competition for power, where two or three effective and contender political parties are encouraged.

We must continue to seek cooperation with the United States, but not be subordinate to its foreign policy. We must always be ready to put forward our own strongly held views, immune to blind prejudice or envy or jealousy.

Canadians are innately decent people, wanting to do the right thing at home and abroad; tested many times in wars and world calamities, but always responding well to such challenges; willing to assist those in need at home and abroad; challenged again now to regain the respect and influence we formerly had by devoting more resources to effective military capacity – not only to help maintain peace and security abroad, but to protect our own coastal waters and territory as a sovereign state must; prepared to support our diplomacy abroad morally and financially; prepared to help through effective and well-financed aid programs; determined to resist terrorism and to improve our national security; determined to remain economically efficient and productive and competitive, and to encourage entrepreneurship, initiative and self-reliance.

We must continue our efforts to live successfully in a complex federal system in a country of strong regions and provinces with diverse peoples, and we will continue to be successful if we understand how lucky we are to be Canadians – even with the problems and difficulties we have in managing our own country.

As Canadians, we had forebears who pioneered in overcoming the continental wilderness by clearing and developing our natural resources; building business and industry and infrastructure; creating a great trading nation and an important farming and fishing country; proving themselves skilled in dealing, through compromise and conciliation, with sensitive political issues caused by language and race, or by regional rivalries and aspirations; responding successfully to the emergencies of war, terror and poverty; absorbing many peoples of different nationalities and cultures; and allowing us to survive as an independent nation, proud and free, next to a benevolent but assertive giant neighbour.

Canadians surely realize how lucky they are to have profited from such opportunities and advantages, and to have overcome such challenges. In considering our future actions, we should keep in mind the thoughts and advice of sage thinkers who preceded us, such as Aristophanes, who wrote, "The country of every man is the one where he lives best."

Or as Thomas Jefferson put it so well in the early nineteenth century: "We should let the love of our country soar above all minor passions."

Or as Cicero wrote in 63 BCE: "The budget should be balanced, the treasury should be refilled. The public debt should be reduced, the arrogance of officialdom should be tempered or controlled lest we become bankrupt."

We must remember as well what Disraeli said: "In a progressive country change is constant, change is inevitable."

Canadians are far from perfect, and often appear too politically correct and inclined to move with the current fashionable thinking of the social and cultural elites. To achieve our real potential as a people and a country, we must resist any tendency to follow herd or mob mentality or attempts to enforce certain patterns of thought that might be fashionable from time to time.

A Canadian need never be afraid to express views that differ from the views of the majority or from current popular ideas, or to participate in vigorous and vehement debate to advance whatever ideals and causes he or she may believe in.

Finally, keep in mind that our Constitution exists to serve us and our country, and that neither we nor our country exist to serve the interest of any particular constitutional theorist or fanatic.

St. John's, Newfoundland and Labrador
Copyright © 2006 by John C. Crosbie

John C. Crosbie

John Carnell Crosbie, PC, OC, QC, is chancellor of Memorial University of Newfoundland and counsel for the law firm of Patterson Palmer. He was elected to the House of Commons in 1976 and held a number of senior cabinet posts in the Clark and Mulroney governments. In the ten years prior to his election to the House of Commons, John Crosbie held a range of portfolios in the Newfoundland House of Assembly. He is also the author of a political autobiography, No Holds Barred. *He was appointed an Officer of the Order of Canada in 1998.*

AUDREY McLAUGHLIN

A CANADIAN IS ... someone who lives in a nation on trial.

Is it our identity that is in question or, in fact, is it the very essence of the country itself? I begin by a comment on our image outside the country.

Having spent time abroad in the past few years, I find that our often benign reputation is somewhat embarrassing to one who has seen our flaws from the inside. Our modesty is legend, but perhaps tempered with the slight suspicion that we have nothing to brag about, and that we are simply minor Americans who just have not made it.

I am surprised, however, by the number of Americans who tell me that they claim to be Canadians when travelling abroad. How curious that we seek our identity and place in the world, while others borrow it!

So why are we a country on trial? To quote Gloria Steinem: Like art, revolutions come from combining what exists into what has never existed before. This summarizes our challenge and our opportunity. In this difficult world, can a reasonably rich and stable country with an educated, multiethnic population become a model for what has never existed before, drawing lessons from the past and inspiration from our privileged state?

In fact, we have begun, if we only realize the potential. Through the creation of Nunavut, we have accomplished something virtually unheard of in modern history. We have changed the geography of our country – without a war, by constitutional means, under one flag, recognizing the reality of culture, language and history.

As a Northerner, I think that this achievement demonstrates why, while we have both the burden and privilege of living next to a superpower, we should spend as much time looking north as emulating our neighbour to the south.

Canada is an Arctic nation that has not fully grasped this profound identity. While Ottawa has created the position of circumpolar ambassador, one wonders whether this was a mere gesture or a commitment based on a new vision, and indeed how many Canadians are even aware that such a position exists?

Canada has much more in common – geographically, culturally and politically – with circumpolar nations than with our southern neighbour. Certainly, the bulk of our economy rests in the south, but if we move beyond merely looking at the world as a market, but also as a home, could we not also expend considerably more effort in linking with the North, to our mutual benefit?

We are, of course, part of an increasingly globalized world, but wherever one looks the merging of world economies reinforces, rather than distracts from, the need of people to find a place they can call their own.

Pride of place is still alive. But what contributes to pride of citizenship? I believe it is the values we hold in common and exercise through our political system.

And this is the reason why we are on trial.

It is now common to hear that Canadians reject politics, but to do so is, in many ways, to reject our identity. Cynicism is the best weapon of any enemy, and a lack of faith in our institutions is our worst ally.

Canadians are extraordinary in that we constantly have to rethink who we are. Are we Northerners, Westerners, Maritimers, Newfoundlanders, Quebeckers, immigrants, First Nations, Inuit, Central Canadians? Of course, we are all of those, for each part forms the whole. In each of us, there is a bit of the immigrant, the First Nations, the Inuit, the francophone, the anglophone, and of the furthest East, West and North.

In recent history, the values that bind us together rest on two primary factors, in my estimation: the recognition of a multiethnic citizenry and the principle of cooperative sharing. This principle of cooperation is embodied in programs such as a public health care system, which demonstrates that through collective responsibility we can promote individual freedom.

Internationally, our present is not as proud as our past. Our drive to tie foreign policy, and particularly our foreign aid, with Canadian business interests has eroded our power and influence as a force for justice. Indeed, I would suggest we are on the edge of losing those values that, in the eyes of the world, have brought us respect.

There is a song sung by the Rankin Family that says, "We rise again in the faces of our children." And it is our children who will be the jury in this trial. Will they ask how we came to lose this sense of cooperative sharing; why our health care system was eroded; why young people began to leave the country in search of greater opportunities?

Tommy Douglas mused that a nation is not judged by the height of its skyscrapers, but by the way in which we treat each other. If politics is the way in which we implement our values, then politics has to change. We need a system that more accurately reflects the will of voters. We need voters who are participants in our system, not mere recipients and critics.

Changing politics is not the responsibility of politicians alone. Canadians value freedom, but we must also learn to take responsibility for it. Democracy, freedom and justice are not given; they are earned. If we allow our political system to be reduced to a situation comedy, where one-liners and facile solutions – rather than thoughtful debate – are the order of the day, then we are all guilty.

When we stand before the jury of our children, will they ask whether we paid as much attention to peace, social justice and the environment in the world as we did to the World Trade Organization? Will they ask how Canada became a vision of what never existed before, or will they simply ask where we were when the meaning of being Canadian was reduced to just not being the citizen of another country?

Perhaps it is more difficult to inspire citizens when we have not been through a war or major loss. But the erosion of our values through death by a thousand cuts will have the same result. We have the technology to wage war and, in fact, destroy the world, but have we the intellect and passion to change it?

Every July 1 in Whitehorse, Yukon, a citizenship ceremony takes place on the banks of the Yukon River. This ceremony includes new citizens and officials, and is observed by Canadians and visitors, young and old. As I look over the crowd, I see up to fifty people smiling: they are new Canadians. These smiles may have originated in the United States, Africa, Asia or Europe, but these smiles become the face of Canada.

At the end of the ceremony, all of us repeat the oath of citizenship. Many of us have tears in our eyes. This is not reckless nationalism. This is the pride of home in one small town in a remote part of Canada.

In this era of globalization and increasing homogeneity, what must triumph is the power of belonging, the symbolic smile – the hope and belief in a nation to become better.

Do we as Canadians have the determination to live up to the promise, or will we simply let this hope dissipate through apathy and cynicism?

We are a nation on trial.

Rabat, Morocco
Copyright © 2006 by Audrey McLaughlin

Audrey McLaughlin
Audrey McLaughlin served as leader of the New Democratic Party of Canada from 1989 to 1995, and was the first woman elected to lead a federal party in Canada. She was the federal member of Parliament for the Yukon from 1987 to 1997. She is currently working in Morocco as the director of political party programs for the National Democratic Institute. In 2004, she was appointed an Officer of the Order of Canada. In addition to numerous articles, she has also published an autobiography, A Woman's Place: My Life and Politics.

ROY MacGREGOR

A CANADIAN IS ... 32,146,547 different things altogether – and count-
ing. A far more telling question, perhaps, might be *What is Canada?*, for
this is a place where the country defines the people as much as the people
the country; perhaps far more so.

I used to think I knew the answer. I have, after all, been a journalist
operating almost exclusively in this country for more than thirty years.
A friend and I once sat down, over pen, paper and beer, and tried to cal-
culate just how much free living we had been able to run through
expenses; my tally worked out to more than a million miles, and somewhere between $2 million and $3 million. I have watched dawn rise at Cape
Spear, Newfoundland, and stared across the pink Atlantic toward Ireland.
I have body-surfed with my children at Long Beach, Vancouver Island,
and told them there is nothing but open water all the way to Japan. I have
stood, shivering, on the north shore of Ellesmere Island, and squinted
across the chopped ice toward Russia.

The moment I realized I knew nothing came one bright June day in
2005 while flying back from the tip of Ellesmere in a military Twin Otter.
The story assignment had to do with the last trip north by outgoing
Governor General Adrienne Clarkson, and the trip from the base at Alert
to weather station Eureka was long and slow – but never slow enough,
given the clear day, the spectacular scenery and the low flight path.

The pilots, bless them, picked up a number of strategically dropped
hints and invited me up into the cockpit for the run down Archer Fiord
and along the Dodge River that twists along a spectacular mountain
range. With most of the passengers in the noisy plane hooked up by
intercom, the comments quickly began steamrolling over each other as

dramatic sweeps of ice breakup would be overtaken by a sudden turn past a rock face that seemed virtually within reach.

An hour into the flight, the pilot suddenly took the plane higher to run over an icefield. The commentary also rose – *"Extraordinary!"* *"Beautiful!" "Outstanding!"* – but then, as a sense of the *size* of this icefield gathered, the entire earth now so white bare eyes could not look at it, the plane turned completely silent, but for the roar of the engines. The plane seemed to shrink, now little more than a mosquito flying over a vast white shoulder of a country with more faces than even Statistics Canada can document. Not a single passenger or crew dared speak – every single one struck with his or her utter insignificance in a land so large and diverse that not even the imagination seems capable of capturing it.

I remember vividly my own silent feelings at that moment. The first was a question – "Where *am* I?" – and the second a shocking sense of my own ignorance, the arrogance of ever daring to presume I knew anything at all about this place world maps define with a single splash of colour.

It seems foolhardy to think that there might be a single, identifiable "Canadian" in a land filled with such contradiction. In an instant, we had flown from jagged rock face and fractured ice to a crown of snow so seemingly smooth and endless it had, in its whiteness, somehow erased any sight or thought of other existence. The day before, I had been snow-mobiling across frozen rivers; a week from this moment, I would be swimming in what one southern part of this vast country naively calls a "northern" lake.

Contradiction is perhaps the only rule of this land. It is not just the prairies and the mountains, not just the three shores – the high rocks over the Atlantic, the thick ice over the Arctic, the inviting beaches into the Pacific – but contradictions that run, as well, through the people and their fractured views of the county in which they live.

The best example of this I ever encountered on assignment was aboard the funeral train carrying Pierre Trudeau from Ottawa, where the former prime minister had lain in state, to Montreal, where he was to be buried. All along the tracks, people stood and saluted and cheered, the most powerful moment coming in the small town of Alexandria, Ontario, where the train slowed and the people surprisingly stepped forward to place their bare hands on the passing cars. That squeak of human hands on metal is the strangest sound I have ever heard. Some reporters inside burst into tears at the sound of the hands, and yet these same misty-eyed reporters knew only too well that this very same train on a much different track in another part of this country would cause hands to reach out only to raise a middle finger.

Journalism gives you, as author Mordecai Richler once so neatly put it, an entrée into worlds into which you would never otherwise be allowed. The Trudeau funeral train is a prime example, but this entrée would also include the major political, cultural and sporting events that are the front page of any country that is made up so much more of back pages or no mention at all.

The access that has delighted this journalist is far more into the lives of everyday Canadians, none of whom seem to suffer the fretting and angst and self-absorption that the first three words of this essay suggest.

This past year alone, I have spent time with Betty Fitzgerald, the mayor of Bonavista, and listened to this former nurse plot out how her lovely little town on the eastern shore of Newfoundland need not disappear just because the cod has. I have sat with Gerald Merkel, a young farmer in Raymore, Saskatchewan, and heard him talk about the frost that killed his crop, the accident that almost killed his father – "She's beyond crying" – and yet he was still mapping out planting plans for the coming season, the banks willing. I had coffee in Saskatoon with Matthew Dunn, a brilliant mechanical engineering graduate and National Aboriginal Achievement Award winner who hopes to become an astronaut, and simply accepts that he will need to go away to accomplish this. I have been invited by Shirley Chan into the basement of her Vancouver home to see the small shrine she has built to her mother, Lee Wo Soon Chan, who, well into her eighties, was known as the "Mayor of Chinatown" and left behind a sense of pride and belonging that was most assuredly not there when she first arrived in this country. I have stood at the foot of the statue to Marie-Madeleine Jarret de Verchères that stares out from the south shore of the St. Lawrence River, and listened to young Marie-Eve Lainesse talk about how her generation has given up on politics, but never for a moment on who they are and where they live. I have visited with Larry Audlaluk of Grise Fiord, Nunavut, and listened to his story of how his family was forced to come to this place where they did not even know how to hunt the available animals, where the hardships were almost incomprehensible, and where, over time, they stopped fretting over the past and came to love this stark place as "home."

And when I was not working, I was home myself, several evenings each week off in cold arenas and stinking dressing rooms where, believe me, the national game is *not* self-analysis.

How can you possibly say "A Canadian is . . ." when the personality you are trying to define speaks two official languages, hundreds of other tongues, and is made up of faces in shapes and colours more varied than in any other country in the world? How can it be that a country so vast and so blessed with natural resources could shift, in seventy years, from a place where four out of every five lived on the land to a place where four out of every five now live in cities? This, in fact, is a society that has changed so rapidly that even if you could properly say "A Canadian is . . ." your definition would be out of date before the sentence could be completed.

Perhaps this is why we cling to the generalities. The northern cold, Robertson Davies once said, "breeds caution," and while this is not exactly true of Canadians in war or in sport, it is certainly somewhat true in personality. Some might be tempted to add suspicion, cynicism and, perhaps, that odd, often misinterpreted sarcasm that is at the essence of most Canadian humour. And yet, once you fly past the icefield that surrounds so many who live here in this massive country, it is also generally true that there is a generous spirit to be found, as well as that quality that is so often held up for applause when speaking of Canadians: tolerance.

It could be, of course, that tolerance is natural in a place so isolated by weather, by distance, by language, by background, even by inclination. But it could as easily be said that Canadians have decided to apply a collective Trudeau shrug to those matters that do not directly, or locally, affect their own lives.

Such contradiction must leave others scratching their heads. How, they must wonder, can a people apply such ridicule to government – even to Confederation – and yet take such pride in being annually named one of the very best countries in the world to live?

A strange people, rejecting every definition, yet continually in search of one. Or so it seems.

All we are certain of is that this gnawing question of identity is rarely given much peace. Centennial Year brought on such a frenzy of belly-button examination that it lasted well into the 1970s and became its own cottage industry. George W. Bush has now created another round of picking through the lint, and it may one day even be argued that no one in history has ever made Canadians see themselves, and their difference, more clearly. It is so often argued that this endless – some might suggest pointless – soul-searching goes on because Canadians, whatever they are, are at the core insecure and lack identity.

But since we are playing here with contradictions, what if this is nothing but a clever ruse? Canadians simply *pretend* to have an identity crisis in order to talk about ourselves, virtually endlessly; that, in fact, there is a smugness and self-righteousness here that plays off wonderfully, and conveniently, against America and is, in many ways, an understandable residue left over from a past of British and French rule and a Loyalist elite. This self-obsession, in fact, could suggest what poet Earle Birney said more than half a century back when he defined Canada as "a high-school land frozen in its adolescence."

Or, it could be something quite apart.

Al Purdy once wrote about visiting Roderick Haig-Brown, the British Columbia judge who considered fly-fishing to be the ultimate court of decision. It was the early 1970s. The two men were sitting in Haig-Brown's Campbell River retreat, and the judge was smoking his pipe, while Purdy was going on and on about the elusive Canadian Identity.

The fly-fishing judge cut him off. "That," he said, "is a question man-ufactured by writers and intellectuals."

I have travelled enough backroads – including the one that leads to Haig-Brown's cabin – to know there is some truth to this. Unless I pose the question, the answer is not even a consideration. People are getting on with defining their lives, not with any unnecessary definition of who they are.

As for the country, it merely defines itself, as it always has. A whole with far too many parts, both in people and places, to ever be regarded as a single, knowable entity.

Kanata, Ontario
Copyright © 2006 by Roy MacGregor

Roy MacGregor
Raised in Huntsville, Ontario, Roy MacGregor is a columnist with the Globe and Mail. *He has covered Canadian politics, culture and sport since the early 1970s. He is also the author of thirty-six books, both fiction and non-fiction, including the internationally successful Screech Owls hockey mystery series for young readers. He lives near Ottawa.*

CHARLOTTE GRAY

A CANADIAN IS ... likely to suffer from historical amnesia. The American writer Edith Wharton once described her country as "a land which has undertaken to get on without a past," but as we embark on the twenty-first century, it seems a more apt portrayal of this country than the United States.

When Canadians are quizzed about our history, our shaky grasp on the past is obvious. Who was Canada's first prime minister? Barely half of those polled in a recent Dominion Institute survey could summon up the name of Sir John A. Macdonald, the canny Kingston lawyer who presided over the creation of Canada in 1867. Which Canadian won the Nobel Peace Prize in 1957? Only one in eight of Canadians knows that our premier peacemaker was Lester Pearson. Dig a little deeper, and we enter the territory of glassy-eyed indifference. Which Shawnee war chief was an important British ally in 1812? Why are the "Famous Five" famous? Ummm ... Dunno.

The good news is that nearly 50% of Canadians *do* know that Sir John A. Macdonald was Canada's first prime minister. The bad news is that a shaky grasp of political history obscures total ignorance of almost any other history – social, cultural, ethnic. We Canadians are such laggardly travellers along highways into the historical hinterland that the twisting byways or dangerous dead ends of the past remain completely unexplored.

Let me cite three examples of the kind of historical curiosities that I love, and that bring our history to life:

- One of the oldest and most eerie British Columbian Native artifacts is the Yuquot Whalers' Shrine, which features whale carvings, puzzling human skulls, and eighty-eight strange, sightless, carved wooden figures. Captain Cook, who was intrigued by its profound mystery and spirituality, was the first person to reveal its existence to non-Natives, in 1788. But no one today really understands who established this weird temple, or what local Nootka chiefs did in it before they led their people on dangerous whale hunts. And for the past century, its power and magic have been entirely suppressed. Since 1904, it has been stored and ignored in a backroom of the American Museum of Natural History on the island of Manhattan.

- One of the first pieces of pornography in North America was published in Montreal in 1836. Maria Monk's *Awful Disclosures of . . . Five Years as a Novice and Two Years as a Black Nun in the Hotel-Dieu Nunnery at Montreal* was a sado-Gothic (and almost certainly fictional) account of sexual corruption in the Roman Catholic Church. More than three hundred thousand copies of this slim but sensational Canadian volume were sold, and it was the all-time American bestseller until 1852, when *Uncle Tom's Cabin* was published.

- One of the greatest, and most lucrative, Canadian innovations of all time was Pablum, developed in the 1930s by researchers at Toronto's Hospital for Sick Children. In the previous decade, around one in six infants died, often as a result of malnutrition or intestinal-tract diseases. Pablum reduced infant mortality rates dramatically because it was a wonder food: easily digested, containing all of the calories required by growing babies, plus iron, copper, and calcium, and vitamins A, B_1, B_2, D and E. One of its most important qualities, noted its inventor, Dr. Fred Tisdall, was that cooking the mush at high temperature destroyed "the insect eggs which are present in all grains." The royalties on worldwide sales of Pablum triggered an explosion of medical research at the hospital.

Maybe these fascinating factoids smack of MacHistory – easily digested nuggets bearing scant relation to the broader themes of our past. When I disinter gems like these from the sludge of "proper" history, I often feel like a jackdaw, attracted to shards of shiny glass. Yet each illustrates an important aspect of Canadian history. The tale of the Yuquot shrine is a vivid example of the way that native peoples have seen their culture dissipated. Maria Monk's *Awful Disclosures* illuminates both the power of the Catholic Church in Quebec, as well as the nineteenth-century obsession with Gothic horrors. The story of Pablum is part of the larger story of Canada's rapid transformation from an impoverished and scattered rural society into a sophisticated urban nation with first-class intellectual institutions.

Other nations incorporate the colourful quirks of their histories into founding mythologies. Americans treasure the image of feasting pilgrim fathers, on which they base their Thanksgiving rituals. The French revel in Marie Antoinette's Diorissima elegance, as she ordained, "Let them eat cake." The Brits enjoy a cornucopia of folklore, whether it is Sir Francis Drake laying his cloak over a puddle for Queen Elizabeth I, or Guy Fawkes setting eighteen hundred pounds of gunpowder under the Houses of Parliament. But Canadians? Laura Secord leading her cow through enemy lines in 1813 is about the only picturesque (and probably false) detail of our history that most of us can summon – and that's largely because a candy manufacturer has kept her name alive. Yet without these details, history becomes a drab social science, lacking the intellectual rigour of economics, the societal insights of sociology or the drama of good literature.

Why is today's Canadian so recklessly indifferent to this country's evolution? All kinds of explanations have recently been offered for our historical amnesia, from bad teaching in high schools to disdain for narrative in universities. There is also the uncomfortable truth that, for thousands of years, there have been vicious power struggles on our continent, featuring ruthless winners and savaged losers, and gallons of spilled blood. Since contemporary Canada prides itself on its feel-good inclusiveness, we seem to have decided that past conflicts are best forgotten. The promise of the 1867 *British North America Act* was "peace, order and good government." Since Confederation, Canada has enjoyed an extraordinary growth in prosperity and civic harmony. As a country, we have made compromise and accommodation a political art form. But we are being Pollyannas if we choose to ignore less salubrious elements in our history that do not fit the "good government" label. We suck the life out of our history when we politely ignore systematic extermination of Native peoples, angry confrontations between French speakers and English speakers, labour riots, suppression of French-Canadian culture and pervasive racism. We also make it boring – and forgettable. No wonder our critics like to scoff that Canada is a sort of "decaffeinated America."

Our historical amnesia is doubly strange in that it is a form of cultural death. Our history is partly what makes Canada unique in the world, distinct from other nations with different populations, traditions, political systems, myths and landscapes. There are plenty of Canadian nationalists today who worry about the gradual erosion of our culture in other fields. Artists, writers and filmmakers lobby fiercely for the preservation of the "Canadian voice," despite the onslaught of American books, films and visual arts. Sadly, they are not always effective – but at least they are making the argument.

However, each generation of artists behaves as though it must reinvent the country from scratch, both to inform its audiences and to justify government subsidies. Ignorant of what went on before, most of our artists cannot draw any sustenance from cultural roots within Canadian soil. In some cases, this is because they or their parents are recent arrivals here. They have been given little opportunity to understand that there is more to Canadian history than a civics lesson in levels of government. But in most cases, people whose families have lived here for generations are equally unaware that our history is a colourful tangle of individual struggles, powerful movements and collective pluck. More than half a century ago, Prime Minister Mackenzie King said, in a much-quoted remark, that Canada had too little history and too much geography. Nothing has changed since he spoke – neither the majesty of the Rockies, nor the Canadian inclination to downplay the history that helps define our distinct identity.

Ottawa, Ontario
Copyright © 2006 by Charlotte Gray

Charlotte Gray

Charlotte Gray is the author of four bestselling books of popular history. She is also an adjunct research professor in history at Carleton University. In

2003, she was awarded the Pierre Berton Medal for distinguished achieve-ment in popularizing Canadian history, and her biography of Pauline Johnson, Flint & Feather, *won the University of British Columbia medal for biography. Her latest books are* The Museum Called Canada *and* Reluctant Genius: The Passions and Inventions of Alexander Graham Bell.

HUGH SEGAL

A CANADIAN IS ... the most fortunate, demanding and indebted person in the world.

Fortunate for the resource wealth, land mass, space and opportunity Canada provides as a common birthright; demanding because of what we expect from ourselves, our society, our allies and neighbours; in debt to a history of sacrifice, determination and service that preserved and built the best for the inheritance we call Canada.

There is a generosity of spirit that keeps us from drawing lines in the sand between competing Canadian histories. The British made room for and institutionalized French Quebec's language, religion, education, and culture after the fall of Quebec in 1759. The *Quebec Act* of 1774 was the opposite of a line in the sand; it was a bridge over European rivalries to a Canada where French and English aspired to better. When the excesses of the American Revolution – excesses around guns and a propensity to violent solutions that can still drive many Canadians away – propelled Empire Loyalists north, the new Canadians would build a responsible democracy that kept both Crown and representative institutions, without one crushing respect for the other. French, English, Irish, and First Nations Canadians stood with British regulars (the Royal Irish among others) to repel American incursions (spurred by "manifest destiny") into Canada during the War of 1812 and issued a firm "no thank you" to absorption by the United States.

The evolution to responsible government and the advent of elected legislatures in Nova Scotia, New Brunswick, Upper and Lower Canada was largely without violence – and only a country as peaceable as Canada would have taken historical note of skirmishes as minor as those accompanying this period of transition.

The good fortune we share is very much a result of who came before, and of how they managed the good fortune they inherited. From the seventeenth century onwards, the sacrifices of First Nations – often imposed upon them by the arriving Europeans – and of those whose pioneering courage shaped the communities and life we call home, created a hard-won culture of good fortune. But this was also very much a culture of demanding more from ourselves and future generations. Sacrifice will do that for those in whose name the sacrifice is made. The men who took Vimy Ridge with a Canadian patch on their shoulder sent a signal for the ages about know-how, can-do, design, planning and leadership. As did their forebears who built the CPR, or the subsequent generations that stormed Juno Beach, took Ortona or liberated the brave Dutch nation. The tradition of punching above your weight, sacrificing for faraway peoples and for down-home principles became part of who we are. We were, in the Second World War, a million under arms for a nation of 11 million: by 1945, ten percent of Canadians armed to engage the enemy, with millions more on the home front supporting those at war.

Demanding Canadians insisted on homes and college opportunities for the returning veterans – and schools, roads, hospitals, and jobs for their children. Today's boomers who demand the best for their ageing parents are the very grandchildren and great-grandchildren of those who confronted Hitler – on land, at sea, and in the air – making sacrifices beyond belief for beliefs that we would not sacrifice. The result became the core of a profound good fortune we owe to the sacrifice of others, and a demanding series of expectations we make of ourselves and our institutions. It is because we demand so much that we are so easily disappointed with the minor institutional failures that any living and multilevel governing tradition will, perforce, yield. Indeed, the pettiness that we often see Canadians embrace – Does the prime minister have a government plane, God protect us, with a shower *and* a cot? Is his limo larger than a Honda Civic? – is really a proxy for the unyielding demands we make of institutions and the people who secure them. We want to be worthy of our elders' sacrifices, and when human failings intervene, as they must, we sometimes exhibit a pettiness that is especially unbecoming of a mature nation's regard for those we choose to govern us.

It is because we are so profoundly not a corrupt society in our private and public institutions that we hyperventilate at even the most modest evidence of malfeasance. This trait is endearing and virtuous – especially because it can be naive and profoundly hopeful – two key parts of being truly demanding and deeply Canadian.

As Canadians, so much of our good fortune was made real by the very ancestors and immigrant parents and grandparents whose individual acts of courage and foresight shaped that fortune. Those two national qualities – courage and foresight – those two compelling shapers of who we are, as common to the suburbs as to the inner cities, define in turn the indebtedness we share as a people. We share a debt to the grandparents and parents who kept us free and emigrated to freedom, so that we might have better lives; a debt to allies and neighbours who partnered our great global battles and anchored a common economic space and opportunity; a debt to those less fortunate among us, whose economic rights we need to respect and make real; a debt to an international stability in which we cannot afford to disinvest: all of those debts define much of who we are in the context of our future.

The sense of obligation and debt, to the past, to allies, to neighbours, is complex. Hence the neuroses about our American neighbours – neuroses that are too much a part of the identity of so many. America is the least imperial of great powers, but because we share debts and obligations to each other, and are dwarfed by all but their land mass and national resources, being Canadian means embracing the angst of envy, often expressed as condescension. There is a reason that George Bernard Shaw chose envy as the worst of the seven deadly sins, because its effect was to deny the sinner any hope of happiness. However fortunate one may be, however wealthy, there is always someone wealthier and more fortunate. For some, this envy and condescension define our view of Americans. But not for all. The hundreds of thousands who lined up to give blood on September 11, 2001, or mourned on Parliament Hill with the American ambassador to Canada, or who opened their homes to stranded and rerouted US-bound passengers in the thousands underlined a generosity of spirit that we cannot suppress. It is who we are at the turn of the century, and not even the small-mindedness of the far right or the institutionalized envy of the far left can diminish that part of our heritage. But the repayment of debts – to less-developed parts of the world (ironically by wiping away mere monetary debts they owe us), by building a more dynamic military and humanitarian deployability, by increasing our development aid on the ground – will be a large part of defining who Canadians are in the decades to come.

At any big city hockey arena early on weekend mornings, you can find pint-sized hockey players, from every race, colour and creed on the planet, desperate to become part of the great Canadian proxy for life itself: hockey. Their passion for the game is at once about team achievement, loyalty, pulling your weight, and assisting or being assisted by others. It is about the transition from local to regional to national to global; it is about the mix between skill and brawn. It is about practice, hard work, good fortune, and demanding more of oneself and one's teammates; it is about how you play, not where your mother and father were born.

Anyone can be a star. Anyone can be a bum. We can be exhilarated and deflated, ostracized or humiliated. The same dynamic takes place on swim teams, on soccer pitches, on tennis courts, and baseball diamonds – but not in the same emotional and visceral way. Watching the mosquitoes or peewees play hockey can be like attending a citizenship court ceremony, except that it is even more emotional.

How we sort our mixed attributes of being fortunate, demanding, and in debt will change by generation and by circumstance – and the proportionality of each will matter.

A Canadian heart is resolute in its fairness and decency, determined in its engagement with those less fortunate, and prone to the selfish and self-centred only when its institutions and leaders aim too low – choosing to pontificate rather than listen and explain.

At the turn of the century, our choices are no less compelling than they were when the Cold War or the First World War grasped at our psyche. Can we be the Canadians who choose to reach over to our own hemisphere to eradicate poverty and make social and economic freedoms determinants of a better future? Can we be the Canadians who face up to a world of economic injustice, and make available the real support that we can offer?

Will we face our own inequities and challenges and embrace First Nations and others outside of the economic mainstream – as fellow travellers in a nation of good fortune? Will we let generosity of spirit and resolve to preserve the best define how we manage diversity and shape a truly integrative citizenship as we build our own tomorrow? Can we build a new nationalism – one rooted in values and interests, and not in anti-Americanism?

I believe that, whomever we elect or criticize, whomever we praise or denigrate, in the end we will embrace the identity of obligation, good fortune and paying back the debt that has brought us this far. I say this because I believe in the essence of the Canadian spirit – a spirit that understands duty and obligation, balances freedom with responsibility, and is unafraid of the joys and burdens of loyalty. Loyalty to the core tolerance and conciliatory framework that made Canada real; loyalty to those who built and shaped this most compelling of multinational countries; loyalty to the values of respect for the law; respect for the heritage we embrace; respect for the democratic principles of fairness and opportunity. And, as has been the case for all our prior generations, deep in the Canadian soul is the burning fire of opportunity: opportunity for personal growth, economic success, social justice, new frontiers – of the planet, of the mind, of knowledge – in the struggle for rights and decency. Engaging that sense of opportunity, doing everything wise to enhance it and realize its benefits for all, doing nothing unwise to diminish or dilute its promise: that is what we expect from ourselves and from our leaders. That is who we are. Sir John A. Macdonald wasn't called "Old Tomorrow" for no reason. He was less than perfect in many ways: he was a bit of a hard-drinking scoundrel, but he was *our* hard-drinking scoundrel; a man who so well reflected who we are and who we would and could become that we trusted him to shape the architecture of a confederation that would itself embrace the diversity, common cause and the superstructure of respect that moves our nation still.

To be Canadian at the dawn of a new century is to embrace the obligation, opportunity, duty and promise of this country and make it our own, while ensuring that the mainstream we share always has room for those less fortunate, among both our fellow citizens and those who would come from afar to build it with us. We eschew complacency but embrace civility. We recoil from hubris but engage with pride. We have no imperial goals but we seek a better world. We are the envy of many and the enemy of few. We owe as much to our future as to our past, and we will always be unkind to those who avoid their debts.

Montreal, Quebec
Copyright © 2006 by Hugh Segal

Hugh Segal

Hugh Segal was appointed to the Canadian Senate in 2005 as a member of the Conservative Party of Canada. He served as president of the Institute for Research on Public Policy (IRPP) from 1999 to 2006. He is a senior fellow at Queen's University, Kingston, and chair of the Walter and Duncan Gordon Foundation. He also sits on various corporate and community service boards. He has authored, co-authored or edited five books on different aspects of politics, policy and public life. Prior to his time at the IRPP, Hugh Segal was chief of staff to Prime Minister Brian Mulroney. He holds an honorary doctorate of laws from the Royal Military College and is a Member of the Order of Canada.

JANET McNAUGHTON

A CANADIAN IS . . . a person whose national history and personal past may have very little overlap.[1] We are, for the most part, a nation of immigrants, of people who cling to this country with shallow roots. Canadian history has no personal connection to me, for example, until the first decades of the twentieth century, when my father's family left Glasgow, Scotland, because skilled carpet weavers were needed for a factory in Guelph, Ontario. The first generation of McNaughtons remained passionately connected to Britain. When the First World War began, my grandfather's older brother, John, enlisted with the 48th Highlanders. He died in the battle of St. Julien in the spring of 1915, a battle so terrible it left no body to recover. He was eighteen. Soon after, my grandfather lied about his age and enlisted. He was sixteen and tall, but he continued to grow throughout the war. Soldiers were not supposed to be growing boys, so he had no excuse to ask for larger boots. By the end of the war, his feet were so deformed that he had to have one toe removed from each foot. A survivor of the battle of Vimy Ridge, he also carried shrapnel to his grave.

While Canadian-born anglophones did enlist to fight in the First World War in greater numbers than their francophone counterparts, the real difference in enlistment was due to the large numbers of British-born immigrants who joined up. Like my great uncle and grandfather, these men were drawn by historical ties so compelling that they were willing to risk their lives for the country of their birth. It has been said that the First World War made Canada a nation. I suspect that fighting in a Canadian battalion alongside British troops may have transformed my grandfather from a British immigrant to a Canadian as well. He never talked about that war, but his loyalty, when I knew him, was to Canada.

At the end of the 1920s, my mother's family, the McIvors, came to Toronto over a period of years. The first immigrants to arrive were my mother's teenage sisters, who were able to gain reduced passage because moneyed Canadians regarded British girls as highly desirable domestic servants. Native-born Canadian girls preferred to work in shops and factories where their employers could not control their lives so completely. In industrial Lanarkshire, where my mother was born, the daughters of most coalminers entered domestic service as soon as they left school, around the age of thirteen. When my mother's oldest sister Jean was dying, her sister Barbara came to visit while I was there. Jean could no longer speak, but Barbara reminisced about the trouble they got into after they left school by going to the local playground when they should have been looking for work.

The Canadian government did not encourage child labour, and girls had to be seventeen before they could come to Canada as domestic servants on the reduced passage program. In 1928, Jean and Barbara were joined by their sister Jenny, who sailed on her seventeenth birthday. The girls had to agree to remain in domestic service for at least three years to repay their reduced passage to Canada. They were paid twenty-five dollars a month. They kept five dollars for spending, and sent the rest home. In October of 1929, my grandparents immigrated to Canada with seven more children, escaping the coal mines that had already claimed the life of their oldest son.

October of 1929 was not the most auspicious time to come to Canada but, in spite of the deprivations of the Depression, Toronto proved to be a better place for the McIvors than Airdrie had been. Even when work was scarce for men, British girls were still in demand as domestic servants and my mother's sisters earned steady, if small, incomes. Jean and Barbara would remain domestic servants for the rest of their working lives, but Canada was already changing the younger girls, making them less willing to accept such a deferential occupation. Although Jenny was seventeen when she arrived, her strong, independent nature had caused her siblings to nickname her "the battleaxe" well before. The new ways of doing things suited her, and she left domestic service as soon as her three years were over. Upward mobility was almost non-existent during the Depression, so the job she took, in a factory woollen mill, hardly seems better by today's standards, but it allowed her to be her own person.

In 1933, when my mother, Isabel, was twelve, her father enforced the old ways on her, and she was made to leave school to become a domestic servant. My mother was an intelligent, sensitive child, who loved learning and had wanted to become a nurse. Unlike most of her older siblings, she lost her Scottish accent and rapidly became indistinguishable from the Canadian children around her. Leaving school at twelve was a terrible blow, made worse by the fact that my grandfather allowed her older sister to continue her education. As a Canadian girl, my mother hated domestic service. In one job, as a "mother's helper," she was required to cater to the whims of a very spoiled child. In another, she was accused of stealing. After she was dismissed in disgrace, the "stolen" money was found in the house. Ontario laws would not allow her to work in a factory until she was sixteen, but she followed her sister Jenny into the Paton and Baldwins wool mill as soon as she could. Eventually, she would train as a bookkeeper and be quite successful, but she always deeply regretted her forced lack of formal education.

So my personal past does not intersect with Canadian history until the twentieth century. In Ontario in the 1960s and 70s, Canadian history was an important part of the curriculum. In a working-class suburb of Toronto, we learned about French-Canadian fur traders, early missionaries, and United Empire Loyalists without ever knowing anyone who could trace their ancestors back to those times and places, and we never gave that a thought. I fell in love with early-nineteenth-century Canada. When I was fifteen, I set my first, unfinished historical novel in the Rebellion of 1837. Later I worked for the Toronto Historical Board in sites that dated to the same era. As the child of recent immigrants, the line between personal past and Canadian history did not exist. As a Canadian, this was my past.

Yet, when I tried to write my first novel as an adult, it was the personal past that drew me. Not the nineteenth century, but the twentieth. Not the pioneers, but the teenaged Scottish domestic servants who sacrificed so much to bring their families to Canada. That first attempt became my second published novel, *To Dance at the Palais Royale*. When I go into schools and libraries across Canada to talk about this book, I see children whose personal pasts connect them to every part of the globe. These children look at someone like me and assume I have always belonged here. But when I talk about my family coming to Canada to escape poverty and create a more hopeful future, I see recognition of a common past.

Coming to Canada presents a unique opportunity to leave behind the old ways that confined and limited children in the past. This is not to say that people must change when they come to this country, but they can if they choose to – and in the case of the children they certainly will. My mother pushed me to do well in school and, although neither of my parents finished high school, I completed a PhD. It is unrealistic to think that immigrants might replace the history of their own countries with Canadian history, but certainly their children will if they are allowed to. Canadian history is, for the most part a mild, civil, bloodless story. We tend to characterize it as boring, without stopping to consider how rare and precious a thing it is on this planet for a country to have a history so peaceful as to be boring. The children who are absorbed into this gentle current of history can leave behind the bitterness and hatred of those other pasts, the suffering that drove their parents or grandparents to make the momentous decision to leave and come to Canada.

A Canadian is, I hope, a person who accepts all other Canadians as equal citizens, regardless of how far they might have travelled to come here, or how recently. A Canadian is a person who knows that our collective future is more important than our divergent pasts.

St. John's, Newfoundland and Labrador
Copyright © 2006 by Janet McNaughton

Notes

[1] While trying to find a topic for this essay, I discovered that a Canadian is, above all, a person who defies generalization. My opening statement will not apply to Native Canadians, most French Canadians (both Acadian and Québécois), United Empire Loyalists, African-Canadians who were brought here as slaves, and probably a few other groups.

Janet McNaughton

Janet McNaughton was born in Toronto, Ontario in 1953. She completed a BA at York University in 1978 and moved to St. John's, Newfoundland, where she did a master's degree and a doctorate in folklore. She has written five young adult novels, ranging from historical fiction to science fiction and fantasy; one junior novel; and one picture book. Her books have won ten awards to date, and have been translated into Dutch, Danish, French, German and Portuguese. She currently serves on the board of the Canadian Children's Book Centre, and is an active member of the Writers' Alliance of Newfoundland and Labrador.

SUJIT CHOUDHRY

A CANADIAN IS . . . a participant in an ongoing constitutional conversation. Our constitutional conversation is rooted in Canada's past. Our past structures and makes intelligible our governing institutions and political practices. It furnishes the symbols and language that equip us to speak to each other about the kind of country we should be. But although the past constrains us, we are not imprisoned by it. Canadians, both old and new, have the right to be the authors of their constitutional future. The changing makeup of our country – our growing ethnic and cultural diversity, increasingly concentrated in our polyglot urban centres – is giving rise to a new constitutional narrative. And this new Canadian constitutional identity may profoundly challenge our prevailing sense of self as a multinational, federal political community in ways we have only just begun to comprehend.

I

The past exerts a powerful hold over Canadian constitutional thought, in two distinct but related ways. The first is the familiar idea that the framers of the Canadian Constitution agreed to a federal constitution for Canada in 1867 in order to further a set of widely understood and shared political objectives. Canada, we teach our children in school from the time they are small, was a union between two founding peoples, English and French. Federalism was a deliberate institutional choice to protect Canada's French-speaking minority from assimilation. Our Constitution recognizes and protects the French fact by creating a province, Quebec, in which French speakers constitute a majority, and by assigning jurisdiction to the provinces over matters integral to the survival of Quebec's "distinct society," such as education, culture, and language. Modern champions of this view of the country, such as Alan Cairns and Will Kymlicka, refer to Canada as a multinational federation. The particular genius of Canadian federalism is the idea that the territorial boundaries and powers of Canada's internal political communities track, accommodate and institutionalize ethnocultural and linguistic differences in order to reconcile unity and diversity within a single nation-state.

The second and somewhat less familiar idea is that court judgments handed down in the late nineteenth and early twentieth centuries define the legal terrain within which governments today exercise their powers under Canada's Constitution. For the first eighty years of Canada's history, our final court of appeal was the Judicial Committee of the Privy Council, which sat in London, England. As with most other constitutional documents, Canada's bracketed disagreement over the respective scope of federal and provincial powers through adopting open-ended constitutional language is open to competing interpretations. It soon fell to the Privy Council to settle disagreements among governments over constitutional meaning. The Privy Council quickly set out a vision of Canada in which the scope of provincial powers was large, the scope of federal powers small, and each level of government was confined to its respective "watertight compartments" of jurisdiction, with no overlap allowed. These interpretive choices were permitted, but not required, by the constitutional text. They therefore reflected the Privy Council's vision of Canada – a country with strong provinces and a weak federal government, in which the provinces had jurisdiction over the major aspects of social and economic policy.

These stories of Canada's constitutional origins and development are often understood as having etched the grooves of our constitutional law and politics, and having preordained the future paths that Canada can take. They are frequently strategically deployed as baselines or benchmarks against which political and legal change is measured. For example, during our recurrent cycles of constitutional introspection, reform proposals such as the Meech Lake and Charlottetown accords were often criticized or supported for departing from or honouring the legal and political architecture of the federation as laid down in the past by politicians and judges.

II

As a constitutional scholar, I have chafed against the hold of the past on our constitutional fate. In doing so, I have drawn upon an established scholarly tradition within the English-Canadian legal academy. The apogee of the Privy Council's decentralist vision of Canada was a series of decisions handed down in the late 1930s, which struck down our version of the New Deal – laws designed to alleviate the social and economic upheaval of the Depression by regulating markets and creating the beginnings of the Canadian welfare state. The academic reaction to these decisions in English Canada was fiercely emotional. Frank Scott, Vince MacDonald, William Kennedy – the giants of Canadian constitutional law in their day – publicly attacked the Privy Council for robbing Canada of the ability to deal effectively and quickly with its pressing social and economic needs. The needed solution was a new court of final appeal, the amendment of the Canadian Constitution, or both. Without these changes, it was thought, Canada could not be a true nation, and would be incapable of controlling its destiny.

As a student reading these articles over a decade ago, I was deeply and profoundly moved. When I teach these materials to my students, I still feel the sense of uncomprehending anger, the bitter disappointment, the rage that jumps off these pages. In anchoring social concern to constitutional analysis, these articles are exemplars of engaged legal scholarship. I often understand my work as a continuation of the constitutional project they launched. The 1930s gave us a new court, but not a new constitution. As a scholar, I've therefore argued for expansive interpretations of the federal government's powers over economic and social policy, in furtherance of a vision of a strong, united Canada – a "community of fate" – of the kind of which the Privy Council deprived Canada during the Depression.

But I have not just taken on the Privy Council's niggardly views on the scope of federal power. I am an ethnic immigrant to Canada, and cannot trace my ancestry to any of Canada's founding nations. Grounding the legitimacy of Canada's constitutional arrangements in a set of historical agreements, compacts and legal texts among ethnic communities to which immigrants cannot trace their ancestry suggests that immigrants enjoy a less than equal status in the Canada of today. These challenges have been raised in a variety of arenas. The mobilization of so-called Third Force Canadians against the Royal Commission on Bilingualism and Biculturalism is a famous example. Another is the debate over the "distinct society" clause in the Meech Lake Accord, and its replacement with the Canada clause in the Charlottetown Accord. And so I have argued that the Canadian Constitution, working from the liberal values of equal dignity and non-discrimination, should not discriminate among different ethnocultural groups on the basis historical priority.

III

Taken together, these commitments sketch a modern stance toward Canada and its constitutional order that treats the past as undeserving of respect simply because of its "pastness." To be legitimate and relevant, Canada's fundamental law should reflect our nation's contemporary needs and sense of self. I am quite confident that I am not alone in holding these views, and that outside of the rarefied confines of the academy, where I spend most of my time, an increasing number of Canadians of my demographic – young, urban, ethnic, immigrant – share them.

But I have also come to appreciate that these positions cut deeply against the grain of much of our way of constitutional thinking, and stand in the way of comprehending and articulating the logic inherent in our constitutional arrangements and political practices.

As is so often the case, I had to leave Canada to grasp this point. My moment of constitutional revelation occurred in Sri Lanka, which I recently visited to participate as a foreign constitutional expert in a series of public presentations on the characteristics of federal forms of government. My suggestion was that the Canadian system of ethnocultural accommodation was a potential model for Sri Lanka to deal with its own ethnic conflict among the Tamils, Sinhalese and Muslims. A common theme in our presentations was the potential desirability of some form of territorial autonomy for the Tamil minority in the northeast of the island, within a united Sri Lanka, analogous to Quebec's position in Canada. In the process of explaining why federalism was a potential solution to Sri Lanka's problems, we were often met with the challenge that federalism in Sri Lanka would set the stage for secession, much as almost occurred in Quebec in 1995, and may yet take place.

As someone who has challenged the according of preferential constitutional treatment for territorially concentrated minorities such as French Canadians, I could have been receptive to these claims. But to my amazement, I found myself making the case for Canadian federalism with gusto, through simultaneous translation into Sinhalese. I argued that Quebec had been created because of the failure of Canada's first experiment in unitary government, the united Province of Canada. For twenty-five years, predominantly French-speaking Lower Canada and English-speaking Upper Canada attempted to live together in a legislative union which ultimately proved unworkable. Indeed, dividing Canada into Ontario and Quebec was the solution to keeping the country together. Far from Quebec posing a threat to Canada's viability, had Quebec not been created in 1867, there would likely be no Canada today.

Over the course of my visit to Sri Lanka, I found myself repeating this argument time and time again. This was one of the most astonishing experiences of my academic career. My own experience tells us something in microcosm about constitutional culture writ large. When citizens live under a constitutional order, we are engaged in highly complex and elaborate social practice. That practice emerges from the concrete political history of a society, a history that explains the origins of our governing institutions, why we have them, and how they operate. In liberal democracies like Canada, when we make constitutions work, we engage in a conversation that uses our shared constitutional culture as a common basis for communication. Engaging in the practice of constitutionalism reinforces these dominant accounts of the purpose and rationale of a constitutional order in the minds of its citizens, even among sceptics like myself. And to depart too far from settled constitutional meanings would be more than just suggesting constitutional change. It would be to step outside the constitutional conversation itself, and be unrecognizable by others as an acceptable constitutional argument.

IV

So are Canadians forever doomed to move along the paths charted by our constitutional past? Can we exercise collective choice about the kind of country we want Canada to become? I think that the answer is yes. Let me first speculate on what the emerging Canadian constitutional narrative might be.

Despite our self-description as a country spread thinly across the vast Canadian expanse, Canada is increasingly becoming a country of city dwellers, due to migration from rural areas and immigration. And the increasing importance of cities has given rise to the "cities agenda." Cities now argue that they require the finances and legal powers to deal with their particular challenges and needs, ranging from social housing and public transportation, to immigrant settlement. We do not understand the implications of the emergence of cities for Canadian federalism. But underlying the cities agenda is a message that strikes at the very heart of Canada's self-understanding. Since Confederation, the national project has been understood to include the building of strong regional communities through the buttressing of provincial capacity. The cities agenda suggests that this interpretation of the nation-building enterprise should be drawn to a close, replaced by a new national project which holds that Canada's prospects in the twenty-first century depend largely on the growth and vibrancy of its principal urban centres. On the legal terrain, this points to a massive redistribution of legal powers, with newly empowered municipalities partnering with a stronger national government, squeezing out provinces in the middle.

The second piece of the new national narrative is Canada's growing ethnic diversity. The impact on federalism of Canada's increasing ethnic diversity and the concentration of that diversity in Canada's urban centres is a question that has largely remained unexplored. My sense is that federalism is in for a bit of a shock, because many recent immigrants do not identify with Canada's self-description as a federal political community.

They have not taken to federalism in the same way that they have embraced other aspects of our constitutional identity, such as rights and the rule of law. The difficulty here is that federalism offers up a conception of the Canadian political community with which immigrants find it difficult to identify. Conventional accounts of which communities Canadian federalism is about – founding nations to which immigrants, for the most part, do not belong – make it difficult for ethnic immigrants to feel that this institutional, constitutional and political project is about them.

The constitutional vision of the New Canada – and the New Canadian – remains incomplete. But in making the case for the New Canada, its proponents must reckon with the dominance and durability of the conventional constitutional perspective, and its entrenchment in our institutions and political practices. The challenge will be to persuade Canadians that the new constitutional narrative is better than the old. And it is the right of all Canadians, both old and new, to engage actively in that national conversation.

Toronto, Ontario
Copyright © 2006 by Sujit Choudhry

Sujit Choudhry

Sujit Choudhry is an associate professor at the University of Toronto's faculty of law, a senior fellow of Massey College, and a member of the University of Toronto Joint Centre for Bioethics. He holds law degrees from the University of Oxford, the University of Toronto, and Harvard Law School. Prior to joining the faculty of law, he served as law clerk to Chief Justice Antonio Lamer of the Supreme Court of Canada. Professor Choudhry's principal research and teaching interests are constitutional law and theory, and health law and policy.

ARITHA VAN HERK

A CANADIAN IS . . . a quiet conundrum, self-abnegating, even mysterious. A Canadian is a believer, committed to this miraculous and impossible country. Attempting to characterize a Canadian is an exercise similar to chasing chimeras, the essence of Canadian so strongly imaginary, almost intangible.

I am a Canadian by birth, born somewhere in the middle of the last century in the middle of a muddy May in central Alberta. I cannot imagine not being Canadian, but I never take the good fortune of my citizenship for granted. My parents are Canadian by choice, and the choice that they dared to make has taught me that "being Canadian" is not so simple a condition. Their progress toward citizenship was one that, like many journeys, required determination, hard work and sheer luck – those accidents that together comprise any life's pilgrimage.

In my parents' childhood in the Netherlands, some eighty years ago, "Canada" was a vague reference, a country full of scenery and wildlife, mysterious and elemental, home to the fabled Indians. They knew of a few people who had immigrated to Canada at the turn of the century, but their departure and disappearance were folkloric and inexplicable; what had happened to them was a mystery. Home was the flatlands of Holland, green short winters, Holstein cattle, and bicycles that perambulated along the sandy roads. But that orderly calm would change with the cataclysm of the Second World War, tearing apart the fabric of peace.

My father, who had served in the army, was called up to defend his country in the face of Hitler's invasion, but as history already knows, the small Dutch army was defeated in mere days, and Holland capitulated. The years that followed were hard ones. My father survived the military defeat, and he and my mother married so that he would not be sent to work in the munitions factories in Germany. But life in occupied Holland was hellish, not only because of the oppression of living under an occupying force, but because of the sheer challenge of day-to-day survival. As the war progressed, food and other goods grew scarcer and scarcer, and starvation became the primary enemy. My parents supported the Resistance, but knew little except that the Allies were working to liberate them; that British, Canadian and, later, American soldiers were fighting on their behalf. But it was a long, miserable war, and simply trying to survive, trying to help others, and trying to feed their small children made my parents acutely aware of the slender thread of existence.

By the spring of 1945, although the war was almost over, it seemed the war would never end. The first Canadian my family encountered has become a myth of its own: a tall, well-fed, good-looking soldier who swung down from his tank on the verge of the road in front of my parents' farm. My oldest brother had been told not to play in the road, not to stray too far away, but tanks are irresistible to small boys, and of course he wanted to see their lumbering progress. He couldn't understand the words of the tall soldier who smiled at him and held out his hand and said, "Hey, kid, here's a chocolate bar." The soldier climbed back up, waved, and vanished. He probably made it home to Canada.

My brother took the chocolate bar inside to my mother and said, "Look. A soldier gave me a stick."

My mother started to cry. "It's good," she said. "You can eat it." My brother was almost five, and he had never had a bite of chocolate.

Canadian soldiers liberated Holland. Canadians swung into that small and broken country bringing their energy and engagement – large, laughing men who had chocolate and white bread and energy to spare, even though they were tired and homesick themselves.

They shook their heads at my father's small farm, and said to him, using that universal mixture of hand signals and scattered words, "What are you doing here in this tiny country? We have a lot more space. Come to Canada – it's much better for farmers there."·

Canada. It was a mantra of tantalizing wealth, size, and mystery. Canada, where it seemed that dreams might have a chance of fulfillment.

Canada, far away from the anxious tensions of Europe, of terrible conflict, of hunger and privation.

The immigration offices that sprang up after the war came out of a mutual agreement. The Netherlands was a devastated country, worried about supporting its population; because there were so few resources, they encouraged emigration, while Canada, seeing a horizon of development, was eager to embrace a new wave of immigrants.

My parents went to meetings about Canada, watched films that depicted a Canada of wealth and bounty. They saw pictures of prosperity, huge fields being harvested by five combines in a row! To a farmer, that looked like nirvana, and so my parents decided to uproot themselves and their by-then three children, and set out to become Canadians.

But it is hard to become a Canadian. A Canadian is someone whose love for Canada must always live beside an old and ineradicable yearning for another, earlier home.

The journey to becoming a Canadian is full of turns and twists. For my parents, getting immigration approval was only an initial aspect of this transformation. What they did not anticipate was the adversity they would face, their homesickness, the sheer physical difficulty of their lives, the work they would do. The voyage by ship was easy (except for my mother, who suffered terribly from seasickness), and in Halifax, at Pier 21, Canadian immigration officials were kind and helpful. Every child got a present, and best of all, they could all have a bath, get properly cleaned up.

But then my family boarded the train, which took them across the country, all the way to Wainwright, Alberta, a journey of some five days, sitting and sleeping upright on hard benches, the other immigrants with them mostly Ukrainian women going to join their husbands on the prairies. My mother still talks about how rough that trip was, especially because my brother was sick. When the train stopped, one of the men would disembark to fetch milk and bread, and that was what they ate.

My parents had been guaranteed work and a place to live, a roof over their heads and a chance to start again. But the misery that they confronted was difficult to reconcile. A Canadian can be nasty and exploitative: a Canadian paid my father and mother $60 a month for their combined labour, while he paid his "Canadian" hired man $145 a month. A Canadian put my parents and their three children in a house that was really a granary. The winter of 1949 was terribly cold, and my parents were completely unprepared, didn't have the right clothes for the weather, and were shocked at Canadian profligacy. My father would go to the base in Wainwright to pick up what the military kitchen there threw away for pig food. He couldn't believe his eyes. Canadian pigs ate far better than the people of Holland had all through the war.

But my parents persevered. They worked hard, day and night. They learned English from my brother and sister's grade school readers. They milked cows and sold eggs, and scratched together enough money to buy a farm of their own. There was nothing to do but trust Canadians and hope for the best; my parents never knew whether they would be kind or not. And Canadians were both kind and unkind, as representative of human nature as anywhere else.

I was the first Canadian in the family, born in May of 1954 in Wetaskiwin, Alberta. I knew I was Canadian from my first breath of parkland air, my earliest glimpse of light. And my formerly Dutch parents and two brothers and one sister followed only a few months later, standing in front of a Canadian judge to declare their allegiance to their new home, so harsh and so embracing. A Canadian is an immigrant with hope; a Canadian is a person who sticks out the hard times; a Canadian is someone who believes in the future. A Canadian is a person who chooses Canada, who adopts whatever this nation offers, and accepts its challenges.

I have asked my parents if they had regrets, and they are adamant that they do not. "We were lucky," they tell me. "It was tough to break apart our life, to start again, and in some ways, we were young and stupid. But we never felt sorry. We are lucky."

My parents were cited as examples of what postwar immigrants could do – pulling themselves up by their bootstraps, learning English, working unceasingly, pushing their children toward good educations. Ideal Canadians who came to love Canada passionately. My father died in the spring of 2004, at eighty-nine. When I said my last goodbye to him, I was not surprised that even in his coffin he wore a pin of the Canadian flag in his lapel. He was buried with it; he was a proud Canadian.

A Canadian, then, is a stranger in a strange land, ready to adopt new ways, eager to embrace potential.

But this definition is too simple, an uncomplicated conclusion derived from the myriad of other moments that contribute to the Canadian. For although I am a Canadian, I have never been able to figure out – not quite – who I am. And that too is part of being a Canadian.

And so, that is the question, the question we live with day to day, our quiet conundrum. What is a Canadian? And have you ever met an interesting Canadian? A Canadian is part of a jigsaw puzzle, always trying to find that one missing piece that has fallen behind the wainscoting. We search for ourselves in unlikely places: the rocky east coast of Newfoundland; the sere edge of the Arctic Ocean, a segue to ice; the Pacific coast mild with mist. These borders outline our geography, yes, but a Canadian intent on occupying that geography reads its dimensions in a landscape that is itself a chameleonic force. A Canadian is snow- and wind-resistant, as familiar with tundra as with paved streets.

A Canadian follows a wandering trail of desire in search of home and its opposite. A Canadian looks for pay dirt, but will settle for some scenery, a good wood fire, a patch of ground that can grow carrots and potatoes. No lofty ambitions, just winter vegetables and the stakes of summer tomatoes, with a few sweet peas for beauty. A Canadian, too, is a diehard and dexterous regionalist, a local booster intensely loyal to locality, while still practising a pragmatic nationalism. We are ambivalent nationalists and ardent regionalists, sympathetic to underdogs. We are keepers of a painful democracy, doubtful but determined. We keep checklists and balance sheets; we attend public panel discussions; we are respectful of metronomes, clock-wise and space-foolish. A Canadian is a light sleeper, fond of sheets dried on a laundry line outside, happy to smell the Chinook wind blowing in from the west. A Canadian is a schoolyard swarming with children, an enigmatic snow angel semaphored in a snowy field. A Canadian is no empire-builder, but a contented occupant of a suburban plot, a lakeside cottage, a swell of sky that geese fill with their farewell honking. We are Marco Polos of a large country, impassable, daunting in distance, but somehow intimate.

We are, for all our diversity, a collective, more than we are individuals. A Canadian works within a group rather than alone, and despite the resistant environment, will demonstrate a dry and wintry sense of humour. We tend to be watchful rather than passionate, fond of our small part in history, despite our size; quietly robust, postulant rather than aggressor, an escort more than an official, booksellers and introducers rather than stars. Stewards and breadmakers and butter churners, we practise the small but essential arts of being. We are the conductor on the train, the footman holding a coat. We are the long-forgotten school-teachers and the buckets that make sandcastles. We are the refill inside a ballpoint pen, the zipper that holds a coat together, the pawns that bring about checkmate. We are pawky rather than stylish, soft-spoken but persuasive for all that. We are season-ticket holders, and we mark garbage collection day on our calendars – innocent practical jokers, fond of park benches on cold hillsides. Neither adulterers nor moneylenders, we have an aptitude for faithfulness, practise a kindly humour, and are long-suffering and actuarial rather than risk-taking. But not so cautious as never to throw caution to the wind; rather, cautious is as cautious does, temperamentally unfit for the tango or the trombone, but easy in a kilt, easier still in a parka.

A Canadian is a keeper of impermanence on a base of permafrost, workmanlike rather than flamboyant, without the closetfuls of designer shoes that express personality; no soapbox for him or her, but a neat little footstool and a discreet lapel microphone. Happy with insignificance, we revel in our size, certain that because we are so wildly unembraceable, we must be desirable. A Canadian knows how to romance tundra, to seduce a rock. We are always interested in maps and topographies, but even our permanent committee on geographical names is trumped by the weather, our nemesis and namesake, our pride and joy, our adversary and killer and exhilaration and delight. After an ice storm, we marvel at the intricate beauty of the carvings. After a tornado, we pick up the pieces.

We are denizens of this sprawling, uncontainable country, fragmented by water and geology, and yet strangely cohesive. Canadian Brass, without knuckles. A Canadian is, at a party, the one with the ice-breaker, the

pickaxe, the one lacing up her skates. We are mysterious strangers to ourselves, full of a perverse disquiet, comfortable dissatisfaction. And for all
this retirement, this shuffle and graze, a Canadian is the one you want with
you when you have the flu, when you are afraid of the dark, when you need
to know about the habits of bears. A Canadian will thaw out a story in a
frying pan, then flood the backyard with the garden hose, make the world
one small skating rink. And we're not all good. We too cheat on our taxes,
tamper with mail, listen to cowboy songs, although we never draw our
weapons, preferring the roundabout way, diplomacy and boredom. We
can rubadubdub to death anyone who wants to have a fiery argument.
We'll appoint a royal commission just to keep matters in slow motion.

A Canadian is someone who wants to curl around what is already
there, the fire in the hearth, the trees on the land, the shape of a hill.
Canadians are cool, never hot; we keep a polite distance from ourselves
and one another – the intervention of ice. What do we do with passion?
We worry about it, arm's length. Kissing a Canadian is a complex undertaking, rather like learning to dance in the dark. We are diffident, reserved,
unfunny, although that makes us hilarious straight men, comics to the rest
of the world. The passion for order in our muskeg hearts shines a frangi-
ble beauty. And so we recite a hybrid xenogamy, a mythical monster,
Canada part-husky, part-grizzly, part-coyote, part-moose. But whole for
all that, impatient, immunized and imperfect. A Canadian is the silent hush
after a snowfall, before there are tracks. We wait. We watch. We listen.

Where am I writing from? Calgary, Alberta, as bellicose and breezy as
a bronco barroom. And I am a Canadian.

Calgary, Alberta
Copyright © 2006 by Aritha van Herk

Aritha van Herk

*Born in central Alberta, Aritha van Herk is an award-winning Canadian
novelist whose books include* Judith, The Tent Peg, No Fixed Address: An
Amorous Journey *(which earned a nomination for the Governor General's
Award for Fiction),* Places Far from Ellesmere, *and* Restlessness. *She has*

also published two books of fictocriticism and a history of Alberta. An active public intellectual who provides frequent commentary on contemporary literature and on Alberta regionalism, van Herk also works as an advocate for reading and writing. Her creative and critical work has been widely published and has been translated into ten languages.

L. YVES FORTIER

UN CANADIEN EST ... avant tout un disciple de Lester B. Pearson, l'architecte des Bérets Bleus à qui l'on a décerné le Prix Nobel de la Paix. Un Canadien est un médiateur par excellence dont l'impartialité lui vaut d'être invité à régler les conflits les plus difficiles sur la planète. Un Canadien est un diplomate qui est engagé à part entière au sein d'organisations internationales, telles l'ONU, dont il veut voir accomplir leurs objectifs.

Je me souviendrai toujours de ma première rencontre avec le Secrétaire Général des Nations Unies à l'époque, S.E. Javier Perez de Cuellar. Nouvel Ambassadeur, j'arrivais à New York en septembre 1988 et je devais présenter mes lettres de créance au Secrétaire Général. Je fus accueilli très chaleureusement par ce haut personnage qui, durant tout mon mandat, devint un ami et un allié fidèle.

Après la cérémonie formelle et très protocolaire, le Secrétaire Général invite le nouveau diplomate accrédité auprès de l'Organisation à sabler le champagne dans son cabinet à l'occasion d'un tête-à-tête. Coupe à la main, le Secrétaire Général me confie que lorsqu'il est appelé à donner en exemple le pays qui, à tous égards, contribue le plus à l'ONU, invariablement, il cite le Canada comme modèle.

Grisé beaucoup plus par ce commentaire que par la coupe de champagne que j'ai bue, je rentre à ma Mission particulièrement fier d'être Canadien et en me «pétant les bretelles». J'échange avec mes collaborateurs qui, contrairement à moi, sont tous diplomates de carrière, et, à l'unanimité, ils se déclarent aucunement surpris par les propos si élogieux envers le Canada que le Secrétaire Général m'avait tenus quelques heures plus tôt. Quant à moi, je demeurais cependant un peu sceptique et très curieux. Je pensais qu'il devait dire précisément la même chose à presque tous les nouveaux Représentants Permanents à l'occasion de la remise de leurs lettres de créance.

À l'automne 1988, à New York, le Canada était l'un des pays qui briguait les suffrages pour un siège de deux ans au Conseil de Sécurité de l'ONU. Je savais évidemment que le Conseil de Sécurité était l'instance décisionnelle la plus importante des Nations Unies. Ses décisions lient les États membres et il jouit d'une autorité et d'un prestige exceptionnels sur la scène internationale. Être élu membre non permanent du Conseil permet à un pays d'entrer au cénacle des cénacles de l'ONU.

Pendant deux mois, je m'évertue donc à mousser la candidature du Canada à New York auprès des missions des autres États membres de l'Organisation. Dans toutes les officines de mes nouveaux collègues, la plupart de carrière, je reçois un accueil chaleureux et encourageant. J'entends, à toutes fins pratiques, des échos du discours que m'a tenu le Secrétaire Général lors de la remise de mes lettres de créance.

Je résume ces propos comme suit:

- «Le Canada et les Canadiens sont nos amis.
- C'est surtout par altruisme que le Canada appuie les Nations Unies.
- On peut toujours compter sur le Canada lorsqu'un problème survient qui requiert une solution négociée et non pas un «diktat».
- Le Canada est certes allié des grandes puissances, telles les États-Unis, la France et le Royaume-Uni, mais il est aussi membre de ma «gang»: la Francophonie pour plusieurs, le Commonwealth pour bien des pays, l'OEA pour d'autres et ainsi de suite.
- Monsieur l'Ambassadeur, le Canada peut compter sur l'appui de mon pays aux prochaines élections.
- Mon gouvernement veut voir le Canada siéger au Conseil de Sécurité à titre de membre non permanent».

Et, effectivement, fin novembre 1988, à la suite d'un scrutin à l'Assemblée Générale de l'ONU, le Canada est élu au Conseil de Sécurité de l'ONU avec la plus importante majorité que tout autre pays ait jamais recueilli depuis l'adoption de la Charte à San Francisco en 1945.

Durant les trois années qui ont suivi, maintes et maintes fois, tant au Conseil de Sécurité que dans d'autres instances onusiennes, telles l'UNICEF, le PNUD et combien d'autres, j'ai été à même de constater que Perez de Cuellar avait dit vrai. Les diplomates canadiens étaient de toutes les tribunes onusiennes et multipliaient les interventions. De Chypre à la Namibie, sans oublier la présidence du premier sommet de l'enfance, le Canada était toujours appelé à servir. Et il répondait toujours: oui.

Je déplore que les faits d'armes des diplomates canadiens de carrière ne soient pas mieux connus chez nous. Ces Canadiens nous font honneur. Ces disciples de Lester B. Pearson sont des internationalistes chevronnés. Ce sont de vrais professionnels que ces hommes et femmes que j'ai eu le privilège et l'insigne honneur de côtoyer pendant près de quatre ans et de voir à l'oeuvre quotidiennement.

La tradition diplomatique canadienne veut qu'à la fin de son mandat, le chef de mission livre au ministère à Ottawa le bilan de son séjour et ses recommandations pour les années à venir. En 1992, alors que je me préparais à rentrer à Montréal pour reprendre la pratique du droit, j'étais venu à la conclusion que le Canada ne moussait pas suffisamment la candidature de Canadiens à des postes de commande sur l'échiquier international. Selon moi, contrairement à d'autres pays qui contribuent eux aussi au bon fonctionnement de l'ONU, l'OTAN et d'autres organisations internationales, tels les Pays-Bas, la Suède, la Norvège, la Nouvelle-Zélande – pour ne nommer que ces quatre-là – nos diplomates qui accèdent à des postes de commande n'étaient pas assez nombreux. Et pourtant, comme je l'ai souligné plus haut, nos diplomates canadiens sont exceptionnels. J'étais d'avis que le Canada n'était pas assez gourmand. Cette fausse modestie fait peut-être partie de notre culture!

L'essentiel de mon message à Ottawa était clair: j'étais d'avis que le Canada devait mousser plus agressivement la candidature de Canadiens et Canadiennes qui nous représenteraient à New York, Genève, La Haye, Paris et ailleurs et mettraient ainsi en exergue les talents de nombreux Canadiens.

Même si je ne veux surtout pas en revendiquer la seule paternité, j'ai été particulièrement heureux d'apprendre ces dernières années la nomination de brillants diplomates canadiens à des postes de commande fort prestigieux au sein d'organisations internationales. Enfin, me suis-je dit, les Canadiens vont savoir que plusieurs de leurs fonctionnaires se démarquent vraiment de leurs collègues d'autres pays.

Je pense, entre autres, aux nominations de mon amie Louise Fréchette, comme Vice-Secrétaire générale de l'ONU; de mon collègue Philippe Kirsch, comme Président de la Cour pénale internationale; de ma consoeur Louise Arbour, d'abord comme Procureure en chef du Tribunal pénal international pour l'ex-Yougoslavie et le Rwanda et, plus récemment, à l'ONU comme Haut commissaire aux droits de l'homme; de mon confrère de classe Don Johnston, comme Secrétaire général de l'OCDE; du vénérable Maurice Strong, doyen des internationalistes canadiens, comme conseiller du Président de la Banque Mondiale et du Secrétaire général des Nations Unies; du distingué Général Raymond Hénault, comme premier militaire de l'OTAN; et combien d'autres Canadiens et Canadiennes qui figurent maintenant au palmarès des plus importantes institutions multilatérales. Je suis fier de mes compatriotes dont tous les Canadiens peuvent suivre les faits d'armes dans les médias.

Certes, le Canadien, selon la perspective de chaque personne qui contribue à ce recueil, affiche de nombreuses qualités. Il est polyvalent mais, pour moi, après l'expérience si enrichissante et fascinante que j'ai vécue à New York il y a bientôt 15 ans, un Canadien est d'abord un citoyen du monde. A l'époque où les frontières entre pays s'amenuisent et la mondialisation nous envahit, c'est par sa participation aux hautes instances internationales et sa contribution aux dossiers qui ne reconnaissent pas de frontières que le Canadien se démarque. Je souhaite que ces qualités d'internationaliste soient reconnues et appréciées ici, *a mari usque ad mare.*

Montréal, Québec
Copyright © 2006 by L. Yves Fortier

L. YVES FORTIER

A CANADIAN IS ... first of all a disciple of Lester B. Pearson, the founder of the Blue Berets who was awarded the Nobel Peace Prize. A Canadian is a mediator par excellence whose impartiality qualifies him to oversee the most difficult conflicts on the face of the earth. A Canadian is a diplomat fully engaged at the heart of international organizations such as the UN, and someone who wants to see those organizations succeed.

I will always remember my first meeting with the secretary-general of the UN at the time, S.E. Javier Perez de Cuellar. I had just arrived in New York in September 1988, as our new ambassador to the UN, and I had to present my formal credentials to the secretary-general. I was very warmly received by this august figure who, in the course of my time in office, was to become a trusted ally and a friend.

After the very formal ceremony, the secretary-general usually invites the newly accredited diplomat to come and drink some champagne privately with him in his office, where they can chat. Glass in hand, the secretary-general confided in me that whenever he was asked to give an example of a country that, in every way, makes the greatest contribution to the UN, invariably he named Canada.

Much more intoxicated by these words than by the glass of champagne that I had drunk, I returned to my mission especially proud of being Canadian, so that I was almost "busting my britches." I talked about it with my colleagues, all (unlike me) career diplomats, and every single one expressed a total lack of surprise about the very kind things that the secretary-general had said to me about Canada a few hours earlier. As for me, I must confess that I was still a little sceptical, and very curious. I thought that he must say precisely the same thing to all of the incoming permanent representatives when they presented their accreditation documents.

In the fall of 1988 in New York, Canada was one of the countries soliciting votes for a seat on the UN Security Council for two years. Obviously, I was well aware that the Security Council was the most important decision-making body at the UN. Its decisions are binding on the member states and it enjoys an authority and a prestige that are exceptional on the international scene. To be elected a non-permanent member of the Council allowed a country to enter the innermost circle of the UN.

For two months I worked hard to round up votes for Canada among the missions of the other member states. In all the missions of my new colleagues, most of them career diplomats, I received a warm and encouraging welcome. What I heard, in effect, were echoes of what the secretary-general had told me when I presented my credentials.

I could summarize these remarks as follows:

- "Canada and Canadians are our friends. It's above all for altruistic reasons that Canada supports the UN."
- "You can always count on Canada when a problem crops up that requires a negotiated solution as opposed to a firm diktat."
- "Canada may be an ally of the great powers, like the USA, France, and the UK, but it is also a member of 'my gang': the Francophonie for some, the Commonwealth for quite a few countries, and the Organization of American States (OAS) for others, and so on."
- "Mr. Ambassador, Canada can count on my country's support in the next elections."
- "My government would like to see Canada seated on the Security Council as a non-permanent member."

And, as it came to pass, at the end of November after a vote by the General Assembly of the UN, Canada was elected to the Security Council with the greatest majority that any country had ever received since the adoption of the United Nations Charter in San Francisco in 1945.

During the next three years, on countless occasions, in the Security Council as well as in other important UN organizations such as UNICEF and the UNDP (United Nations Development Program), I saw for myself that Perez de Cuellar had told me the truth. Canadian diplomats were involved in all of the important bodies, and very actively involved. From Cyprus to Namibia, without forgetting our role in chairing the first Summit for Children, Canada was always called upon to serve. And always answered yes.

I think it highly regrettable that these great achievements by our professional diplomats are not better known at home. These Canadians bring us great honour. These Pearsonian disciples are international workers who have earned their stripes. These are the real professionals, these men and women that I had the privilege and honour of serving alongside for nearly four years, during which I saw them in action every day.

Canadian diplomatic tradition requires that at the end of his posting the head of the mission delivers to the minister in Ottawa an assessment of his time in office, along with his recommendations for future years. In 1992, when I was getting ready to return to Montreal to resume my life as a lawyer, I came to the conclusion that Canada did not lobby hard enough to back Canadian candidates for important posts on the international scene. In my view, unlike those other countries that also contributed to the smooth functioning of the UN, NATO, and other international organizations – such as the Netherlands, Sweden, Norway, and New Zealand, to name only four – the number of our diplomats reaching high office was not large enough. This despite the fact that, as I have stressed earlier, our diplomats are exceptionally good. I came to the conclusion that Canada was not greedy enough. This sort of harmful modesty is perhaps a part of our culture.

The gist of my message to Ottawa was clear; I was certain that Canada had to push more aggressively the candidacy of the Canadian men and women who would represent us in New York, Geneva, The Hague, Paris, and elsewhere, thus putting into play the talents of many Canadians.

Even if I have no wish to claim the sole paternity, I was especially pleased to note during these last few years the accession of brilliant Canadian diplomats to prestigious leadership roles at the heart of international organizations. At last, I told myself, Canadians are going to be aware that several of their officials are really rising above their colleagues from other countries.

I am thinking – among others – of the nominations of my friend Louise Fréchette, as deputy secretary-general of the UN (now retired); of my colleague Philippe Kirsh as president of the International Criminal Court; of my sister-in-arms Louise Arbour, first as a chief prosecutor of the International Criminal Court for the former Yugoslavia and Rwanda, and more recently, as the United Nations High Commissioner for Human Rights; of my classmate Don Johnston as secretary-general of the Organization for Economic Co-operation and Development (OECD); of the venerable Maurice Strong, dean of Canadian internationalists as adviser to the president of the World Bank and to the secretary-general of the UN; of the distinguished General Hénault, as the leading military officer of NATO; and so many other Canadian men and women who are to be found high up among the most important multilateral institutions. I am proud of my fellow Canadians, whose achievements can be followed in the media by their compatriots.

According to the perspective of every writer who contributes to this collection, the Canadian has many different qualities. He is versatile, but for me, after my enriching and fascinating experience in New York fifteen years ago, a Canadian is first and foremost a citizen of the world. At a time when the borders between countries are eroding and globalization is overtaking us, it is by its participation in high-level international matters and in its contribution to problems that do not recognize borders that Canada makes its mark. I hope that these international qualities will be recognized and appreciated here, *a mari usque ad mare.*

Montreal, Quebec
Translation copyright © 2006 by Douglas M. Gibson

L. Yves Fortier

L. Yves Fortier is chairman of the law firm Ogilvy Renault. Considered one of the world's leading arbitrators, he has pleaded important cases before all court jurisdictions in Canada, as well as before domestic and international arbitration tribunals. From 1988 to 1992, he was Canada's ambassador and permanent representative to the United Nations. He is a former president of the London Court of International Arbitration.

CATHERINE FORD

A CANADIAN IS . . . a citizen of the world without ever having to leave home. In just over a dozen words, that encapsulates the positive reality of being Canadian. Here we live at the top of North America, citizens of a huge country with a small population of just over thirty-two million people, including about four million "visible minorities," most of us within three hundred kilometres of the most powerful nation in the world. Yet we maintain, despite the critics, a unique nation.

It is Canada's treatment of newcomers that contributes most heavily to the mosaic of race, creed, class and culture. The philosophic of mind would say we are all newcomers, but within the last two generations, the living portrait of Canada has changed. Those four million visible minorities, in the ethnocultural picture of this country as drawn by Statistics Canada, include those thousands upon thousands of Canadians whose heritage from the United Kingdom, Europe, Scandinavia, Central and South America, and the United States allows them to pass unnoticed on any city street. Canada is a Heinz 57 country. We are all the better for it.

A Canadian is someone who believes there is nothing unusual about eating a British breakfast of kippers and eggs, a Japanese noodle lunch and an Indian vindaloo dinner. Multiculturalism has made it possible for us to drink American beer, Scotch whiskey, French bottled water and South African wine. We sleep on Egyptian cotton sheets in Taiwanese-made pajamas. In merely looking at this broad global picture, we might be tempted to overlook what all this really means: that, curiously enough, all of this globalization has made many of us more Canadian than ever.

Despite its detractors, multiculturalism works. When Prime Minister Pierre Trudeau told the House of Commons in 1971 that his government was adopting the recommendations of the Royal Commission on Bilingualism and Biculturalism, he said: "A policy of multiculturalism within a bilingual framework recommends itself to the government as the most suitable means of assuring the cultural freedom of Canadians." He did not say that multiculturalism would ensure the freedom of South Americans or Pakistanis or Chinese. He did not guarantee the supremacy of French or English, but used the two solitudes of this country as a frame large enough to encompass all the realities of Canada. Trudeau talked about ensuring cultural freedom for all Canadians. It is a unique concept in a fractious world, that it is possible to be a Canadian and retain another heritage; a Canadian and wear the hijab; a Canadian and a visible minority. That is the simple beauty of Canada.

Yet, Pollyanna doesn't live here any more. It is clear that many Canadians do not understand or appreciate the complexity that has been made possible within the borders of this country without arguing for a kind of assimilation. In doing so, they disregard the lie their own actions offer: All over the country, Scottish bagpipes lead in the head table of formal dinners without a whisper of complaint; rugby and soccer are common sights on Canadian schoolyards, the latter reaching the popularity of hockey, due to its less expensive demands for equipment and playing room; recreating six-gun shootouts (without injury or bullets) at the Calgary Stampede and at Calgary's Heritage Park is part of the fun, although not a real part of the Canadian west. Ukrainian, Scandinavian and Greek celebrations of Christmas do not jibe with the Canadian calendar, yet there are no voices of disapproval. We make no complaints about these "foreign" culture events. They are part of the Canadian ethnic landscape, as are the cultural celebrations and mores of more "visible" citizens from another country.

Multiculturalism makes us more sensitive to the ways of others, while it presents the problem of relinquishing the stranglehold of "white" culture on public events. Still, a Canadian tries to accommodate the differences. Why? Because we must do so to preserve what is unique about being Canadian. This Canadian garden, as late prime minister John Diefenbaker said of Canada's policies and attitudes toward immigration, takes the best and the hardiest of everything immigrants bring to the country, finds room and lets them thrive.

The challenge of being Canadian means more work than, for example, being American. We have to think about it; they merely live with their nationality and citizenship. Americanism is overt, proud and public: salute the Stars and Stripes, recite the Pledge of Allegiance, fly the flag in front of your home and on all public buildings. Canadianism, although the very word looks and sounds strange, is no less proud, albeit considerably less overt and public. No Canadian is asked to pledge allegiance to the Crown, with few exceptions: the ceremony granting landed immigrants their citizenship being the most notable and, if truth be told, capable of squeezing tears from the most unsentimental Canadian.

We no longer ritually sing "God Save the Queen," and "O Canada" is trotted out to be sung in unison rarely. (Hockey games don't count, although I confess to pride whenever the Stanley Cup is played between and American team and a Canadian one and both anthems are sung.) I believe this reticence to wear one's maple leaf on one's sleeve, regardless of the ubiquitous Tim Hortons ads, makes Canadians more, rather than less, aware of their citizenship.

A Canadian is a citizen of a country that is too big to be contained in one reality: what do the northern Inuit have in common with the farmers of southwestern Ontario? What are the common denominators between the fruit orchards of the British Columbia interior and the fishing villages of Newfoundland and Labrador? There may, in reality, be only one denominator: we recognize that we are all Canadians, albeit separated by regional differences and united in a combined loathing of Toronto's centre-of-the-universe mindset. (Okay, okay, just kidding.) Within that jibe, though, is the dichotomy that is Canada and Canadianism. It is sometimes impossible to define this country without seeking negative comparisons – the most fatuous, if famous, of which is that we are *not* Americans. Since Canadians seem to derive a certain amount of smug satisfaction from comparing themselves, they believe favourably, to Americans, it is fair to say that Canadians recognize the unique qualities of whatever culture they are born into without feeling the need to render it down like so much collected bacon fat, into the melting pot that accurately describes America.

It is how and what we share with each other that make sense, not some philosophical knee-jerk patriotism that at its heart is empty, for all its stirring words. It is actions that count, not words.

In provinces such as Alberta – okay, maybe there is no other province quite like Alberta – that understanding is turned on its head. Perhaps it's so because the largest single – and invisible – minority in cities like Calgary, in which I live, is American. The pull toward our neighbours to the south is strong and compelling. But separation from the greater part of Canada is, and always will be, nothing more than a threat. Indeed, for all the regional differences, even in Alberta we are Canadian first. Sometimes fractious, sometimes angry and discontented, but always Canadian.

The geographic pull may be along a north-south axis, but the heart leans east and west. Even in Alberta, it is important to identify ourselves as Canadian first – despite those who would reject that identification because of regional discontent. Being Canadian first is an important concept because the act of self-identification plays such an important role in how we look at ourselves, at our country and at our affiliations. It is never more important than in today's global village, which invites our children to pay no regard to physical boundaries.

To a student today, the reality of being wired into a chat group coming out of China or Germany – or more likely Oregon or California – can be greater and more fulfilling than anything in his or her own neighbourhood; certainly more than a concept of what it is to be Canadian. Their temptation will be to see themselves as citizens of a global village, as people who can surf the net for information, friends and relationships in Sydney or Johannesburg, but can't find Regina with a road map – and worse, don't care. Our challenge is to show them how being Canadian helps them in their search for identity in that vast network of competing interests. If nothing more, a secure sense of place helps young people understand that there are – to paraphrase the Bible – many rooms in the mansion of citizenship. A Canadian is someone with a key to many more than the one marked North America.

The first challenge is to understand that the differences between

Canadians and Americans – two people separated by a common language – can be as basic as how we define patriotism. Patriotism is a tough word and even tougher challenge, as a concept, in a country such as Canada. It is a touch of long-remembered British heritage that makes Canadians squirm at overt displays of emotion – whether such emotion consists in saluting the flag or a riot of patriotic bumper stickers. One doesn't have to actually be British or have that clinched, stiff upper lip to absorb the lesson of inner emotion and patriotism.

Perhaps Canadians understand that to make symbols the most powerful expression of citizenship is to give them too much power. In the United States, there are never-ending efforts to make any "desecrations" of the Stars and Stripes an offence. Such efforts would never reach the level of serious contemplation among Canadians who understand the power of symbolism and reject any attempts to provide the discontented with an easy target. In Canada, you can wear the Maple Leaf flag on your backside and no Pecksniffian nationalist can order you to cease and desist.

To quote the late, great Pierre Berton, who did more to make Canadians interested in their own country than any other single writer: "A Canadian is someone who knows how to make love in a canoe." Let me add one additional thought, in keeping with our image as the polite inhabitants of North America: A Canadian is someone who knows how to make love in a canoe . . . but doesn't.

Calgary, Alberta
Copyright © 2006 by Catherine Ford

Catherine Ford

Catherine Ford was an award-winning national opinion columnist at the Calgary Herald *whose work appeared in the CanWest chain of newspapers. In 2005, she received an honorary doctor of laws degree from the University of Calgary. Her most recent book,* Against the Grain: An Irreverent Look at Alberta, *was published that same year.*

MARK KINGWELL

Thesis 1

A CANADIAN IS ... an imaginary creature with various mythological traits, some of them charming, some irritating, many of them contradictory.

The Canadian is, famously, able to make love in a canoe; pass for American until asked to pronounce "out"; inflect sentences upward at the end. The Canadian is self-deprecating, ironic, polite and deferential to authority. Also hockey loving, beer drinking, pemmican eating, igloo dwelling. Fond of universal health care, vestiges of monarchy, extra *u*'s, reversed *r*'s and *e*'s, and the sound of something called *zed*. Multicultural, tolerant, civil, clean, mildly socialistic. The Canadian says "Sorry" when you step on his foot.

The most accurate book ever written about the subject of Canadian identity is Anthony Wilden's *The Imaginary Canadian*, a work by an English-born, American-trained, French-influenced Lacanian psycho-analytical sociologist who lives in Vancouver. Wilden argued that the Canadian, like the typical Gen-Xer or classic Piscean, is a categorical fiction, a chimera. The Canadian is a projection of our desires and fears, a straw man or whipping boy, as the case dictates, a notional sum of forces and vectors, just as illusory but a lot less useful than a centre of gravity or statistical mean, and legally of a significance somewhat less than the proverbial man on the Clapham omnibus.

Because he is imaginary, the Canadian is someone we shall forever seek yet never find, for the Canadian is everywhere and nowhere at once. Editorialists and pundits may search endlessly for him by daytime lamplight, like Diogenes the Cynic, and yet he, or indeed she, is right there under our noses all the time, walking the streets. And yet, never there . . .

The confusion here dates back to an ancient philosophical quarrel between two camps called the *nominalists* and the *universalists*. A universalist is someone who thinks categories pick out, or highlight, real similarities in the fabric of existence, beneath-the-surface realities: identifiable traits of independent things. A nominalist, by contrast, is someone who thinks categories are names coined to carve up experience, say, according to usefulness, convenience, similarity of function, or family resemblance. But there is no set of essential features of character or qualities lying, as it were, *underneath* the category. Attempting to define Canadian identity as if it were an essential quality, or set of them, is a classic universalist's error, mistaking creation for discovery, making for finding.

More nominalistically, then, let us say that a Canadian is a citizen of the nation called Canada, former dominion of the British Crown and, before that, two colonies bearing the name in upper and lower modification, plus a few others, who straggled into a loose, and contested, federation around 1867 – also 1905 and 1949 – with much of the territory lying north of the forty-ninth parallel, and a good deal of the population nevertheless living south of it. The Canadian may or may not have been born within this geographical territory; indeed, his parents are more likely not to have been. He or she is sometimes, but not always, a holder of a certain passport or social insurance number issued by this nation-state, which has existed, more or less, since 1867, though certain parts did not join until 1905 and even, in one case, 1949.

The Canadian may be, slightly more usefully, the bearer of certain rights, provisional on certain kinds of behaviour; he or she may be, likewise, the executor of certain responsibilities, given world enough and time – and a duly completed tax return. The nation-state itself, meanwhile, fount of this spectral (anyway mostly legal) identity, remains its own kind of fiction, a federation of regions and *de facto* city-states, themselves with no agreed-upon essences, forever changing as more people arrive on its shores and take up residence within its conventional but unnecessary borders.

Thesis 2

It follows that any definitive sentence beginning *A Canadian is* . . . is always already nonsensical. Such a sentence will possess no determinate truth value; it will be as false as it is true. Still, as Edward Lear, Lewis Carroll and Ludwig Wittgenstein, among others, all knew, nonsense may be of interest. Not all interesting things are true, just as not all true things are interesting.

To be sure, that judgment holds for the present effort no less than the others in this volume. Notice, for example, that, by calling the Canadian *imaginary*, I do not simply mean that the standard clichés about Canadians are untrue – for, indeed, some of them are not; and anyway, that sort of debunking is simply first-order essentialism masquerading as sophistication. Nor am I saying something else that we often hear about Canadian identity, namely that it is composed of negatives, as in: not-being-American or not-being-British or not-being-at-war-with-Iraq. Again, these things may be true, but they are not interesting or helpful.

Not-being-American is, of course, a mug's game, pro or con. No amount of self-abasement will curry favour with a powerful presence that is ignoring you: the jilted-girlfriend manoeuvre. By the same token, no amount of piqued anger will change the indifferent power into an attentive party: the jilted-boyfriend manoeuvre. Like manifestos against manifestos, or theories about the end of theory, these identity discussions quickly collapse under their own weight. Pretty soon you find yourself at the limits of thought, and nobody likes to be there for very long, least of all pundits and thumb-suckers who use definitions of Canadianness for their own purposes. Neither Don Cherry, rabidly pro, nor the *National Post*, rabidly con, makes *any sense at all* to anyone outside Canada. To outsiders, especially Americans, these figures are debating a non-issue against non-opponents within a non-context, where only non-questions can ever be raised.

Indeed, both approaches fail because of what Sun Tzu would recognize as the inevitable defeat of strategic envelopment. When your opponent has all the power, you cannot win for trying. Result: a culture of defeatism. (Wilden notes that a common American slogan during the Second World War was "You can't win 'em all." The comparable Canadian slogan during the same period was "You can't win.") When enveloped, the only recourse is a lateral change in strategy. Walk away, chart an independent course. Instead of this, Canadians engage in an endless and self-defeating round of debate of no concern whatsoever to the supposed target object. We begin to discern here the dismal character of almost all existing discussions of Canadian identity, namely their endless-and-agonizing quality.

Which might lead us to the appropriately self-reflexive definition that a Canadian is someone who forever debates what it means to be Canadian. That may seem unhelpful but it leads, I think, to thicker soup.

Thesis 3

First of all, then, the open-ended sentence *A Canadian is . . .* leads to a debate over *what Canada stands for* – a very different thing from asking who the Canadian is. Asking what Canada stands for presumes not a pre-existing essence to be discovered (an identity), but a future course of action to be justified (a vision). Deliberately confusing these two is one of the Right's favourite tactics, usually as part of a one-two whose first punch is denigration of the country. But let us also agree that we cannot proceed by assuming an air of moral superiority with respect to our southward neighbours or anyone else. That would indeed be thin soup for an essence, and irritating besides. Deliberately confusing smugness with identity is one of the Left's favourite tactics, itself part of a different one-two punch, with the sanctimony usually preceded by a swing of economic wishfulness.

Second, we can see lurking in these flurries of unhelpful blows an even more useful debate – on the nature of justice. And this is where our energy should be redirected. Consider, in other words, how we imaginary Canadians can make a virtue of necessity.

Political philosophers working in the modern era have struggled with the issue of pluralism, frequently arguing that embracing pluralism is the task of liberal justice. But pluralism can mean two different things, and both of them need to be distinguished in turn from relativism, that great conservative bugbear.

Social pluralism is the recognition that more than one ethical life-plan may compel different but reasonable people. That is, we may find that we answer, in different ways, the question "What is the life worth living?"

Pluralism means there are, at a minimum, at least two such answers; at a maximum, millions, one for each distinct person. In real practice, there is a relatively small number of often overlapping answers, most of them variations on a cluster of familiar themes. Liberalism says we can manage social pluralism by finding common ground, where the different answers overlap or, failing that, on procedures of law and deliberation that we hope count as "rational" over and above our differences. Critics of liberalism say this move is either utopian (deluded) or cynical (deluding) – either blowing smoke or a smokescreen for power. But they are too quick in defeat.

Personal pluralism at once complicates and humanizes the political picture. As Isaiah Berlin forcefully argued, it is the recognition that humans are rarely, if ever, motivated by consistent and simple ethical life-plans. Most of us have competing, even contradictory, values affecting our most important decisions (and unimportant ones too). These values do not resolve, nor do they easily rank-order. We struggle for consistency and defensibility, surely, but these are asymptotic goals at best.

Paradoxically, personal pluralism bolsters the argument for the liberal approach to social pluralism, because it suggests, among other things, that conflicting values can be managed, if never eliminated. Despite our differences, there is such a thing as the court of public reason, where we can debate, if never solve, the problems of ethical disagreement. That is just what politics means.

Both forms of pluralism remain importantly distinct from relativism. "I prefer coffee, you prefer champagne. There is no more to be said. That is relativism," Berlin wrote. Pluralism, he said, is "the conception that there are many different ends that men may seek and still be fully rational, fully men, capable of understanding each other and sympathizing and deriving light from each other . . . Ends, moral principles, are many. But not infinitely many: they must be within the human horizon." Relativism is the position that anything (end, ethical claim, life-plan) is as good as any other – a claim, let it be noted, that is non-relative and therefore *prima facie* self-contradictory. ("The man who tells you truth does not exist," the philosopher Roger Scruton said.) But more simply, it is untrue. Ends, as Berlin says, must be within the human horizon: we do not just care about *anything at all*.

Thesis 4

But we can go further: the genuine flourishing of humans embodies, as Aristotle knew, a set of norms – standards that limn the range of good human action. We can – we must – debate what, precisely, that range allows; but such debate shows, always, that there is an answer, if never a final answer, to be articulated.

It was the very same Diogenes the Cynic who first said, when challenged on his identity: "I am a citizen of the world." We might call his attitude *cynical cosmopolitanism* – a wry but positive dedication not to national or ideological traces or programs, but to the possibilities of the human condition. Since, for the time being, nation-states are still the best guarantors of those things that make human flourishing possible – freedom, law, and the chance to belong – let us say that the best nation-states are those with the least fixed identity, fewest distracting myths, no heated debates over patriotism and, instead, an open-ended play of possibilities.

Thesis 5

Liberty, plurality, justice – that is what Canada stands for. In the only sense that matters, then, a Canadian is anybody who too stands for these.

Toronto, Ontario
Copyright © 2006 by Mark Kingwell

Mark Kingwell

Mark Kingwell is a professor of philosophy at the University of Toronto. He is the author of eight books of philosophy and cultural theory and co-author of the bestselling photographic history Canada: Our Century. *He is a contributing editor for* Harper's *magazine and has written for more than forty mainstream publications. Mark Kingwell's writing has been translated into eight languages, and he has lectured to popular and academic audiences around the world. His latest books are* Nearest Thing to Heaven: The Empire State Building and American Dreams *and* Classic Cocktails: A Modern Shake.

SILVER DONALD CAMERON

A CANADIAN IS . . . at the helm of his sailboat, steering up a winding tidal creek in Georgia. The sun is setting blood-red over the brown marshes when the small ketch with the Maple Leaf flag motors into a tiny backwater marina. I bring *Magnus* up to the wharf, where Marjorie tosses the dock lines ashore. Two boys catch the lines and tie them.

"Y'all goin' to the cookout?" one asks.

Hadn't known about a cookout, I reply.

"It's a pig-pickin'. Roastin' a whole hog," says the boy. "Starts at six, in back of the marina." He looks up. "Here comes anothah boat."

I know the new arrival slightly – *Tayo*, a sloop from Montreal, crewed by a charming Québécois family. Like us, they are sailing south to Florida and the Bahamas for the winter, and this morning we started from the same small port, fifty miles back.

At six when I arrive at the pig-pickin', Didier and Henriette and their daughter Catherine are already there, paper plates loaded with barbe-cued meat and baked beans and coleslaw, talking intently with members of the Troup Creek Boating and Fishing Club. A short woman with a near-impenetrable Southern accent is herding the three into posing for a snapshot.

"Get this fella in, too," a tall man says. "He come from Canada, too."

"Yeah," says Didier, with just the hint of an accent. "We're d' Canadian navy."

The three Québécois and I laugh and throw our arms around one another. Flash. Four Canadians, captured on film.

At home we might have been shy with one another, conscious mainly of our differences, as Canadians often are. Francophone, anglophone, allophone, Native. Westerner, Easterner, Maritimer. Sikh, Catholic, Muslim, Jew. Canadians come from everywhere on the globe, and bear their cultural origins proudly unto the twelfth generation.

Abroad, we are all Canadians. After six months cruising down the east coast of the United States from Maine to Florida, meeting numerous other Canadians en route, Marjorie and I have concluded that Canada truly exists not on the map, not in our institutions or ethnicity, but between the ears of Canadians. Canada lies deep in our assumptions, our attitudes, our understanding of social structures.

For example, Canadians have a distinctive social style. Ernest Hemingway once wrote that one of his characters was a Canadian, and (if I recall the quote accurately) "had their easy social grace." When we told an expatriate friend that we had found a very warm and accommodating welcome all the way down the US coast, she said, "Well, you have that Canadian charm. You approach people with that, and they respond. But don't misunderstand. If you approach Americans aggressively, they can do that, too."

We find that we expect to like other Canadians, and usually do – and the Canadian private code includes a wry sense of humour. Indeed, one of Canada's great exports has been its humour, from Leacock to Richler to Red Green, Mike Myers and Jim Carrey. When the crew of *Magnus* meets another Canadian crew, we almost immediately find something to laugh about, and the laughter sounds like home. Laughter is the Canadian social lubricant.

And we differ profoundly from Americans in our understanding of security. Americans seem to think that security can be achieved by unilateral force. You step on my property, and I'll shoot. This gated housing complex is patrolled by attack dogs and armed guards. This gated nation is patrolled by satellites, radar, helicopters, the Coast Guard and the US Marines. A Canadian whose Florida house was demolished by Hurricane Jeanne told me that her sympathetic neighbours had pitched in by offering to lend her some guns so that she could shoot looters.

"Why?" she asked. "It's all trashed anyhow. If someone steals my water-logged television set, they just save me the trouble of lugging it to the dump. Would I shoot a person over a *television set*?"

Canadians, by contrast, consider that genuine security can only be based on sound social relationships. We don't need guns – or even locks on our doors – if our neighbours don't need to harm us. In one of the funniest sequences in *Bowling for Columbine*, Michael Moore goes to Toronto – big, bad, nasty Toronto – and finds one house after another with its doors unlocked. When he opens the door, the homeowners look up and say, "Yes? Something we can do for you?"

My Cape Breton village takes pride in leaving the doors unlocked and the keys in the ignition. Anyone who enters your home in your absence will probably be returning a tool or a book, or dropping off the minutes of the meeting or a loaf of fresh-baked bread. Unlocked doors testify to the health and security of the community. They testify to the fact that it *is* a community.

Moore argues that the American obsession with self-protection and security – most vividly symbolized by the gun culture – is based on fear. Fear of those who have been left out, fear of those who have been humiliated and abused. The poor, the mentally disturbed, Hispanics, blacks, Natives, addicts. Desperate people are roaming the streets, filled with resentment and need. If you do not defend yourself, they will invade your space and take what you have.

They might, too. But the Canadian approach has traditionally been to remove the threat by removing the underlying desperation. Create a decent social safety net – unemployment insurance, street clinics, social assistance.

Fewer desperate people means fewer desperadoes.

Medicare is a perfect example. American ideologues and their intellectual agents in Canada often decry the long waiting periods for Canadian medical services, neglecting to note that forty million Americans will wait forever to see a doctor, because they have no medical or drug coverage at all. Forty million souls constitute an entire nation of desperate people within the United States. Those are some of the people who might well feel the need to rob you, and might kill you in the process.

I don't mind waiting for routine medical procedures if the delay helps ensure that every Canadian has basic health care, and that fewer Canadians are desperate. The welfare state is as beneficial to those who don't need its services as to those who do. Medicare is part of my personal home security system.

From the village to the nation to the international stage, Canadian attitudes are consistent. We are peacekeepers by instinct because we know in our bones that peace provides our only true security. That's not sentimentality; that's realism. In the end, nothing works except peace.

So we don't seek to win fights; we'd rather turn down the rhetoric, sidestep the battle and resolve the basic conflict. I am inordinately proud of my brother David, who has spent much of his time over the last few years working with former Ontario premier Bob Rae to devise a federal system to end the long-running civil war in Sri Lanka. I cheer when Stephen Lewis is honoured for his extraordinary effort to mobilize the world community to deal with the HIV/AIDS crisis in Africa. General Roméo Dallaire, in his public anguish over the UN's failure to stifle the Rwandan genocide, strikes me as a military hero of the very highest order.

Don't fight if you don't have to. Don't let others fight if you can prevent it. Instead, solve the problem.

When Canadians are obliged to fight, of course, they are formidable, as our record in two world wars amply shows. And though we don't wave our flag very much, we are deeply attached to our peculiar home and native land. When I told Marjorie about Didier's jest that we were the Canadian navy, she laughed. Then she said, "Any Canadian would laugh at that. We don't have a navy, we don't have an army, but we still figure we can handle any sonofabitch barehanded on the beach if we need to." A British Columbia fisherman says something similar: "I'd never join the army. But if they were comin' ashore in Powell River, I'd be the first one down there on the beach with a pitchfork."

How did we get to be this way? More importantly, how can we continue to be this way, given the contempt which Canadian values inspire among Canada's political and economic elites?

Northrop Frye memorably described Canadians as "Americans who reject the Revolution." For Americans, the lesson of the Revolution is that violence sanctified by abstract principle provides a perfectly satisfactory solution to political difficulties. You gain independence through revolution, you resolve your internal difficulties through civil war, you expand your territory by conquering your neighbours, as in the case of Mexico, or by threatening it, as with the British Pacific colonies.

Fifty-four forty or fight!

Canadian history teaches a different lesson. We achieved our independence and augmented our territory by the bureaucratic and undramatic process of negotiation, lobbying, pressure, accommodation, federation. We bound ourselves to no official set of values encapsulated in evangelical documents comparable to the Declaration of Independence or the US Constitution.

To the extent that we have solved our internal problems – particularly the knotty problem of creating a proud and independent Quebec within a strong and united Canada – we have done it by accepting most of Quebec's reasonable demands, and talking about the remaining issues until everyone got tired and went home. Not civil war, said the poet Frank Scott, but "a crashing civil bore." The genius and the absurdity of our country are symbolized by the installation in 1993 of the Bloc Québécois, whose official objective is the demolition of the country, as "Her Majesty's Loyal Opposition." Gilbert and Sullivan would have rubbed their hands with glee.

Perhaps Hugh MacLennan struck to the heart of our national character when he noted that Canada was founded by defeated peoples: the Loyalists, who were humiliated in the American Revolution; the Scots, who were rousted from their own glens by the English; and the French, who were conquered at the Plains of Abraham. What they shared was a first-hand knowledge of the bitter fruits of violence, and a deep-seated will to find alternative solutions to difficult problems.

Canada is no longer dominated by those founding groups but, like the drops of water that first trace the bed of an eventual river, they set our odd country on its mysterious course. They established the institutions, passed the legislation and inaugurated the traditions that would define a nation far more complex and colourful than they could ever have imagined. Later immigrants have enriched the nation profoundly, but they have not altered its fundamental character.

Canada is an idea that underlies Canadian assumptions, attitudes and social philosophy. The media barons, the right-wing think tanks, the

Canadian Council of Chief Executives and the corporate political parties all seem determined to lead us into what they call "deep integration" with the United States, which amounts to annexation without the privileges of statehood – a status like that of Puerto Rico or American Samoa. The concept offends the idea of Canada, and its implementation will be a lot harder than the elites suspect. George Bush's imperial administration has freaked our leaders, but it has galvanized a latent Canadian patriotism, which is always more powerful than our leaders believe.

Somewhere in Georgia, there is a photograph of a French-Canadian family with their arms around an English-speaking Scots Canadian. The English speaker should feel more kinship with the Georgians, whose company he obviously enjoyed, and who shared his ethnic heritage and spoke his language. Right?

Wrong, wrong, wrong. *Vive le Québec. Vive le Canada. Et vive le Canada libre.*

Aboard the Magnus, *in the Bahamas*
Copyright © 2006 by Silver Donald Cameron

Silver Donald Cameron

Silver Donald Cameron's work includes fifteen books, numerous plays, films, radio and TV scripts, an extensive body of corporate and governmental writing and innumerable magazine articles. A former columnist with the Globe and Mail, *he currently writes a weekly column for the* Halifax Sunday Herald. *In July 2004, he and his wife sailed from their home in Nova Scotia down the entire US east coast, destined for the Bahamas. His book on the voyage,* Sailing Away from Winter, *will be published in 2007.*

GUY LAFOREST

A CANADIAN IS . . . if this person happens to be like myself – a Québec patriot, first and foremost – inclined to consider our political sphere with a sense of discomfort. This unease has been present since Confederation. The daily revelations, in 2004 and 2005, of the Gomery Commission on the sponsorship scandal are unlikely to alter this feeling.

Nevertheless, a Canadian remains a lucky person on this planet of ours. Notwithstanding all our philosophical, religious, cultural, national, political and ideological differences, all of us reflecting on this issue should at least agree on the fact that we are fortunate to live in Canada, to feel Canadian to various degrees or to care about Canada's destiny in the world.

I was touched when I was approached to write this piece, for one major reason: I am both a citizen of this country and a political exile from within. I carry the passport of a country to which I cannot, at least not yet, give an unwavering, unmitigated allegiance. I shall provide here reasons for this peculiar kind of political exile, not uncommon in present-day Québec. I shall also briefly discuss what could be done to overcome such estrangement, at least in part. But first I will propose a perspective on Canada's political identity. For if we want to avoid an ultra-naive form of idealism on these matters – and I think that we should – our feet must be reasonably grounded on historical and social realities.

Our country is a geographical monster, obsessed by its vulnerability and insignificance vis-à-vis the United States of America, possibly the greatest power in the history of humankind. Canada is a giant seeing a dwarf when looking at itself in a mirror. Correspondingly, a Canadian is, quite frequently, someone who suffers from an inferiority complex vis-à-vis Americans. From this perception flows a deep desire, particularly in the Ottawa–Toronto corridor, where much of the political and intellectual establishment of English-speaking Canada live, to affirm and differentiate us in both discourse and action from the United States.

Canada is, in principle, since the 1931 Statute of Westminster, and in totality since the 1982 constitutional reform, a sovereign state, proud to multiply forms of international activism in the era of globalization. A Canadian is somebody who sees himself or herself as a citizen of the world. Canada's internationalism stands for peace, dialogue, negotiations, multilateralism. Our central governments like the world stage, in part because Canada has been a vulnerable, threatened state, having survived two sovereignty referendums over the last twenty-five years in Québec.

Our political identity has much to do with our British past: Westminster parliamentarianism and cabinet system, rule of law, a limited liberal state with substantial safeguards protecting individuals from the arbitrary hand of authority. Contrary to what many law students are taught to believe these days, as we political scientists like to joke, Pierre Trudeau did not give us *habeas corpus*! Canada was a liberal state prior to the 1982 reform. From this stems the fact, as I often remind my students, that Locke, Burke, Durham, Acton and Mill belong to our philosophical ancestors, whereas Rousseau and his French successors do not.

The Westminster heritage also means that Canada is a constitutional monarchy. Since 1763, without a single day of interruption, Canadians have been the subjects of British monarchs. Although Mr. Trudeau – in truth, the last of our founders, and thus our Lincoln – would have liked it otherwise, the principle of popular sovereignty is absent from Canada's political identity. Considering that the monarchical principle belongs to the category of items requiring unanimity in the workings of the constitutional amending formula adopted in 1982, this will not change anytime soon. Citizenship was nationalized in Canada in the late forties. Technically, however, we remain citizens *and* subjects.

Is Canada a nation? The belief that Canada is a nation is shared by the vast majority of inhabitants of this country. In this context, if we recall as well that expert literature sees the subjective dimension as the prime criterion of nationhood, no one in his or her right frame of mind should doubt that Canada is a nation. The matter is of course made more complex if we add that the vast majority of inhabitants of Québec think that their province is also a nation. Logically, this should not be doubted by anyone in Canada or elsewhere in the world. Things are made even more complex if we add the claims to nationhood of the Acadians, Métis and over six hundred First Nations peoples. In the skies, Canada would be a multinational constellation. Let us not try to settle the issue here. Let us compromise and rejoice over the fact that Canada, throughout its history, has been the land of an altogether civilized debate on one the most perplexing matters of modern politics: the contours of the nation and the forms of allegiance that are owed to it.

I suppose that our ambassadors abroad are frequently asked about the nature of Canada's political identity. What do they answer, and does this diverge from what they should answer? I take it that the official answer is that Canada is a bilingual and multicultural nation-state, originally peopled by our First Nations, with an open citizenship granted on generous conditions to persons coming here with a multiplicity of backgrounds and origins. The elements linked to the British connection and to our obsession with the United States are probably put across rather informally. Over the last decade, a lot of emphasis has been placed on the Charter of Rights and Freedoms as possibly the strongest marker of a distinctive Canadian identity. Although Canada was a liberal democracy prior to 1982, it is undeniable that the Trudeau-inspired reform has tilted the country toward a rights-based regime, placing greater emphasis on our institutional order, on the judiciary power and its interpretive work. In 2002, the federal Justice Department and the Supreme Court of Canada joined forces to celebrate the twentieth anniversary of the Charter. In French, the theme chosen to sponsor the event established quite clearly that this was at least as much about identity as it was about rights: "La Charte, c'est à nous, la Charte c'est nous." I grant that the Charter belongs to us, adding that our political identity should not be reduced to its juridical and normative sphere.

In the Charter era, a lot of people have forgotten that Canada is also a federation, the kind of country where sovereignty is divided between at least two levels of government, where federated political authorities share with the central government the duty to discuss and deliberate about the common good. Canada became a federal dominion under the British Crown in 1867 for many reasons. Only one will concern me here. Federalism implies autonomy (of the members) and separation (from the other members); it also implies participation (of all members to common institutions) and interdependence (between all members of the political community as a whole). The federal principle in 1867 facilitated the re-establishment of Québec as a self-governing political community. Reconciling himself, however reluctantly, to the federal principle for the Dominion of Canada, John A. Macdonald, our first prime minister, reminded his parliamentary colleagues of the times that "it was found that any proposition which involved the absorption of the individuality of Lower Canada . . . would not be received with favour by her people." The federal principle emerged in the nineteenth century as an important element in the political identity of our country in large part because French-Canadian leaders like George-Étienne Cartier, whose support had to be secured, wanted Québec to be self-governing, distinct and free within Canada. It should be a bit clearer by now to the average reader why a Canadian citizen who is a Quebecker first and foremost, like myself, feels like he is living in a kind of interior exile in this country.

Almost twenty-five years ago, in 1982, the Canadian Constitution was patriated and transformed over and against the objections of the government and National Assembly of Québec, without securing the consent of Quebeckers as a political community. Elected representatives from Québec, including Mr. Trudeau, gave overwhelming approval to the reform in the Canadian Parliament. However, in true federal logic, they had no mandate to reduce the powers of Québec, in fields such as education and language, without the consent of Québec. On my understanding, the 1982 reform was, and remains, thoroughly without legitimacy in Québec. The whole matter is made even worse by the fact that Québec had been, since the Quiet Revolution in the early Sixties, the main proponent of major constitutional changes. Successive Québec governments had sought reforms such as a new division of powers between Ottawa and the provinces, the redesigning of central institutions, such as the Supreme Court and the Senate, and the elimination of quasi-imperial elements (such as the powers to reserve and disallow provincial legislation, rarely used, but never abrogated) that have established in law as well as in the larger political culture a clear preponderance of Ottawa over and above the provinces. Most contemporary Canadian politicians buy the mantra that, because the Meech Lake and Charlottetown accords miserably failed, we should not talk anymore about the Constitution. They fail to convince me and they feed my sense of estrangement. They lack the nerve and the backbone required to face the fact that we do not have the institutions that will provide us with justice and stability for the twenty-first century.

What could be done to make somebody like myself politically more at home within Canada? Making changes to the great icon of Trudeau-inspired nation-building, the Canadian Charter of Rights and Freedoms, would be a start in the right direction. The rights of Québec as a distinct society and national political community should be properly placed in the Charter. The Meech Lake Accord would have provided for this through a clause recognizing Québec as a distinct society and acknowl-edging the fact that the government and National Assembly of Québec have the obligation to preserve and promote this distinct society. The federal character of Canada should also be firmly recognized – for instance, through an amendment to Section 1 of the Charter establishing that there are limits to rights in a "free and democratic federation" (rather than a free and democratic *society*). In law, as in politics, words count. They are important. Judges interpreting the Charter should be told clearly about the centrality of the federal principle in Canada's Constitution. It should also be made clear in the Charter that the Canadian brand of multiculturalism is dualistic: people ought to be told that they are invited to live their multicultural heritage in two distinct societal cultures, one of them in Québec, which is allowed to operate its institutional public network mostly in French. This would not solve all the problems I alluded to earlier. However, it would break the current stalemate.

If I were polled today about my political identity, I would gladly say that I am a Québécois (or Quebecker, a synonymous term, referring also to a political community) first and foremost. Some people would con-clude that my loyalty to the country is thus questionable. They would resent the conditionality of my allegiance to Canada. This is a problem that cannot be easily solved. In the modern world, people can have plural identities; they can be loyal to more than one political community. I could be a Québécois first and foremost, and simultaneously quite loyal to Canada.

As matters stand in 2006, I have a sense of solidarity with the land and with the people across Canada, combined with a rather weak sense of loyalty to our current political institutions. I am thus without question also a Canadian, but politically and constitutionally a very unhappy customer. I hope things change during my lifetime.

Québec, Québec
Copyright © 2006 by Guy Laforest

Guy Laforest

Guy Laforest is a professor of political science at Laval University. He has been co-director of the Revue canadienne de science politique, *director of the department of political science at Laval, organizer of the Congrès de l'Association canadienne-française pour l'avancement des sciences and the Fédération canadienne des sciences humaines et sociales, and president of the Action démocratique du Québec.*

MARIA TIPPETT

A CANADIAN IS . . . like an onion – multi-layered, thin-skinned and a product of organic development. For example, I am a Canadian, a British Columbian, a west coaster who lives on Pender Island in the Strait of Georgia. How I choose to identify myself – and how others choose to identify me – depends on where I am. When I'm in Calgary, I say, "I'm from the coast." If I happen to be in Toronto, Montreal, Halifax or in any other city lying east of Calgary, but within two hundred miles of the American–Canadian border, I say, "I come from BC." This revelation conjures up images of mountains and a gentle climate; a culture that encompasses the carvings of Bill Reid and the paintings of Emily Carr; and a political identity that has occupied positions at both ends of the ideological spectrum. It is only when I am in the Canadian Arctic that these reference points cease to work. Whether I am on Baffin Island or in Yellowknife, my regional identity vanishes in the eyes of Northerners. Like everyone else living below the sixtieth parallel, I am simply someone from the South. This can mean anything from an exploiter of the North's natural and human resources to a potential customer for the burgeoning tourist industry.

When I travel abroad, my identity changes yet again. I'm no longer a British Columbian or a Southerner: I am a Canadian. I proudly identify with Canada's peacekeeping forces, with hockey's Team Canada, and with writers such as Margaret Atwood, Antonine Maillet and Robertson Davies, whether I follow the politics of the United Nations, the score of international hockey games or read the books of the world's leading authors. When foreigners embarrass me into singing a typical Canadian song, I can reel out at least one verse of "Alouette" or "Four Strong Winds." And, unless I happen to be in Donegal, Northern Ireland, where my ancestors lived before emigrating to Vancouver Island in the 1870s, my sense of who I am not only embraces the coastal landscape of British Columbia, but the rolling grasslands of the Prairies and the picturesque hamlets along the banks of the St. Lawrence River.

For previous generations of Canadians, identity was a different matter. For example, in the years between the First and Second World Wars, four dancers from Vancouver, Ottawa, Montreal and Nanaimo who joined the *corps de ballet* of the famous Ballets Russes, had to take new names. Respectively, Denise Myers became Alexandra Denisova, Betty Low became Ludmilla Lvova, Jean Hunt became Kira Bounina, and Robert Bell became Boris Belsky. (One can hardly imagine what it was like for these dancers when the Ballets Russes made a tour of Canada in the 1930s.)

During the same decade, a group belonging to the Toronto-based Boris Volkoff Ballet Company distinguished themselves at the Internationale Tanzwettspiele that was held in conjunction with the 1936 Olympics in Berlin. The performance is worth noting because it drew on First Nations culture. Volkoff based his choreography on a Native dance. Ernest MacMillan provided the music by transcribing one of the songs that he had recorded on the west coast into classical European musical notation. And Ottawa's Victoria Memorial Museum, which had bought – or, in many cases, stolen – artifacts from First Nations people, kitted out Volkoff's dancers with costumes, rattles and masks from its permanent collection. Though the dancers got to keep their own names while performing in Berlin, there was something missing: the Natives themselves!

Even in the more recent past, such homegrown luminaries as Peter Jennings and John Kenneth Galbraith in due course relinquished their Canadian identity in favour of another – in both cases American – when they left the country in order to pursue their careers. So what has happened to make Canadians like Margaret Atwood, Wayne Gretzky, Diana Krall and Denys Arcand keep their names and their Canadian identity whether they live on or off Canadian soil?

According to the country's cultural nationalists, the future of our identity as Canadians looks bleak. After the founding of the Canada Council in 1957, dancers, writers, musicians and actors were given what one writer called "the most generous sugar daddy art has ever known." But the

Canada Council espoused an elitist moral vision of culture that was anti-commercial, anti-American and pro-nationalist. This meant that artists, writers, musicians and dramatists who did not belong to the British and, to a lesser extent, to the French charter groups were left out in the cultural cold. Moreover, the people who were lucky enough to receive heavy subsidies from the Canada Council tended to look inward – or, in some people's view, to spend too much time navel-gazing by repeatedly asking "Where is here?" and "Who are we?"

Yet no one can deny the fact that during the 1950s, 1960s and 1970s, much homegrown culture was produced. Indeed, cultural nationalists came to believe that what had been produced prior to the founding of the Canada Council was little more than watered-down versions of British or American art, music, drama and theatre – whereas what was being produced post-Canada Council was somehow more authentic. In its heyday, the Canada Council's support for the production of mainstream culture did enable many of our major writers to flourish in the 1980s and 1990s. But it was rather like the heavily protected and heavily subsidized Canadian wine industry: there was plenty of output, but it was frequently of low quality, and – this is important – it was made for domestic consumption only.

Thanks to – or because of – the subsequent worldwide recession, we don't have the luxury of heavily subsidized culture today. The Canadian Broadcasting Corporation, Telefilm Canada, the National Film Board, the Art Bank and the Canada Council, to mention just a few of the cultural agencies that help to shape our identity, have either had their budgets slashed or been eliminated altogether. Moreover, owing to the global resurgence of ethnic nationalism and the emergence of politically correct thinking, people who had been previously excluded from the cultural nationalists' project have now found a place in mainstream culture.

So are the cultural nationalists right to think that Canadians are losing their identity? Is the world going to become a single domestic space, in which everyone will share a common culture and a common identity? Or are those who espouse "cultural internationalism" right in believing that cultural homogenization will never be complete, because globalization has the capacity to recognize multiple cultural identities?

Cultural internationalism is as familiar to Canadians as cultural nationalism. As early as 1928, the humorist Stephen Leacock announced that the world had become an intellectual unity. During the years before the founding of the Canada Council, writers like Lucy Maud Montgomery, Morley Callaghan and Gabrielle Roy published their books abroad, had them reviewed abroad, and, in some cases, won prestigious foreign book awards. It was no different for the country's musicians, dramatists, visual artists, and, as we have seen, its dancers. Indeed, even though some were forced to play down their Canadian identity, placing their work in the international cultural arena had many advantages. It allayed their feelings of isolation and inferiority. It tested their ideas, and gained them greater financial security through their access to foreign markets. They also got what they wanted most: recognition and respect in their own country.

And this is where we are today. Our writers are winning Britain's Man Booker Prize, America's Pulitzer Prize and France's Prix Goncourt. High-end galleries in Europe, Japan and the United States are selling work by Canadian artists. The voice of Céline Dion launched and sank a very big ship in the film, *Titanic*. Diana Krall is now the top female jazz vocalist in Britain. Canadian compositions and plays are being performed at festivals in Salzburg and Edinburgh. The Cirque du Soleil is as well known outside as inside the country. Northwest Coast First Nations artists are curating their own exhibitions and producing their own plays. Writers of the calibre of Rohinton Mistry are allowing Canadians to share and thereby identify with different experiences and different histories.

Whether one agrees with the cultural nationalists' or the cultural internationalists' view of things, there is no doubt that our writers, artists, musicians, dramatists and dancers are not only allowing us to enjoy a diverse cultural experience, but have given us a more inclusive cultural identity.

After all, it's not like choosing between apples and pears – it's more like onions. But we should not spend too much time peeling an onion – it can end in tears.

Pender Island, British Columbia
Copyright © 2006 by Maria Tippett

Maria Tippett

Maria Tippett is a cultural historian, lecturer and curator who explores the history of Canadian culture. Among her eleven books are Emily Carr: A Biography, *which received a Governor General's Award for Non-Fiction in 1980;* Making Culture: English-Canadian Institutions and the Arts Before the Massey Commission; *and* Bill Reid: The Making of an Indian, *which won a British Columbia Book Award in 2004. A former senior research fellow at Cambridge University in England, Maria Tippett now lives on Pender Island in British Columbia. She is currently writing a biography of Yousuf Karsh, the renowned Canadian portrait photographer.*

E. KENT STETSON

A CANADIAN IS . . . confused. Free to marry whom he or she chooses, a Canadian decides whether it will be a sacred or civil ceremony. If he chooses a man, or she a woman, the question is raised, Do gay men and lesbian women have souls? We suppose all persons have souls; all gay men and lesbians are persons. He and he, and she and she, must consider whether they wish their souls to be united in the presence of the sacred – aka God – and witnessed by the community, upon whose support they, like all social, human creatures, depend. The "go-it-aloners" may choose a simpler civil union, less encumbered by family, tradition and matters of the human spirit. Either way, Canadian gay men and lesbian women suddenly have much to consider. In the post-Christian era, as Canadian values become increasingly complicated, Canadian society becomes more complex.

If a Canadian has a gun, he must, by law, register it, in the same way he registers to vote, operate a motor vehicle, marry, and so on. This is all good. Will he use his gun(s) for recreation, to help feed his family, or to destroy his neighbour? Will his choice enhance his well-being, and that of society, the stage upon which he plays out all the acts and scenes of his life?

Because we belong to a species prone to inexplicable bouts of lethal madness, we like to know who owns a gun. This can lead to resentment: my freedom or your peace of mind? Me or you?

Us.

A Canadian may worship many gods; but not the god of guns.

Despite the Kyoto Accord, Canadians continue to wheeze and gasp their way toward a waste-blighted future. A Canadian knows he is responsible to reduce the pollution he, as an individual, foists upon the choking world. He is urged to reduce his production of cataclysmic vapours by one metric tonne per year.

In the last century, North Americans and Europeans decided that rather than raising cows and hogs in spacious pastures, carefully tended barns, charming farmyards and such, it would be better to cram them together, raise them standing belly-high in their own filth, and feed them offal recycled from others of their species: pulverized, pelletized brain and spinal cord matter replaced grass, alfalfa and grain. We converted herbivores and omnivores to cannibals. This drove some of us, and many of them, mad. The methane produced by man, a natural by-product of his overstressed, overloaded digestive system, is minimal compared with that produced by his favourite foods: beef and pork. Triple jeopardy here; three flatulent animals locked in a perverse, gassy embrace.

This madness is surpassed when man pumps oil from below the surface of the Earth, then, through a complex series of actions, reductions and reactions, uploads poison into the sky. The process keeps him more mobile than necessary, warmer than he needs to be, then kills him.

A Canadian is a gassy creature who, nonetheless, likes to breath clean air and abhors signs that warn, "Don't drink the water/L'eau n'est pas potable."

If a Canadian becomes an international war criminal, engaging in cruelty as defined by the old twentieth-century Geneva Convention (recently eclipsed by belligerent, tit-for-tat principles of pre-emptive strike and terrorist assault), he must submit himself to the rigours of international jurisprudence. He will be required to subvert his national mores to those endorsed by nations of the larger world community, less one. He hopes the larger world itself, not one single rogue state, will adjudicate his individual agony of penalty, regret and redemption. He hopes humanist principles of the eighteenth-century Enlightenment still apply. He is not certain. The possibility of a new world order arising from terrorist assault and pre-emptive strike makes him very, very nervous.

Sensible Canadians assert world peace.

A Canadian has a choice; he may pay his way in the developing world (formerly known as the Third World), or he can continue to exploit those less fortunate than himself, for his own gain. His history shows he has been known to do both. The less-developed world wishes to become encumbered by the stuff that has bloated Canadians to our astonishing state of excess. It is in the nature of a hunter/gatherer to pursue a perpetual state of plenty, but when is enough too much?

Epicurus tells us: "Nothing is enough for the man for whom enough is too little."

Canada is too fat. A Canadian should take more time, use less energy – do more with less. A Canadian should return to the enlightened Highland Scots principles of stewardship: one leaves the nest in better shape than one found it.

A Canadian should always pay his way, and be more abstemious.

A Canadian should switch the gender of his third-person pronoun mid-essay.

A Canadian has the right to determine the fate of her living body. If the society is in good health, the woman likewise, and if she wishes to donate a vigorous offspring to the community and to her family, the best resources of the family and the community – which stands to benefit – should be put at her disposal, then at the disposal of her offspring through her formative years. If a woman feels unable or unwilling to produce new life, or properly nurture a newborn child, she should not be compelled. Her body: her decision.

A Canadian strives to be just.

In a Charter-driven social democracy, people, not God, elect their leaders. In a single-deity, capitalist democracy, melting-pot type situation, the state maintains power by harnessing every individual in the same tack, then pointing them in a single direction. One God for all the people – sadly, a narrowly interpreted Old Testament- or Koran-type God, not one who kicked the moneychangers out of the temple, preached peace, tolerance and forgiveness.

It is better, I think, that a diverse collection of people – a mosaic – elect its leaders in accordance with the solemn principles of all religions, which generally attain the same goal by varied means. The goal is simple human generosity, defined in the collected wisdom of the many: Gods as love.

We hardly know what to make of ourselves, these early twenty-first-century days. It bears restating: Canada is very complex; complexity leads to confusion. Confusion requires clarity; clarity arises from informed debate in an open forum.

We intuit that we have become somewhat good. When someone tells us what they think of us, a friend who knows us, who shares concerns for our mutual well-being in an all too simple us-versus-them world, we are surprised and often pleased.

In March 2003, I was in Havana, researching a new play called *Excess*, which explores the tortuous relationship among Canada, the United States of America and Cuba since the imposition of the American embargo some forty years ago. In an elegant marble office, in a decrepit building on the exquisite Vedado campus of the University of Havana, I sat with a distinguished writer who said: "We see no difference between Poland in 1939 and Iraq in 2003."

Canada had already said no. "First Iraq, then who is next?" our then prime minister, the Rt. Honourable Jean Chrétien, also said: "Terrorism is not caused by religion, but by poverty." This comment resonated with my Cuban colleague. "In the Third World," he said, "all evil comes from the north."

This resonated with me. *We* are the North. "No," he qualified. "You are the Far North. When we look northward, two nations watch and wait. One treats us with respect. The other starves us to death. Canadians are considerate; the Americans are not. Canadians we have come to love, because you are kind. Unofficially kind, but kind nevertheless. You are very sensitive. You watch. You notice detail. You are polite. You are thoughtful. Your own society is complex, so you are slow to judge others. Your concern is genuine; we know this because you ask questions and, when we respond, you actually listen. Then, more often than not, you offer your help on our terms. The United States 'offers' us American freedom. Which would you chose?"

Silence hung. "All we can do is scream and bark at America," he said, "and try to feed our people."

A Canadian, by my Cuban colleague's definition, is enlightened. "O wad some Power the giftie gie us, To see oursels as ithers see us!"

"How did this phase in your history [which I had already come to call the Canadian Enlightenment], this illuminated present, come to be?" he wondered.

I had spent considerable time in Cuba contemplating the contribution France and Scotland had made to the early formation of Canada, with particular reference to the eighteenth-century Enlightenment. A character from *Excess* provided a glib, entertaining answer: "In France, the Enlightenment resulted in Revolution and the Terror; in Scotland, the Enlightenment resulted in Canada."

A more thoughtful character might have uttered a single word: generosity. Canada's climate demands enlightened selfishness. Canadians demonstrate independence by depending on each other. With grit and luck, a Canadian becomes a generous citizen of planet World. Our survival depends upon cooperation.

"As a general guiding principle," I told him, "Northerners do not permit the Other to freeze in the dark." (There are exceptions: Alberta's crabby, energy-crisis malediction that we Easterners could so do, for all they cared, chilled us to the bone. And caught us by surprise.) We Far-Easterners, Maritimers, cast our minds back to the Great Depression, and our grandparents' tales of the trainloads of food and clothing sent west. We wondered at the brevity of gratitude.

We became enlightened because we have had, from the get-go, an intricate history in a dangerous country. Combine hard facts and varied world views with a determination to survive; realize your survival and well-being will be greatly enhanced by accommodating not only your tribe, but older tribes who know more than you about the place you live . . . You can't help but become a better Canadian.

The philosopher John Ralston Saul – spouse of former governor general Adrienne Clarkson and a most excellent gentleman, indeed – provides us with a defining national vision. He conceives a triangular base underlying Canadian society: the formative social and cultural contributions of the French, the British, and the peoples of the First Nations resonate backward through our early history and suggest our future.

I propose three pillars rising from Saul's triangular base. The British pillar was fortified, would not have stood, I contend, without the exquisitely carved, precisely fitted stones of the Scottish Enlightenment. The eighteenth-century Enlightenment suggested the early template for Canada; the Scottish Enlightenment provided a notable particular: the principle of universal education, a Scottish invention, chief among them.

The *coureurs des bois* and sturdy Scots cartographers/explorers survived the North by living with the Inuit and Woodlands peoples, adapting their ways, inter-marrying, trading, discovering who they were and how they lived. In the beauty of our great frozen mysteries, Scots and French explorers, in the presence of the First Nations, redefined themselves while inventing us. In these very early days, the Canadian Enlightenment took root, flourished and continues to thrive.

The French had turned themselves inside out. The best of what they had discovered in their twofold agony, first in the bloody Revolution, then in the bloodier Terror, gave them the urge to begin anew. The newborn soul of purified France took root in the French-tilled soil of Canada. The Auld Alliance was refreshed and reinvented in the New World by Highland Scots and French adventurers, whose survival of climate and geography depended on the goodwill of First Peoples.

One does not wish to whitewash horrors perpetrated by certain of the First Peoples on the Europeans, or the horrors perpetrated by certain of the Europeans on the First Peoples. Cruelty mars, but by no means defines, our shared histories. Given the choice of outright slaughter to secure territory, or acclimation, the English, Scots and French chose, by and large, to moderate, not annihilate.

The English were less clever than the Scots and the French in their approach to colonization and discovery. Canadians carry the image of Sir John Franklin frozen solid, his monogrammed napkins and Royal Navy flatware within reach of his rigid hand, members of his crew mutually cannibalized. Noble, and savage . . .

The British underwrote much of the great Canadian experiment, and governed fairly, often wisely. The British served and protected. In 1812, Britain, with the assistance of French, Scottish, Irish and, most importantly peoples of the First Nations, the great Tecumseh chief among them, said no to American territorial ambitions, asking: "First Upper Canada. Then who is next?" We restate this position two hundred years on. A Canadian is blessed with a long memory in a cold climate.

No matter how great our desire that it be otherwise (there is comfort in simplicity), as former governor general Adrienne Clarkson said, in the days following September 11, 2001, the world is no more or less complex than it ever was. Stasis and restraint are not chief among the gifts to humanity portioned out by the world's various gods. To aggrandize one's misfortune then impose misfortune on another; to impose narrow values or a simplistic vision upon a society not your own; to pre-empt a another people's right to define themselves – these are the greatest human evils.

It seems to me that the great breakthrough in eighteenth-century human thought, ascendant when Canada was born, is simply this: societies flourish when the needs of those least favoured are foremost in the hearts and minds of those most blessed.

One great Canadian, Tommy Douglas, not at all confused by his adopted country's complexity, said it beautifully: "We believe that every man is his brother's keeper. We believe that those who are strong ought to help bear the burdens of the weak. We believe that any society . . . is measured by what it does for the aged, the sick, the orphans and the less fortunate that live in our midst . . . I believe that love is stronger than hate, that the outstretched hand is more powerful than the clenched fist . . . that, in the long-run, feeding the hungry and clothing the naked and lifting up the fallen will do more to establish peace in the world than all the bombs and guns we can ever make. This is the policy of humanity first."

Our complex society produced a compassionate Christian social democrat parliamentarian, rooted in the best traditions of the Scottish Enlightenment. Tommy Douglas told us what we had become, and assured us that, for the good of all, ours is a very good way to be.

Douglas absorbed the long history of this country, understood the confusion and the cohesiveness of the thousands who had come before – thousands upon thousands of Canadians bound to each other by climate, geography and a profound sense of common decency.

Our Tommy put Canadian words to transplanted European ideals of human social and cultural excellence that formed, and still form, Canada's conscience.

I recant my opening remark: a Canadian is not confused. She is enlightened.

Havana, Cuba; Montreal, Quebec; and Charlottetown, PEI
Copyright © 2006 by E. Kent Stetson

E. Kent Stetson

Author of a dozen plays and several screenplays and essays, writer/director and Prince Edward Island native E. Kent Stetson has an extensive oeuvre that includes the award-winning The Harps of God. *Trained in screenwriting and direction by the British Broadcasting Corporation and the Canadian Broadcasting Corporation, Stetson co-founded, and has written and directed for Charlottetown's independent film company Points East Productions, the National Film Board of Canada, and a wide variety of independent film and television companies. He has taught introductory and advanced playwriting.*

LOUIS BALTHAZAR

UN CANADIEN EST... une personne qui vit au nord de l'Amérique sans être citoyen des États-Unis. Voilà une manière plutôt négative de décrire l'identité canadienne. Certes, on serait plus positif en rendant compte des traits de ceux qui ont été les seuls à s'appeler Canadiens pendant environ deux cents ans, soit les Canadiens de langue française. Si l'on considère cependant l'histoire et l'évolution du Canada moderne dans son ensemble, il faut bien constater que le refus de se joindre à l'expérience américaine dite révolutionnaire et républicaine constitue le trait majeur de la genèse de notre pays, l'orientation fondamentale sans laquelle il n'y aurait pas de Canada.

Le Canada que nous connaissons aujourd'hui est donc fondé pour l'essentiel sur deux refus. Celui des premiers Canadiens (anciens colons français) qui ont été quelque peu tentés par l'invitation faite à plusieurs reprises par le Congrès continental américain et par Benjamin Franklin, venu à Montréal en personne au printemps de 1776. Pourquoi ces Canadiens n'ont-ils pas voulu se joindre aux révolutionnaires américains pour se détacher de la domination britannique? D'abord et avant tout parce que l'Acte de Québec de 1774 leur conférait une reconnaissance identitaire, la légitimation de leur religion et de leurs anciennes lois civiles françaises. En d'autres termes, les premiers Canadiens ont voulu maintenir une existence séparée des États-Unis d'Amérique et demeurer sous l'autorité britannique parce que cette autorité leur assurait le maintien de leur identité comme *société distincte* en Amérique du Nord.

Le second refus, c'est celui des Loyalistes qui, pour des raisons plus conjoncturelles qu'idéologiques, n'ont pas cru bon de s'engager dans la révolution. Non pas qu'ils répudiaient l'expérience américaine comme telle, mais ils ont estimé que cette expérience pouvait se poursuivre dans le cadre d'un empire qui s'avérait, pour l'époque, relativement bienfaisant. Ces Américains authentiques n'ont pu continuer de vivre dans le cadre de la République, étant victimes de nombreuses tracasseries. Ils sont donc venus dans ce qui restait de l'empire britannique en Amérique du Nord grâce au consentement des premiers Canadiens. Ils se sont longtemps appelés *Britons* ou *British North Americans* avant d'adopter peu à peu l'appellation de *Canadians* vers le milieu du 19e siècle. Leur refus des États-Unis est essentiellement fondé sur l'amertume d'avoir été rejeté par les révolutionnaires et le désir, accentué par leur exode, de s'inspirer de la grande tradition britannique.

Ce sont ces deux groupes qui ont constitué une entité politique semi-autonome en 1867. Les autres habitants du pays, les plus anciens Canadiens, ceux qu'on appelle aujourd'hui les Premières Nations, habitant ce pays depuis des millénaires, ont malheureusement été exclus, marginalisés au moment de la fondation du Canada moderne. C'est là un phénomène navrant, révoltant, mais c'est une réalité dont il faut prendre acte. Il nous est possible aujourd'hui de corriger cette aberration, mais notre bonne volonté n'effacera pas cette réalité historique. L'identité politique canadienne a d'abord été façonnée par les deux communautés britannique et française, bien que les mœurs et la culture profonde des Canadiens (surtout les francophones) aient été marquées par la coexistence avec les autochtones.

Il en est résulté une culture politique bien particulière, nord-américaine et distincte de celle des Américains. Il s'agissait de poursuivre une évolution assez semblable à celle des États-Unis, mais sans jamais le déclarer solennellement comme avaient voulu le faire les révolutionnaires en se proclamant indépendants et en se donnant des institutions républicaines. Les Canadiens ont aussi voulu s'affranchir de la domination britannique, mais peu à peu, de façon graduelle, sans trop faire de bruit. À ce point que bien peu de Canadiens pourraient dire aujourd'hui à quel moment précis de l'histoire le Canada est devenu indépendant. Les Canadiens ont chéri la liberté, les droits humains, le suffrage universel, la démocratie, mais sans jamais le proclamer trop fort. Leur constitution, qui est demeurée longtemps une loi du Parlement britannique, a été fondée sur les bases de «la paix, de l'ordre et du bon gouvernement», contrairement aux grandes déclarations américaines: «la vie, la liberté et la poursuite du bonheur».

En conséquence, les Canadiens ont conservé un grand attachement aux institutions gouvernementales de type britannique et ont volontiers autorisé l'État qui les régit à intervenir dans la trame de leur société. Le haut-fonctionnaire, au Canada comme au Royaume-Uni, est toujours demeuré un personnage prestigieux et influent. Les Canadiens ne sont pas obsédés par la méfiance de l'ordre politique, comme le sont les Américains. Ils en ont développé un profond respect pour les procédures et un style de tolérance qui leur est propre: une grande réticence à régler les conflits par la violence, une préférence marquée pour l'accommodement social. Ainsi, les Canadiens, tout autant que les Américains, ont accepté très tôt la diversité ethnique et ont accueilli d'assez bonne grâce les immigrants qui se sont joints à eux. D'abord sans doute, tout comme aux États-Unis, des Européens exclusivement, mais peu à peu aussi des personnes venues de tous les coins de la terre. On a dit que le Canada est essentiellement un pays d'immigrants et cela est bien vrai, même dans cette société longtemps repliée sur elle-même du Québec francophone où des Écossais, des Irlandais, des Juifs, des Italiens et bien d'autres se sont intégrés à ladite «société distincte». En fait, les Canadiens issus de l'immigration récente, comme les autres, ont voulu s'intégrer à un style de vie nord-américain sans pour cela devenir des Américains.

Le Canada est donc fondé sur le *respect* des personnes et aussi, bien davantage qu'aux États-Unis, sur le respect des communautés auxquelles appartiennent ces personnes. Cela s'est manifesté dans un multiculturalisme différent de l'*ethnic revival* américain, car le Canada a conservé un sens de l'appartenance communautaire qui le démarque du culte de la liberté individuelle à l'américaine.

En raison de tout ce qui précède et sans doute de la longue tradition monarchique qui a présidé à l'évolution du pays, le Canada n'a pas donné lieu à de grands ralliements nationaux. On s'est très peu référé à une nation canadienne avant une période toute récente. Le Canada n'a pas eu de drapeau distinctif avant 1967, pas d'hymne national officiel avant 1979. Pas d'*Uncle Sam* pour faire appel à la loyauté des citoyens, à leur patriotisme.

Pas de *pledge of allegiance*, comme c'est le cas dans toutes les écoles américaines depuis la reconstruction qui a suivi la guerre civile.

Cet esprit canadien a inspiré un fédéralisme bien différent de celui des États-Unis. Même si les Pères de la Confédération canadienne ont voulu conférer au gouvernement central assez de pouvoir pour échapper aux dangers qui ont donné lieu à une horrible guerre civile aux États-Unis, c'est un fédéralisme très décentralisé qui a prévalu, d'abord dans les interprétations du Comité judiciaire du Conseil privé de Londres, puis dans la sagesse de la plupart des Premiers ministres et la volonté autonomiste de certaines provinces, toujours en raison d'un régionalisme intense et de l'évidente asymétrie de la structure du pays. Bon nombre de nationalistes et de socialistes canadiens auraient souhaité qu'il n'en fût pas ainsi et ont fait pression pour que le Canada devienne un État-nation homogène et centralisé. Ils n'ont eu gain de cause que d'une manière mitigée.

Le principe canadien du fédéralisme a été ainsi défini récemment par la Cour suprême du Canada dans son jugement relatif à la sécession du Québec (août 1998):

«Le principe du fédéralisme facilite la poursuite d'objectifs collectifs par des minorités culturelles ou linguistiques qui constituent la majorité dans une province donnée. C'est le cas au Québec, où la majorité de la population est francophone et qui possède une culture distincte. [...] La structure fédérale adoptée à l'époque de la Confédération a permis aux Canadiens de langue française de former la majorité numérique de la population de la province du Québec, et d'exercer les pouvoirs provinciaux considérables que conférait la *Loi constitutionnelle de 1867* de façon à promouvoir leur langue et leur culture» (par. 59).

Ce principe est foncièrement non américain. On n'a jamais pu imaginer, aux États-Unis, qu'un des États de l'union se fasse garant «de la poursuite d'objectifs collectifs par des minorités culturelles». Même la Louisiane, jadis française et toujours dotée d'un code civil particulier, même le Texas, jaloux de ses traits culturels propres, ne se définissent pas ainsi.

En fait, du point de vue du Québécois qui écrit ces lignes, la grande tragédie du Canada contemporain, c'est qu'un très grand nombre de

Canadiens n'épousent pas en fait ce principe du fédéralisme, que nos gouvernements ne l'appliquent pas toujours de bonne grâce, que le Canada s'approprie souvent des comportements et d'un patriotisme à l'américaine. Les Canadiens se disent souvent très fiers de ce qui les distingue par rapport aux États-Unis, mais plusieurs d'entre eux ont une façon de s'affirmer, de brandir le drapeau et de bomber le torse qui les ramène à des attitudes qui relèvent d'un ethos typiquement américain. C'est là ce qui agace tellement de Québécois et entretient chez eux des sentiments réfractaires à l'endroit de leur pays. Si le Canada devait devenir une «république une et indivisible», je crains bien que les Québécois n'y trouveraient plus leur place comme d'ailleurs aussi bon nombre d'autochtones, de Terre-Neuviens, d'Albertains et d'autres.

Si seulement le principe du fédéralisme demeurait une réalité indiscutable au Canada, les Québécois seraient les plus loyaux des Canadiens, les plus fiers d'appartenir à un pays qui permet de multiples appartenances.

Être Canadien, pour moi, c'est pouvoir être Québécois en même temps que Canadien. C'est appartenir à une nation québécoise sans remettre en cause l'appartenance à une nation canadienne.

La beauté d'être Canadien, c'est de pouvoir l'être de diverses façons!

Québec, Québec
Copyright © 2006 by Louis Balthazar

LOUIS BALTHAZAR

A CANADIAN IS . . . someone who lives in North America and yet is not a United States citizen. That may be a rather negative way to describe the Canadian identity. Certainly it would be more positive to explain the special characteristics of the people who were the only ones to call themselves "Canadians" during almost two hundred years – that is to say, French-speaking Canadians. Yet if you consider the overall history and evolution of Canada, it is important to note that the refusal to join in the American "revolutionary and republican" experiment is the key moment in our country's beginnings, the basic decision without which Canada would not exist.

The Canada we know today was based on two refusals. The initial one was that of the first Canadians (former French colonists) who were somewhat tempted by the invitation extended several times by the American Continental Congress and by Benjamin Franklin, who made a personal visit to Montreal in the spring of 1776. Why did these Canadians not want to join the American revolutionaries in breaking free from British rule? The first and the greatest factor was the Quebec Act of 1774, which gave them official recognition, and established both their religion and their original system of French civil law. In other words, the first Canadians wanted to keep apart from the United States and to remain under British authority because that same authority had promised to maintain their identity as a *distinct society* in North America.

The second refusal was that of the Loyalists, who, more out of happenstance than ideology, chose not to join in the revolution. It was not that they rejected the American experience as such, but rather that they believed that comparable freedom could be enjoyed within the framework of an empire which showed itself to be relatively benign, for that particular period. These old-style Americans could not continue to live within the framework of a republic, having been the victims of frequent harassment. For that reason, they came to what remained of the British Empire in North America, courtesy of the original Canadians. For many years they called themselves "Britons" or "British North Americans" before, little by little, coming to adopt the name of "Canadians" toward the middle of the nineteenth century. Their rejection of the United States was based on their bitterness at having been thrown out by the revolutionaries, and by their desire, strengthened by their forced emigration, to benefit from the great British tradition.

These were the two groups who created a semi-autonomous political entity in 1867. The other people who lived here, the oldest Canadians of all (known nowadays as the First Nations, since they occupied this land for thousands of years) were unfortunately excluded in 1867, marginalized right from the moment when today's Canada was founded. This is a fact that is distressing, even sickening, but it is a reality that we must recognize. Today it is possible for us to correct this mistake, but our goodwill cannot erase the historical reality. From the start, the Canadian political identity was shaped by the two groups, British and French, while the customs and basic way of living of the Canadians (especially French-speaking Canadians) were influenced by their intimate coexistence with the Aboriginals.

From this emerged a very distinctive culture, one that was North American, but different from that of the Americans. It developed along lines fairly similar to those of the USA, but without ever formally announcing it in the way that the American rebels chose, proclaiming themselves independent and giving themselves republican institutions. The Canadians, too, wanted to free themselves from British domination, but, little by little and very gradually, without ever making too much noise about it. In fact, very few Canadians nowadays could pinpoint exactly when Canada became independent. Canadians prized freedom, human rights, universal suffrage, democracy, but without ever saying so too loudly. The country's Constitution, which for many years remained a law of the British Parliament, was founded on the pillars of "peace,

order and good government," as opposed to the great American declaration in search of "life, liberty and the pursuit of happiness."

As a result, Canadians have remained very attached to the British
style of government institutions and have willingly allowed the state that
governs them to become deeply involved in the details of their lives. The
high-ranking civil servant, in Canada as in the United Kingdom, has
always been a respected and influential person. Canadians are not
obsessed with defying the political system, as Americans are. They have
developed a deep respect for the proper procedures and a very special style
of tolerance; this involves a great reluctance to handle conflict by violence,
and a marked preference for social adaptation and accommodation. So
Canadians, much like Americans, very early on accepted ethnic diversity
and were properly welcoming to the immigrants who joined them. At
first, of course, just as in the US, these immigrants all came from Europe,
but gradually they also included people from every part of the world. It
has been said that Canada is at its heart a country of immigrants, and that
is certainly true. It is even true of French-speaking Quebec, a society that
for so long has supposedly withdrawn into itself, when in fact it has
absorbed Scots, Irish, Jews, Italians and many others into the so-called
distinct society. Indeed, recent Canadian immigrants, like their prede-
cessors, have wanted to become part of the North American lifestyle
without becoming Americans.

Canada is founded on *respect* for people and also, much more than in
the US, on the respect for the communities to which these people belong.
This is revealed in a multiculturalism that is very different from the
"ethnic revival" south of the border, for Canada has kept a sense of belonging to a community that is in marked contrast with the American cult of
freedom of the individual.

Because of everything that has gone before, and no doubt because of
the long monarchical tradition that has overseen the country's evolution,
Canada has never been the setting for great patriotic rallies. References
to "a Canadian nation" were few and far between until very recently.
Canada did not get its own flag until 1967, or its national anthem until 1979.
We have no Uncle Sam figure to appeal to our loyalty, our patriotism,

and no pledge of allegiance such as has been found in every American school ever since the Reconstruction that followed their Civil War.

This Canadian approach has inspired a form of federalism very different from the American one. Even though the Fathers of Confederation wanted to give the central government enough power to avoid the dangers that produced a horrible civil war south of the border, in fact what has taken root is a very decentralized form of federalism. This is the result, first, of the legal rulings of the Judicial Committee of the Privy Council in London, and, second, of the wisdom of most prime ministers linked with the desire for more independence to be found in certain provinces, always inspired by intense regionalism and by the obvious lack of symmetry in the country's structure. Many Canadian nationalists and socialists would have preferred it if the country had been set up differently, and have worked to make Canada a more homogenized and centralized nation. They have made very little progress.

The Canadian principle of federalism was recently defined in this way by the Supreme Court in its judgment relating to the secession of Quebec (August 1998):

The principle of federalism facilitates the pursuit of collective goals by cultural and linguistic minorities which form the majority within a particular province. This is the case in Quebec, where the majority of the population is French-speaking, and which possesses a distinct culture. This is not merely the result of chance. The social and demographic reality of Quebec explains the existence of the province of Quebec as a political unit and indeed, was one of the essential reasons for establishing a federal structure for the Canadian union in 1867. The experience of both Canada East and Canada West under the *Union Act, 1840* (UK), 3-4 Vict., c. 35, had not been satisfactory. The federal structure adopted at Confederation enabled French-speaking Canadians to form a numerical majority in the province of Quebec, and so exercise the considerable provincial powers conferred by the *Constitution Act, 1867* in such a way as to promote their language and culture.

This principle is fundamentally non-American. It is impossible to imagine, in the USA, that one of the states should declare itself the protector of "the pursuit of collective goals by cultural and linguistic minorities." Even Louisiana, formerly a French colony, and still using a distinctive civil code, and even Texas, fiercely protective of its special culture, do not make any such claims.

In fact, from the viewpoint of the Québécois who writes these lines, the great tragedy of today's Canada is that a very great number of Canadians do not actually believe in this federal principle, that our governments do not always apply it willingly, and that Canada often seems to adopt American behaviour and even American-style patriotism. Canadians talk all the time about how proud they are of the things that make them different from Americans, but many of them puff up their chests and wave the flag in a way that, ironically, leads them very close to something that seems typically American. This is what so greatly irritates the Québécois, and leads us to refractory feelings about the place of Quebec in the country. Indeed, if Canada were to become "a republic one and indivisible," I am very afraid that the people of Quebec would no longer feel at home in it, along with a good number of Aboriginal people, Newfoundlanders, Albertans and others.

If only the principle of federalism could become an indisputable and undisputed reality in Canada, the Québécois would be the most loyal Canadians of all, the proudest of all to belong to a country that allows many different ways of belonging.

To be Canadian, as far as I am concerned, is to be able to be Québécois at the same time as I am Canadian – to belong to a Quebec nation without that particular belonging in any way undermining belonging to a Canadian nation.

The beauty of being Canadian is being able to be so in different ways!

Quebec City, Quebec
Copyright © 2006 by Douglas M. Gibson

Louis Balthazar

Louis Balthazar was a professor of political science at Laval University and has taught in several other Canadian, American and French universities. He has been retired from the faculty since 1997, but continues to teach, with his research mainly focused on American foreign policy and Canada–US relations. He currently is the president of the Centre for United States Studies at Université du Québec à Montréal (UQUAM). He is the author of several books and he holds a doctorate in political science from Harvard University, as well as a master's in French literature from the University of Montreal and undergraduate degrees in philosophy and theology from the Jesuit Faculties.

JOY KOGAWA

A CANADIAN IS . . . a transplanted snail called James who sat down on
a brick. A Canadian is a big fat street party on the Danforth in Toronto,
2004. A Canadian is hockey night in Canada on a small patch of ice
created by buckets of water in the backyard. A Canadian is a plane full of
people from Vancouver flying to Quebec with signs saying: "WE LOVE
YOU." A Canadian is the wind on the prairies that who has seen. And a
red-headed girl in a green-gabled house on an island with red soil. And
the Mounties who always, always get their man. A Canadian trusts the
law. And since we generally rank either second or third or fourth or whatever, we try harder. But weren't we proud when Gorbachev said, "Look
at Canada. They don't kill people there." Or something like that. That's
because a Canadian is, if nothing else, decent. Isn't that the adjective that
most commonly comes to mind? We're as decent as the day is long, are
we not – fair-minded, peaceable, not demanding guns to defend ourselves,
abhorring and resisting the culture of violence we are virtually force-fed
by the fee-fi-fo-fuming giant close by. My Canadian friends who travel a
lot say we don't know how lucky we are. I think a lot of us do know it. I,
for one, am a Canadian who loves Canada more than words can say.

My love is not cheap. It's been tested, and it endures. I can thank my
parents for this. And I can thank the community from which I came, and
which was destroyed by the particular brand of 1940s racism in my childhood. I can thank my grade two textbook, *Highroads to Reading*, that I
practically memorized when we were living in that once-upon-a-time
space called Slocan (British Columbia). Books were precious and few.
I can thank the CBC that I listened to when we were finally allowed to

have radios again, after we were moved east of the Rockies. That's when a Canadian became the Green Hornet, *The House on the Hill, Share the Wealth, Terry and the Pirates,* Johnny Wayne and Frank Shuster, Rawhide, and that beautiful blonde skater, Barbara Ann Scott. Other Canadians from my community who were exiled missed out on all that. A Canadian is a group of Japanese Canadians who were exiled for no crime. Oh sweet democratic country that I love. Some people are tired of this drumbeat.

At some point our flag stopped being bold red, white and blue inter-secting slashes, and became a red pointy leaf on white, with two red bands. At some point we stopped singing "The Maple Leaf Forever" because Wolfe the dauntless hero was being impolite in planting Britannia's flag on Canada's fair domain. In Coaldale, Miss McVeety tried to teach us French, but it was a hard row to hoe. I don't think she actually spoke French. She assigned us things to memorize from a textbook. "Mercy buck-ups," the kids said. We all soldiered on. Mr. Connors and Mr. Bryant taught us about the crazy kings and queens of England, but we didn't learn about Canadian history. A Canadian is someone who probably doesn't know much about Canada.

There was a year of patriotic pride when we sang with great gusto, "It's the hundredth anniversary of CON-fed-er-a-tion." And there was no cloudy doubt in the clear blue air that Canada would last as long as the planet did. There was also no doubt that everyone in Canada was white, including me. My parents were another matter. I couldn't really whiten them.

Years later, I discovered that I wasn't completely white, and for that I received an Order of Canada. One of the most memorable moments of that day occurred when a fellow recipient who was sitting beside me leaned over to make small talk as we waited for the ceremony to begin. "I have been to your beautiful country," he said. I was so Canadian and polite and smiled and nodded. He went on to tell me things about my country – Japan – and I kept nodding. He was French Canadian. I don't know what his name was, but if we were arranged alphabetically, maybe his name started with K. Anyway, as I say, a Canadian is someone who probably doesn't know much about Canada, including who a Canadian is.

About a year ago, I was visiting Thorold, a small town near St. Catharines, Ontario, when my son introduced me to one of his acquaintances, who looked to be about thirty years old. The man glanced down at this old white-haired Asian foreigner from his not-so-great height and said, "Does she speak English?" I ought not to have been surprised. It wasn't so long ago that only white people were Canadians. I was a bit put off, but answered politely, "Yes, I speak English," and left it at that. A Canadian is a foreigner who isn't a foreigner.

A few miles away, in the most multicultural city in the world, every subway ride is a trip through the United Nations. I suppose it's our role, as Torontonians, to trumpet the news that humans from all over the world can, generally speaking, live together in peace. It's one of the things that makes me happy about this country. Our ancestors might have fought each other, but we don't have to.

In my untypical Canadian childhood, because I was related to the country of my ancestors, I was "a stench in the nostrils of the people of Canada." Today, another Canadian child goes through that wringer, running home from school with her books clutched tight to her chest, and after supper she's fighting with her parents about what she will or will not wear on her head. And somewhere in a high-rise elevator, a gentle Canadian boy is aware that, even though he is no longer wearing his turban, the old woman has moved aside anxiously. All these little moments of life are the mirrors that tell us who we are.

These days, I'm more worried about the children on the streets, in temporary shelters, in transitional housing – the children who are living on the hungry side of life in a worldwide apartheid, where the dividing line is as black and white as the rich and the poor. The mindset to be dismantled is the powerful faith that money is everything. In its name and for its sake, we are giving our all, sacrificing our lives, our peace, our children and our neighbours as ourselves. Like others all over the planet, we are drifting in the miasma of a dream of riches that has turned murky. Is there, as Jane Jacob's book title says, a *Dark Age Ahead*? Does our country have the kind of enlightened citizenry and moral leadership to guide us through the nightmare of greed?

There was one among us who died recently – a man who helped to shine the light of hope into the darkness of injustice and apartheid in South Africa. Ted Scott, the former primate of the Anglican Church was, as the title of his biography states, a man of "Radical Compassion." Joe Clark called him "an almost perfect representation of Canada."

I was sitting behind a pillar during Ted Scott's memorial service, leaning this way and that, trying to get a glimpse of Desmond Tutu, who was in the pulpit at St. James' Cathedral. He spoke warmly about Ted Scott, about the gratitude of South Africans. At one point, I could see his left hand as he stretched out his arms and repeated the word *all*. "All – all – all. Arafat. Saddam Hussein. All. All. All. *All*." He was including every single person on the globe in the human family – the blacks, the whites, the Aboriginals, the old, the rich, the despised, the admired, the tyrant, the remorseless psychopath. All. All. All.

And so a Canadian is part of the All that includes our Ted Scotts and our Paul Bernardos, our Conrad Blacks and our neighbours sleeping and dying on the streets.

These days, I am working with some of the neighbours in my corner of the world, in Toronto's Old Town surrounding the St. Lawrence Market. We are trying to demonstrate, through the work of a community currency, the Toronto Dollar, that the power of caring is still alive, and that we can work together to make a difference. We are trying to connect the streets and the towers, trying to bridge the horrible gap between rich and poor. It's a hard row to hoe, as hard as trying to learn a language from a text-book. But we do what we can.

Nelson Mandela says he comes from a culture of *ubuntu*, a philosophy based on belonging where the essential identity of a person is based not on "I think therefore I am," but on "I am because we belong." The enemy, then, is not someone to destroy, but someone to embrace.

I think Canada is closer to a culture of *ubuntu* than many other countries. *Je suis. Nous sommes.* Where we fail, I'm thankful that mercy bucks us up.

Toronto, Ontario
Copyright © 2006 by Joy Kogawa

Joy Kogawa

Joy Kogawa is best known for her novel Obasan, *which has won a number of national awards. She has seven honorary doctorates from Canadian universities, and is a Member of the Order of Canada. She has been working for a number of years in the field of community currency and is part of the Toronto Dollar project. Her latest novel,* Emily Kato, *was published in 2005.*

WADE MacLAUGHLAN

A CANADIAN IS . . . lucky. The challenge for the Canadian is to act on Stephen Leacock's famous quip: "I'm a great believer in luck, and I find the harder I work, the more I have of it." We Canadians need to work at getting the most out of being Canadian, at truly understanding how lucky we are, and embracing how our "luckiness" defines our identity as Canadians.

In terms of war or national insecurity, which preoccupy so much of the world, and which mark most national identities, the Canadian enjoys a measure of peace that is known by few people in the world. We have not engaged in all-out hostilities for sixty years, and have not fought a war on Canadian soil for almost two centuries. Our nation has no enemies.

Canada's nature is bountiful, and wondrously beautiful. Notwithstanding the fact that Canadians often deny rather than embrace our "nordicity," this country's nature is not severe. We do not live in fear of natural disasters, unless you count winter. Sure, we must pay attention to the elements, but we have significantly more technology and resources at our disposal for this purpose than is true for most of the world, or than were available to our forebears. Indeed, the Canadian is the world's largest consumer of energy.

A Canadian is wealthy, compared to just about anyone else in the world. We work and buy in an advanced market economy, supported by systems of credit, property rights, financial institutions and infrastructure. The greatest underlying institution for Canada's wealth is its system of education, research and innovation. A Canadian is part of a learned nation, although we seriously underestimate how hard we must work to stay lucky in this regard. A Canadians is a trader; his country enjoys persistent positive balances of trade. And in spite of the fact that most of the world takes a friendly view of trading with Canada, the Canadian must work at this too.

The Canadian is healthy, with one of the highest life expectancies in the world and a remarkable system of health care. We have a lot of knowledge about our health. We know that we could have even better health if we did a better job of looking after ourselves. But, instead of taking obvious steps to avoid preventable diseases, the Canadian complains that more money should be spent to support one of the best-financed health care systems in the world. Medicare (which has become a proxy for anxiety that our health care system is failing us) is now claimed to be a primary element of Canada's national identity. The Canadian knows that we are in trouble when an unrelentingly expensive "free" service is claimed to be a national icon.

A Canadian enjoys abundant natural resources. We have lots to eat, at a price that is arguably too affordable. We have more water than anyone else in the world. We have ample open space, more than any other country, although a surprisingly small number of Canadians really take advantage of our great spaces.

A Canadian is, or should be, rich in culture. The whole world knows about our fiction and our popular music. We do not do so well at sports, beyond hockey and curling. We are not as good as we should be at history. As Jane Jacobs reminds us in *Dark Age Ahead*, memory is a fundamental building block of society. Canadians spend too much time and resources amusing themselves through television, Internet, cell phones, and so on, and not enough truly engaging with their history, their culture, or their national and local communities.

Canadians are rich in diversity. We have invested a great deal in our standing as a bilingual, multicultural society. In this, the rest of the world can learn from Canada. We have invested in our heritage and the realities of our First Nations. In this, we still have much to learn for ourselves, and not much to teach the world. Diversity is and must continue to be one of Canada's outstanding features, but we have to be careful not to work so hard at embracing our diversity that we render it artificial or insincere.

With all of these advantages and rich possibilities, what is a Canadian?

Let me begin by considering my own situation, for each Canadian has his or her own possibilities and context as we engage with this wonderful country. My world is different from that of my parents; some might say dramatically so. My world is different from that of a young First Nations woman; from that of a Western farmer; from that of a new immigrant or refugee; or from that of a big-city power-broker. This is not a comment about hierarchy, but about context.

There is no single answer to what it means to be a Canadian. This is a deeply autobiographical question. It means coming to terms with one's own time, place, heritage and identity; with one's community or communities, and one's sense of well-being. In turn, one must locate these autobiographical elements in the larger historical, geographic, economic, sociological, cultural, environmental and other frames which constitute Canada in the world and which give Canada meaning.

In effect, to be Canadian is to engage in an unrelenting negotiation between the *particular* and the *grand*. The *particular* should not be self-indulgent or self-serving, but we do have to put ourselves into it. The *grand* should not be invented or forced, but Canada is so grand that we have to make a serious effort at truly knowing and loving it. Coming back to the autobiographical, I believe that to know and love Canada, we have to know and understand ourselves – notably, through the lenses of *place* and *time*.

Place: I am a native Prince Edward Islander. I grew up in a rural community – Stanhope – where my ancestors have been settled for almost two hundred years. PEI was the first point of landing in Canada for all of my ancestors, and PEI has been their home ever since. All sixteen of my great-great-grandparents were either born on PEI or emigrated here at a young age, and therefore spent their productive lives here. One of my great-great-grandfathers was born on the ocean during the transatlantic migration. None of my direct ancestors has left PEI for more than a sojourn.

So, that pretty much settles the primary question of *place* for me: Prince Edward Island – a place you can get your arms around. I come from a remarkably tight rural community and a large extended family. My first eight years of education were in a two-room rural school – a very good school, with talented and dedicated teachers who enjoyed the full support of the community. My parents both came from large families, producing a huge network of uncles and aunts and other close relatives, including a total of almost seventy first cousins. On the day of my installation as president of the University of Prince Edward Island in October of 1999, I indicated that some of my family were present. When I asked them to stand, a total of 155 people stood up.

My partner and I live in a wonderful home on a special point of land that extends between two bays on the north shore of PEI, overlooking the dunes of PEI National Park. This is where I grew up; you can see my grade school across the Bay. We share this magnificent place with the foxes, crows, eagles and other wild creatures of our neighbourhood, and spend a lot of time communing with and enjoying nature. We live with the outdoors, and we have a sense of community with our neighbours. Of course, we still do not do enough of this, but we count ourselves very, very fortunate to have this extraordinary sense of local place.

Let me turn to my engagement with my larger place: Canada. I have done more travelling than my ancestors. At a young age, I developed a hunger to see all of Canada, beginning with a school-bus-and-sleeping-bag visit to Expo '67 with my Wolf Cub pack as a twelve year old. By the time I was twenty-two, I had worked as a bus-tour guide on trips to coasts, the longest being a twenty-three-day excursion from Southern Ontario to Vancouver Island and back. I had spent a winter as a rough-neck on the oil rigs in north-central Alberta, a summer as a labourer in a road construction camp in the far north of Quebec, and a season as a front desk clerk at Jasper Park Lodge. I participated in a summer French-language exchange program in rural Quebec, and subsequently mastered French, which permitted an eight-year stint as director of the Common Law–Civil Law Exchange program. I continue to travel to all parts of Canada, and take an active part in various national bodies.

Time: My engagement with Canada was, and is, a product of my time. I had the good fortune to stay in school through university studies (which my parents did not). I came of age during the year of Expo '67 and Canada's Centennial. On PEI in 1964, when I was nine years old, we celebrated the centenary of the Charlottetown Conference. I was at a good age to join in the initiatives and the spirit of engagement that followed publication of the report of the Royal Commission on Bilingualism and Biculturalism. I wore a Trudeau button in 1968, at the age of thirteen. It was a time when it was okay to be "turned on" to Canada, all the more so because of our anxieties about national unity. For me, this same spirit of engagement has continued for more than three decades.

What is more, we were expected to travel – and to do it on a rudimentary budget. In one eighteenth-month period (1976-77), I hitchhiked twenty-five thousand miles across Canada, the United States, Europe and even Asia (until I found that I could afford the Asian trains). Amazingly, I earned enough along the way to put some money in the bank. Much more importantly, I learned an enormous amount about life, and about Canada in the world, in the many places that I visited, and from the people I met.

Quebec sociologist François Ricard writes in *La génération lyrique* about the "lyricism" of the generation of people who were born in the first nine years after 1945, in a spirit of liberty, optimism and bountiful opportunity. I was born at the end of 1954, just managing to squeeze into the lyrical generation, and I count myself lucky for that too. As Canadians, we should think of ourselves as the lyrical country. We have good reason to be.

For me, my "place" in Canada is both intensely local and proudly national. I say this with a great deal of humility. While I embrace my sense of place, both local and national, I know that I should do more to fully nourish these two dimensions, and to negotiate the relationship between the particular and the grand on a continuing basis. I want to spend more time kayaking on the Bay at home, and reading more local history. There are many, many places in Canada that I want to see, and to see again. There is so much more that I want to read. This struggle with time and place and scale captures the "agony" that comes with truly embracing Canada.

One of my greatest concerns about Canada today is that we do not know what it is to work at being lucky. We exercise our citizenship more by insisting on entitlements than by making a special effort to know, explore and contribute to our wonderful country. We are more likely to get up in the morning objecting to something that is not being done for us than we are to smile and tell ourselves how incomparably lucky we are to be Canadians. I say this because, unless we make individual and collective decisions to change this situation, and to do it in a spirit of lyricism, our luck may run out.

MacMillan Point, Prince Edward Island
Copyright © 2006 by Wade MacLaughlan

Wade MacLaughlan
Wade MacLaughlan is president of the University of Prince Edward Island. He is a lawyer by training, and his field of teaching and research is administrative and public law. Since becoming president of UPEI, he has been a successful advocate for new investments in R&D and innovation, as well as for core funding of higher education. He also serves on numerous community and public service boards. Wade MacLaughlan teaches every student at UPEI by offering a lecture on "The Importance of Effective Writing and Communication" to each section of English 101, a required English composition course.

DOUGLAS GLOVER

A CANADIAN IS . . . someone born in the country called Canada or someone born to a Canadian parent outside of Canada or someone who has immigrated to Canada and become a citizen. No other definition makes sense. Any other definition is contentious, because it leaves someone out, or it involves a chimera or a polymorph; I, for example, am not multicultural, French, bilingual or Aboriginal. Any definition that touches those notes does not play me. Somewhat mysteriously, even to me, I don't even live in the country; I am a Canadian expatriate, though I feel fiercely Canadian. If this doesn't seem to make perfect sense, remember that Canada is a country that numbers among its citizens (including some members of Parliament) people who are dedicated to dissolving the country. Canadians are, among other things, people who do not live in the country, who think that the country should not exist and, of course, people whose ancestors lived in Canada for thousands of years before it became Canada, and thus might feel themselves to be only tangentially or at best accidentally Canadian.

We should always remember that being a member of a national, linguistic, racial or ethnic group is largely a matter of accident, the accident of birth. Relatively few people actually choose a nationality, language or ethnicity (race is a bit different, I suppose – never a matter of choice). When they do choose a new nation, often their reasons are practical rather than sentimental: many people in the past came to Canada for cheap land or because it was easy to slip across the border into the United States or, more recently, just because the standard of living is better than the place they come from and the government generally more benevolent and stable. Nevertheless, because they actually choose to become Canadians, there is a sense in which these immigrant Canadians are more Canadian than the Canadians who didn't choose. My mother and father used to call them "New Canadians," which, in those days, generally meant people from Eastern Europe. We were the Old Canadians, I guess, and the Iroquois on the reserve down the road were the even older Canadians (although, in fact, they came to the country in the 1780s, at about the same time as my Loyalist ancestors; both groups chose to come to Canada because it was British, not because it was Canadian).

I grew up in a part of the country, southwestern Ontario, where the concession roads have names belonging to those early Loyalist settlers, where towns were named for English colonial officials (Simcoe) or famous natives (Brantford) or even Iroquois tribes (Cayuga); where the geography is inscribed with the history of that first wave of political refugees; where the countryside itself is a repository of cultural memory. The names of the concession roads are mostly English and Scottish, but by the time I was a teenager farms up and down those roads had been taken over by immigrant Ukrainians, Hungarians and Belgians. I had Christmas at home, and then a few days later would go to a friend's house and celebrate Ukrainian Christmas. I think my parents felt vaguely threatened; the known world was changing around them, their sense of continuity and identity vaguely challenged. I was alternately puzzled and fascinated by the strange customs in my friends' houses, the smells of foreign cooking, and the thick, sometimes incomprehensible accents of their parents and grandparents.

The girl I went out with in high school was Ukrainian, born in Canada of first-generation immigrants, "New Canadians." Her father had arrived during one of those inter-war cycles of migration, only to find himself whisked to the Prairies to perform what seemed to him like slave labour building railways. He loathed Canada, espoused a brand of Marxist socialism somewhat to the left of Joseph Stalin, and would hold meetings with compatriots at which the men would make florid toasts and declaim Ukrainian poetry. (Apparently, the RCMP would make friendly visits every year just to check on him; he compelled his daughters to join the local Baptist church instead of the equally local Ukrainian Orthodox church, so as to make himself less visible.) After his wife died, he decided to return to the old country, to shake the dust of Canada from his feet, to abandon our capitalist Babylon. But after a short time he returned, even more disillusioned (then I learned about the intricacies of Ukrainian retirement homes, the communist homes and the anti-communist homes). He and his wife are buried in Canada, though in life he was clearly a man who had become neither one thing nor another. And I think this is how you become a Canadian, by birth and burial, by accident and the generational accretion of graves and those minute adjustments of assimilation, like sending your daughters to the acceptable church instead of the one in which you were raised.

Identity – which is different from choice and accident – grows out of continuity and familiarity and a sense of difference; we are what we are familiar with, which, first of all, is the place where we are born, the habits of our parents and our childhood peers. Being a Canadian, which might in the end be a process rather than a state, since most of us are in one sense or another new Canadians, means being available to certain influences, threads of discourse, sentences, if you will. For example, Canadians grow up aware of the oppositional nature of their social construct, the uneasy coexistence of two languages, which creates a fundamental relativity in the notion of Canadian identity. Likewise, we are a nation without a single history, except on the meta-level, where we can all basically agree on dates and places and characters involved, even if we can't agree on the meaning of events: Was the Battle on the Plains of Abraham a defeat or a victory for Canada? What we know on the meta-level is that something important to our story happened there; the continuing conversation as to the nature and meaning of that event is part of what it means to be a Canadian. Accepting this condition puts a premium on interaction with the other, on dialogue, on rhetoric, on persuasion and influence, on irony, on change itself. In Canada, there are no fixed positions. And accepting this (again, many of us accept it with irritation and ill-grace), we accept that lack of a final answer, the messianic vision of, say, our neighbours to the south, and their image of themselves as a melting pot, with its Anglo-Protestant-hegemonic subtext. For sure, we are also not-Americans (though, of course, as with all Canadian sentences, one immediately has to backtrack, because within Canadianism there is a thread of discourse about wanting to be American).

A year ago I took my boys swimming at the beach at Port Dover on Lake Erie, where my grandfather built a family cottage, and where I spent many a summer day as a child playing in the shallow waves. When I was young, the beach was monochrome white, and everyone spoke English; my aunt and uncle, who had taken over the family cottage, knew almost everyone in town by name. We called the people in Quebec "Kewbeckers" and took our British connection for granted (we were, by descent, Loyalists; my mother's father was an Englishman). But last summer the beach was crowded with a new generation of young families, like a colony of seabirds, mostly ignoring the single darkly tanned bare-breasted woman with gilt nipple paint, whose presence testified to the retreat of Ontario's old moralizing Tory heart. From the blankets and beach chairs, nearby conversations wafted toward me in the sullen heat, reminding me of the old days. But then I noticed that the people around me weren't speaking English. Their words were unfamiliar, foreign – Slavic, mid-European, I thought; the speakers were stocky, practical-looking men and wide-hipped mothers in bikinis enjoying a new material splendour – the newest new Canadians. Out on the sandbar, a woman in a sari skimmed her palms across the water. And, as the sun began to set, I noticed a lean Indian man in shorts and a T-shirt standing with one foot against his thigh, a yoga pose he assumed with unconscious grace, still as a photograph, the very image of a pilgrim washing in the Ganges, but translated to southern Ontario. And I thought how much the old Canada I had grown up in had changed.

I could have felt threatened by this, I could have mourned, but, recalling that, yes, my ancestors too had come as refugees from another country and, without thinking, had casually displaced those who were already dwelling here, I chose instead to wonder how living amid the concession roads named for Loyalist ancestors would eventually change this man and, conversely, how his presence would inevitably change the descendants of those Loyalists. How, I asked myself, would his children and his children's children alter over the generations? How would their loyalties change as the spiritual anchor of ancestral graves began to take hold? How would dwelling among the Inuit, Cree and Ojibway change him? What effect would living in a bilingual country, where we can read history in at two (or more) different and opposite ways, transform the structure of his thought? And when he had joined the threads of his own memories, allegiances, and dreams to the sentences which already inhabit this strange and mysterious land, what would we be become?

Wilton, New York
Copyright © 2006 by Douglas Glover

Douglas Glover

Douglas Glover is an award-winning author whose bestselling novel, Elle, *won the 2003 Governor General's Award for Fiction, was a finalist for the IMPAC Dublin International Literary Award, and has been optioned by Igloolik Isuma Productions, makers of* Atanarjuat *(*The Fast Runner*). His stories have been frequently anthologized and his criticism has appeared in numerous publications. He was recently the subject of a TV documentary in a series called* The Writing Life, *as well of a collection of critical essays,* The Art of Desire: The Fiction of Douglas Glover. *Douglas Glover has also taught or been writer-in-residence at several colleges and universities.*

LORNA MARSDEN

A CANADIAN IS . . . one who is distinguished by being able, during the past century and a third, to contribute to the definition of this country and its culture; to create rather than simply to accept; to form and reform rather than being merely formed.

Being a Canadian is a deep feeling, but not just that; a citizenship, but not only that. Being Canadian is an impetus to action.

Throughout my lifetime, our history has been one of the increasing, incremental strength of independence and identity of Canada and as Canadians. As a child of immigrants, used to the long and often emotional discussions about the "old country," it has been a joy and a privilege to feel part of the rise of Canada's independent voice in the world. My first vivid memory of this is hearing on CBC Radio, one morning, news of Newfoundland's vote to join Confederation, and rushing out of the house to tell my parents, who were digging in our vegetable garden, this great news. Newfoundlanders had chosen to become Canadians! As Vancouver Islanders, we especially rejoiced that the other island had joined. In the aftermath of the tensions and tragedies of the Second World War years, this decision epitomized growth and hope.

Why were my friends and I all so pleased, as we looked across the Strait of Georgia to Mount Baker shining on the US shores, to know that we were Canadians and not Americans? It was not that we did not admire Americans and study them all the time, but we knew that we were different. So we would go down to the dock after school to see the ferry arrive from Anacortes with its passengers with American accents and strange licence plates. That our dollar was worth more than theirs was, at the time, a source of chauvinistic pride.

The voice of Lester Pearson, his recognition at the UN and his Nobel Prize; the ambitious dreams of John Diefenbaker for the North; James Bannerman and CBC *Wednesday Night*; the Carson family drama at lunchtime on weekdays, for which we raced home from school – all on the CBC Radio, our chief source of news, music and entertainment. The CBC developed in listeners like me a sense of what we stood for in Canada. We had a restrained and deprecating sense of humour, we depended heavily on external trade and the decisions of other countries, and we took seriously speaking properly, music, books and drama. We heard that more Canadian poets, artists, scientists and intellectuals were needed to build this country, and felt that we should be part of this work.

So it was not surprising, many years later, when the CBC broadcast the public hearings of the Royal Commission on the Status of Women as it travelled the country, that we and our mothers were mobilized to action about the inequality of women. We felt strong bonds with women all across the country and in all walks of life; with women attempting to divorce brutal husbands and support their children; with Aboriginal women; with immigrant women; and, indeed, with the commissioners trying to get the ear of governments to enact better laws. The values that underpinned our understanding of the world were much greater than our differences, despite the divisions in the country. We set about to do something about those inequalities, and it never occurred to us that we might not get the changes that were necessary. We did get a great many of them.

Back in the 1950s, probably because of Mr. Pearson, the UN was both important and interesting to us at school. The Cold War was the war of my generation, and we followed the spying, the weapons competition and the standoffs avidly. As Canadians, we might not have been able to prevent the dropping of the bomb, but we knew that we would play a role in the aftermath. During the tensions of the Cold War, strangely enough, we felt efficacious.

In all these years since the end of the Second World War, we have seen growing differentiation of Canadian values, styles and policies from those of other countries and cultures. Quite regularly, Canadians have elected leaders who have enhanced this differentiation – most notably Lester Pearson and Pierre Trudeau. The Canadian flag, the Canadian Centennial, the patriation of the Constitution, have each symbolized the determination to promote Canadian values through peaceful means. Official bilingualism, peacekeeping, the Charter of Rights and Freedoms, joining the G8, the Free Trade Agreement, and the "fish wars" were all determined measures to promote independence through action. Action was equally determined by the entrepreneurs and artists, the scholars and scientists who advanced our presence. Marshall McLuhan wrapped it up by looking at the world, at technology, and finding the global village.

Canadians do travel. We all know as we grow up that we'll survive only by trading and by understanding the rest of the world. Like those *Two Innocents in Red China*, Jacques Hébert and Pierre Trudeau (one of the seminal books of my generation), we leave Canada to come to understand the *them* and the *us*. Indeed, many among us go further and absorb ourselves in other cultures, but that is transitory. Most will return to Canada.

Nothing causes one to feel quite so much solidarity with other Canadians as being stuck in a hot and endless passport lineup at some foreign airport, and being pushed around by a belligerent official. Or finding a Canadian in some small village far from Canada. At home, we may be squabbling or critical of Albertans or Quebeckers, of pinstripe "suits" or long unwashed hair, but in that foreign setting an enormous solidarity emerges among Canadians, regardless of language, ethnicity, creed or age.

Then we return to Canada to complain. A Canadian is a champion complainer. We have a comparative advantage in complaining. Nothing is ever quite right. We would be embarrassed to stand with our hands on our hearts pledging allegiance, but we happily drone out our national anthem in both languages. We would rebel against the class structure of other societies, but we seem eager to preserve our own. We do not like people to be too rich or successful, or too poor or excluded. We rail on about our sports teams, but spend millions on them. We dislike most politicians and forms of government regulation, but expect governments to do much more for us than they do. And the weather? We are permanently outraged by it, except on those few days when it is perfect and we live in the best country in the world.

I live among fifty thousand young Canadians studying at York University. Among them, we estimate, they speak about ninety-five languages. They are of every known ethnicity and religion. They live in the age of terrorism, but are determined to do something about it. They squeeze in and out of our crowded classrooms together; they travel all over the world; they have wonderful humour; they disagree over ideas and beliefs and theories; they want to change things and do so frequently; they are champion complainers in the best Canadian tradition, and I am happy that they will inherit this country.

Toronto, Ontario
Copyright © 2006 by Lorna Marsden

Lorna Marsden

Lorna Marsden is president and vice-chancellor of York University in Toronto, and a former senator. She is the author of three books and over one hundred articles in her field of economic sociology. From 1975 to 1977, she served as the third president of the National Action Committee on the Status of Women. In the 1970s and 1980s, she served on the executive of the Liberal Party of Canada. She was appointed a Member of the Order of Canada in 2006.

SAEED RAHNEMA

A CANADIAN IS . . . someone who finds it difficult to define, without reflection, "What is a Canadian?" The simple fact that the question needs to be asked is an indication, in and of itself, of the challenge inherent in answering it, and the answers are inevitably contradictory in nature. National identity, particularly for a nation like Canada, is not static, and continually takes shape and is moulded through constant debate and reflection, not to mention changing configurations. Part of being Canadian is the desire and freedom to partake in this dialogue. Indeed, Canadians, like no other nation in the world, are willing to question themselves and, for this reason, Canadian national identity is more flexible and evolving than most others. This is a great strength and not a weakness of Canadian society.

From one perspective, anybody carrying a Canadian passport is a Canadian. But not every Canadian passport holder shares a set of perspectives that could differentiate her or him from citizens of other countries. It is difficult to generalize on attributes of nationhood, and we, as Canadian men and women of all ages, with diverse life stories and social and cultural backgrounds, are different in our aspirations, ideologies and politics, have different tastes and dance to different music. Yet it is possible to identify some of the dominant characteristics of the typical Canadian.

There are curious aspects to Canadian identity in that positive values, such as moderation, modesty, tolerance and peacefulness can, in the extreme, actually have the opposite effect. A Canadian is, generally speaking, a moderate individual. The tendency toward moderation and avoiding extremes is more or less universal among Canadians. However, at times, this tendency is pushed to extremes, which in fact can lead to inaction. A Canadian also tends to have an aversion to major change. To a certain degree satisfied with the status quo, Canadians, for the most part, tend to be conformist, preferring minor changes brought about in a slow and gradual fashion.

A Canadian is modest, though there can be contradictions in the way this modesty is selectively expressed toward different people and countries. Most Canadians are modest toward Americans. This may derive from degrees of self-underestimation, combined with lesser recognition of Canada and Canadians' abilities, potentials or achievements. One could think this particularly natural when one lives in close proximity to such a forceful and domineering neighbour. Yet Canada has everything it needs – geographically the second largest country in the world, endowed with enormous natural resources and wealth, a most prosperous and vibrant economy, the most multiethnic population of any country in the world, and for years at the top of the United Nations Human Development Index – despite its cold weather, to make its citizens proud and self-confident. It is therefore puzzling that, despite all of these amazing resources and capabilities, Canadians tend to be self-deprecating. For while it is a virtue not to be boastful, showy and arrogant, self-doubt can hinder the full use of the country's resources and capabilities.

This brand of modesty often disappears and turns into a certain degree of self-congratulation and even self-assurance when it comes to Canadians' dealings with nationalities from less powerful and less privileged countries. New immigrants are particularly appreciated when they are deemed vulnerable and needy. The mild-mannered and truly polite Canadian is always ready to help the new immigrant, but often only until the latter attempts to become equal and take up competitive space.

A Canadian is tolerant. Tolerance is a Canadian characteristic, with both positive and nullifying aspects. Living in the most multiethnic, multicultural society in the world exposes Canadians to different cultures and modes of behaviour. While this great mosaic makes for a large number of hyphenated Canadians, budding identity crises and tensions of different sorts, it also creates great potential for the country, though one that is not fully exploited or utilized. Walking on Yonge Street in downtown Toronto, touching shoulders with people of all colours and nationalities, feels like walking on the globe. But move to the next block on Bay Street, and up the elevators of the high-rises, and colour and diversity begin to diminish. In the Canadian social pyramid, the base is the most colourful, but as we move to the apex colours fade away. Being tolerant of ethnoracial minorities and living under a formal policy of multiculturalism has not made Canadians immune to racism. Though vehemently denied, implicit and systemic racism, and at times even explicit manifestations of it, exists and is practised every day. Tolerating "others" is no doubt better than rejecting, avoiding, or ignoring them, but in the overall continuum of race and ethnic relations, tolerance is only the first step toward the acceptance, appreciation and celebration of difference.

Being moderate, modest and tolerant, and being aware of having such positive qualities, can also make Canadians complacent, not seeing the need to make an effort to recognize existing problems. That might be the reason why one witnesses this complicity even among otherwise progressive Canadians, whose commitment to social justice may not include a serious effort to improve their own understanding of racism. Lack of appreciation of others is not only harmful to ethnic minorities, but is most damaging to Canada itself and to all Canadians. As a result of the country's immigration policy, and contrary to the claims of right-wing institutes and laments about Canada's brain drain, Canada is blessed with massive brain gains from all corners of the world, attracting highly educated and talented individuals, whose education and training have been paid for by other countries. Yet their talents and expertise are not always recognized and employed, forcing many educated new immigrants either to work in low-paying and low-skill jobs, or to eventually leave the country for better opportunities, often in the United States, or simply back in their original homeland.

Even for those visible-minority immigrants who can make it in Canada, there is a glass ceiling. This is especially true for those newcomers who do not accept such limits or recognize the lines that they are not meant to cross. I can vividly see this among many immigrant communities, including among my compatriot Iranian-Canadians. A relatively new community, mostly immigrating to Canada after the 1979 revolution and the establishment of the Islamic Republic, Iranian Canadians, like other immigrants, are striving hard and taking advantage of the opportunities in Canada. They are contributing to Canadian society in different industries, businesses, trades, media, arts, sciences, academia, law, medicine, social services and government. Yet despite their remarkable capability to adapt to new conditions and to succeed in their fields, many of them feel the limits imposed on them because of their ethnic and national origin. The tragedy of September 11, 2001, and the stereotypical reactions to all peoples coming from Islamic societies, whether religious or secular, has drastically worsened the situation for these immigrants. Indeed, secular people coming from Islamic countries are in an even more difficult and confusing situation, and are in a sense doubly alienated. Not only do we face the same discriminatory treatment as our religious compatriots, but the dominant culture can sometimes mould us into something that we are not: we are expected, even pressured, to represent the cultural/religious values and practices that were not even ours in our home countries, and are even less so here in Canada.

No doubt the situation is changing, though slowly, and the new generations brought up together in Canada will have a better chance, and the glass ceiling will eventually crack. As time passes, particularly for the new generations, the signs and symbols of ethnic difference gradually fade away. Different accents, different behavioural patterns, even different tastes will submerge under the dominant "Canadian" patterns. Yet the most visible sign of ethnic and racial difference – that is, the look and colour of skin – will remain, and as long as racism persists and barriers to race equity are not removed, non-white Canadians will continue to be only tolerated, and therefore in a disadvantageous position.

Canada's multiculturalism policy, while providing opportunities for different ethnic and cultural groups to maintain and celebrate some of their traditions, does not counter racism. If overemphasized, it can actually contribute to the reduced cohesiveness and greater fragmentation of Canadian society. In every social system, the more cohesive the subsystems (in this case different ethnic/cultural/religious minorities), the less cohesive will be the overall system (Canada), and vice-versa. There are advantages and disadvantages either way, and no doubt an optimal mix is required. So far, multiculturalism has meant the celebration of different ethnic cultures, costumes, food and music. Still, as racism lingers on, and ethnic minorities remain marginalized, they tend to fortify their communities (ghettoized multiculturalism), and in some cases the religious and conservative elements attempt to revive otherwise dying traditions, where possible taking advantage of loopholes in government policies to impose their agenda on the community. The best case in point is the manner in which religious communities took advantage of Ontario's *Arbitration Act* of 1991. After the Jewish community began to formally use *Halacha* (Jewish law) for arbitration, the conservative Muslim leaders tried to use *Shari'a* in their community. The irony is that such tolerance of different religious interpretations and permitting their entry into the secular Canadian legal system end up jeopardizing the universality of human rights of some Canadian citizens, particularly women, and reinforcing notions of second-class entitlement for some Canadians.

A Canadian is also a pacifist and a peaceful individual. Despite an unmerciful beginning – the very dark chapter of what the founding fathers of Canada did to the Aboriginals and First Nations of this land – and in spite of being dragged into several imperialist wars, Canadians in general care for peace, are antiwar and abhor violence. In fact, to the rest of the world, Canada's most identifiable international role is its continuing legacy of peacekeeping in unstable areas of the globe. Although this legacy was tarnished when, in the early 1990s, Canada joined the US-led coalition in the Persian Gulf War, and regained when Canada refused to join the second invasion of Iraq, the world recognizes Canada as a major peacekeeper and promoter of human rights.

In terms of identity, Canadians in general prefer to be differentiated from Americans and definitely want to remain independent of their southern neighbour. Though recognizing that both societies have much in common, Canadians' national identity debates are often defined by what Canada is *not*, vis-à-vis the United States. While both are highly advanced market economies, with sharp class differences and growing income inequalities, Canada is a more equitable, humane, tolerant, peaceful and secular society than the United States. With the growing influence of neo-liberalism, the expanding power of neo-conservatives on both sides of the border, and the continued domination by the United States of the Canadian economy, society, culture and media – a legacy of the Canada's own neo-con policies – the differences between the two can increasingly get blurred.

In an increasingly globalized world, traditional national identities are at bay everywhere, yet this may seem to be more true for Canada than other countries because of the continuous influx of new immigrants from all parts of the world. These new immigrants, no longer from European countries, now come predominantly from East and South Asia, the Middle East, Africa, and Central and South America, changing the ethnic configuration of the country. Right-wing conservative Canadians constantly give heed to this changing demography, and point to the different value systems that the new immigrants bring to Canada. No doubt these new immigrants bring their different perspectives, and traditionalist elements within every community try to keep or revitalize their way of life but, in reality, these do not have much chance of survival and will eventually submerge under the dominant Canadian values. In other words, they will melt away in the low-temperature and slow-cooking Canadian melting pot. One only needs to compare the attitudes and perspectives of second-generation Canadians, or the very young new immigrants raised in Canada, with those of their parents.

The greatest challenge to traditional Canadian values of moderation, modesty, tolerance and peacefulness comes from the southern neighbour's increasing embrace of neo-conservative and religious fundamentalist values, and from Canada's own homegrown equivalents, and not from the growing and diverse immigrant population. The majority of immigrants to Canada ironically choose this country because of its long-standing values, and are now finding themselves faced with new "values" of intolerance and injustice, espoused by the Canada's homegrown neo-cons. The demanding task ahead for both new and old Canadians is to stop the encroachment of the New Right that is trying regressively to change the meaning of "What is a Canadian?"

Toronto, Ontario
Copyright © 2006 by Saeed Rahnema

Saeed Rahnema

Saeed Rahnema is a professor of political science at York University. Rahnema came to Canada in 1984 as a political refugee from his native Iran. He is a frequent commentator in Canadian and international media on Middle East issues, and he has published several books and numerous articles in English and Farsi. He has been cited three times in the Maclean's University Guide *as a most popular professor, and has won the York University excellence in teaching award.*

DENIS STAIRS

A CANADIAN IS ... a liberal. The assertion is flatly put. It may be thought that its purpose is to give comfort to the Liberal Party of Canada, and to discourage its adversaries. It is not. Nor is it designed to evoke the concept of a "liberal" that commonly prevails in the United States as a partisan who sits vaguely on the centre-left of the political spectrum and advocates big government and the generous use of state revenues to cure the ills of society and to relieve, where possible, the miseries of the unfortunate.

The comment is aimed instead at drawing attention to the fundamentals of Canada's political culture and to the central importance of its political institutions – institutions that not only enshrine the dominant Canadian public philosophy, but give it practical expression through government policy and legislation, and thereby reinforce it politically. In the Canadian context, the institutions include, among others, the mechanisms of representative and responsible parliamentary government, an independent judiciary, and a professional public service recruited and organized on meritocratic principles. They also include a peculiarly Canadian application of the concept of federalism, which reserves certain responsibilities for the central government, allocates others to the provinces and territories, and through processes of intergovernmental bargaining ensures that some of each, and others too, are shared jointly by both levels. The system as a whole is buttressed in part by a written constitution that includes a Charter of Rights and Freedoms. It also depends, however, on practices and norms that remain unwritten, but are nonetheless deeply and profoundly imbued. Some things just are not done. Other things just are.

Taken together – for they are certainly interwoven – our political culture and public institutions account for our strength as a community, and for the civility with which we conduct our public affairs. They are helped along by our wealth, and the wisest and most self-aware of Canadians understand that they might not work nearly so well if our citizenry at large were impoverished or beset by other immutable forces of darkness. But the Four Horseman, so far, have galloped only rarely on Canadian soil, and the quality of the collective life that results explains why so many "from away" would like to join us.

The cultural fundamentals at issue are not, of course, exclusively Canadian. They are derived largely from a tradition of political philosophy born in Great Britain, and touched up here and there by influences grounded in the eighteenth-century French Enlightenment. At the level of political praxis, they are represented by our attachment to individual freedom, political equality, the rule of law, the separation of church and state, and respect for private enterprise and property. They are manifested, too, in the use of the regulatory, administrative and fiscal powers of the state to provide reasonably equal access to public services and at least a modest redistribution of wealth. Without these measures, we collectively assume, the brutalities that would flow from unfettered commercial competition – from a market left too much to its own devices and logic – would be inconsistent with the other requirements of a civilized liberal order. On these matters, there are, of course, differences among us on how far we should go, how much the government should do, and how it should go about doing it. But these are the differences of a normal and pacific politics. They reflect differences of interest, and different assumptions about what makes human beings tick, and about how we commonly respond to different kinds of opportunity and incentive. Such differences are the stuff of democratic debate, but the debate itself is grounded in, and protected by, the liberal premise.

Some might think such observations obvious and unremarkable. The same premise applies, after all, to most of the OECD world, and to other bits and pieces, too. But it is far from applying everywhere, and even in the "New World" of the Western Hemisphere, there are other European fragments (some of them rich in resources and opportunity) in which the liberal idea has had a rough ride. Ask any student of Latin America. Making the idea work is therefore not a small thing.

Referencing the liberal idea, moreover, is not simply another way of referring to democracy, nor is the liberal premise expressed in exactly the same manner in every society that adheres to it. Our earlier observation warrants a restatement here: It is the interweaving of the idea with the institutions that express it that makes the difference. More specifically, it is these institutions that make it both possible and necessary to develop public policies that well-heeled minorities – captains of industry and finance, professional and bureaucratic elites, those who by inheritance or other means have acquired great wealth – would not otherwise be inclined to support.

Our institutional arrangements also ensure that the principle of majority government does not become the source of minority oppression. In effect, they compel those who rule to take the pluralism – the diversities – of their constituents into account, and in so doing they give the political leadership a powerful incentive to cultivate the values of tolerance and a love of diversity among the citizens whom they are attempting (in their own electoral interest) to serve. It is this process – and this interest – that forges the link between the liberal idea and the political institutions it helps to foster on the one hand, and a civilized political practice on the other. In such a context, the oppressive politics that elsewhere seems to flow all too readily from the construction and exploitation of identity-based nationalisms has difficulty finding root. Canadians freeze when they see what they think are signs of it.

It can be argued that there is a downside to the conduct of political life in a society so profoundly inculcated with pluralist assumptions. It lends the greatest political return, after all, to those who are skilled in the pragmatic habits of wheeling and dealing, of compromising right, left and centre, of sometimes abandoning too easily the public good for the sake of the politically workable. That being so, persons of principle in such a polity may come to think that principle never wins. And there are many in Canada now, by all professional accounts, who find their country's political praxis hard to take, and hold in consequence a cynical view of the political process. They may even believe that it doesn't matter very much. If it does matter, they might be tempted to think, it is only because it delivers so little good – which is hardly the right way for it to "matter."

But we can dismiss the politics of compromise too easily, particularly when, as individuals or members of small groups, we become preoccupied with narrow issues of our own choosing. Paradoxically, such a dismissal can be especially bitter when the issues themselves are related not so much to our assessments of our own vested or sectoral interests, but to what we are convinced is the public good when nationally – or even globally – conceived. For it is here that the failures of government to do what we think is right seem most egregious. It is therefore here that we are most sorely tempted to think that things would be a lot better if only the politicians got out of the way.

In response, it has to be conceded that neither the system itself nor those who operate it are perfect. Some of the interests, classes, regions and attitudes that compete for favour in the political contest "win" more often than others. In the constant attempt to moderate such distortions, reforms are certainly possible – to the electoral system, for example, or to the principles of representation in Parliament, or to the composition of the courts and the public service, as well as to the way their members are appointed. But, in the final analysis, none of us can expect to win all of the policy games all of the time, and it may be hard to win even a few of them completely. In a world in which resources are limited and interests diverse, the thoughtful Canadian understands that, with occasional exceptions here and there, balance is required, tradeoffs are essential and righteous indignation, like identity-based politics, is usually a menace in public debate. Canada is thus not a state in the tradition evoked (albeit unsuccessfully) by Arizona Senator Barry Goldwater in his pursuit of the American presidency some forty years ago. Certainly few Canadians would want to say, as he did, that "extremism in the defence of liberty is no vice."

The acceptance of compromise as a tolerable and essential, if sometimes distasteful, ingredient of Canada's collective political life is thus a part of the price that Canadians pay – and must continue to pay – for the unity and civility of their country. Politicians who are adept in the arts of give-and-take thus warrant our sympathy more than our condemnation. There are limits even here, and it is true that the occupants of public office sometimes deserve the opprobrium they receive. But their behaviour is more commonly a reflection of who we are and what our diversities kick up. It is the largely unavoidable result of how we think the job of government should be done, and of the institutions we have created to do it.

As admirable as the Canadian political community may be, there is one other danger (in addition to taking its perquisites too lightly or too cynically) to which Canadians can succumb. It is the danger of assuming that what works for us can work for everyone else, too, and that our behaviour abroad should therefore be informed by a messianic mission – by the desire to transport our political institutions and practices overseas, and to induce others think about politics like we do. Sadly, the world is too complicated to accommodate so simple-minded an aspiration, however well intended. The emphasis in the foregoing has been on Canada's public philosophy and political culture and on the institutions of government that express them. But these are the product of a particular time, place and history, and of an extraordinarily hospitable set of geopolitical and other circumstances. Perhaps others can learn from us here and there. We need to recognize, however, that they will have to do the translating for themselves.

If we fail to make this recognition, we will have become unCanadian. We will have allowed our vanity – fed by thoughtless presumptions of superiority – to take over. Such hubris has consequences. They will quickly follow.

Halifax, Nova Scotia
Copyright © 2006 by Denis Stairs

Denis Stairs

Currently McCulloch Professor in Political Science at Dalhousie University, Denis Stairs attended Dalhousie University, the University of Oxford and the University of Toronto. He specializes in Canadian foreign and defence policy, Canada–US relations, and similar subjects.

A former president of the Canadian Political Science Association, and a member for six years of the Social Sciences and Humanities Research Council of Canada, he was the founding director of Dalhousie's Centre for Foreign Policy Studies from 1970 to 1975. He served as chair of his department from 1980 to 1985, and as Dalhousie's vice-president, academic and research, from 1988 to 1993.

A Fellow of the Royal Society of Canada, he is a member of the board of directors of the Institute for Research on Public Policy, the board of visitors of the Canadian Forces College in Toronto, the advisory council to the Canadian Defence and Foreign Affairs Institute, and the academic advisory council to the deputy minister for International Trade.

VALERIE HAIG-BROWN

A CANADIAN IS . . . one of 32 million people – all different from each other. We say there is such a thing as an Albertan or a Newfoundlander or a Canadian and, while there may be a lot in common within each group, there are probably more differences. We've all had the experience of a fellow Canadian saying, "Oh, you're from . . ."; "You must hate . . ."; "You must eat a lot of . . ." Well, not necessarily. About the only thing we can truly say of a Canadian is that he or she lives in Canada.

It is possible to characterize Canada and, from that, something of the people who live here. Most of us spell *honour* with a *u* most of the time – even in Quebec, where we spell it *honneur* – except when we spell it *honor*, thus reflecting that our original sources of Canadian English have been tempered by our gigantic next-door neighbour. We know who we are when we are away from home, even if we aren't sure how to spell it. But we certainly don't always agree among ourselves when we are at home. Nor are we as "nice" as the jokes would have it. (How do you get fifty rowdy Canadians out of a Montana bar? Ask them politely.)

My father, Roderick Haig-Brown, was writing a book of essays called *Measure of the Year*, published in 1950, when he asked me what I thought about Canada. He was working on an essay titled "Canada," and I was sitting nearby. I was probably thirteen or fourteen, and to his initial question, "Do you think Canada is a good country?" I replied, "Of course it is."

Not letting me off lightly, he asked, "Why?" to which I answered, "Because it's a young country, not all used up. It's got a long way to go." *She thought for a moment*, wrote my father. *It's a good outdoors country, there aren't too many people. It's a varied country, two oceans, mountains, prairies, lakes and forests. The United States will have to come to Canada more and more for everything, because they're using up all they've got.*

"What else?"

"Well, it's got old, old things in it, historical things. Quebec is an old thing in itself. Canada has a lot of history, and then it's got new places, like Vancouver – grown up so quickly."

"What about Canadian laws?"

"Except for duties and things like that," remembering an unhappy moment in customs, "Canada has good laws. Not too many restrictions. There's no segregation in Canada."

"Anything else?"

"Canadian jobs don't pay as well as American, but they're likely to be more interesting. They aren't so set – there's more future in them."

My father wrote: *That seems a very modern, very rational statement of love of country, yet the essential convictions are there. It is a loyalty without fears or hatreds, without sense of guilt or false pride. It is the sort of loyalty that can be taken to world councils and used effectively within them for effective world government. It is not likely to respond to jingoism; it will be able to yield, yet will never accept domination or oppression.*

A lot has changed in the fifty-five years since I made those statements, but they seem to me to reflect an understanding of Canada that still holds in many ways. At that time, I was growing up in a small town on Vancouver Island, and had travelled no farther than Seattle, where my grandmother lived. I hadn't even been to Vancouver. The world is, as we say, a lot smaller, and Canada is less innocent (and so am I), but the nature of Canada in relation to the rest of the world is much the same. A Canadian abroad is likely to have a certain credibility, for all our faults, as a citizen of a small country with good intentions. The variety of Canadians has increased enormously as we both need and want so many people from so many other countries that have less opportunity for those "more inter-esting jobs" I felt Canada offered back then. Why I thought that, I do not know, but I have no doubt that many of the people who have arrived here since 1950 came with the hope of exactly that, and often found those jobs.

In his essay, my father wrote, "Canadians are not great flag wavers – we have no flag to wave, no anthem we have learned to sing with true conviction." We do now have a flag to wave, and sometimes we do it with great conviction, but we still aren't too good at singing "O Canada" with great conviction. Maybe we need a more rousing anthem. Still, most of the rousing anthems have been battle or revolutionary songs in the beginning and, since we have had neither on our way to becoming a nation, we should perhaps celebrate "O Canada" for its rather ponderous pace that perhaps derives from being chosen by the proverbial committee.

In 1950, I said, "There's no segregation in Canada." Obviously, I had the US in mind. My father agreed with me, and stated that Canadian law showed greater tolerance toward minorities than any country he knew. But he went on to say that, as individuals, Canadians themselves could be as intolerant as any of groups that seem different, whether because of nationality, race, religion, or activity. His list was long and concluded: "Pacific Coast hatred of the Japanese, founded on economic jealousy, used the war to strip them of homes and property and liberty; there is no comparable shame in Canada's history." Canadians are not much different now from what we were then, but I believe that we do better than most of the world. Perhaps it is human nature to mistrust difference – some primitive residue of needing to be wary of anyone outside the tribe, but that is no excuse for the people of a country that thinks itself enlightened.

"I am not happy about Canada's treatment of Canadian Indians," wrote my father. "It was benevolently conceived, paternalistic, in some degree protective; but it is hopelessly outdated, it is narrow, based on ignorance and misconception, and at this stage of the twentieth century, it is oppressive." He believed "that change was long overdue and that every delay is shameful to us." Unfortunately, we are now in the twenty-first century, and that change is far from achieved. The change that has occurred is that our Native people have found their voice and are going about making their own solution in spite of the outdated, benevolent policies that still exist, often in law if no longer in the attitudes of administrators and politicians.

My father was "afraid for the unity and greatness of a country that trusts its civil liberties to the petty legislatures of ten provinces…I believe that a nation whose central government does not stand always ready to define and protect the human rights of its citizens must be unsure of itself and short of true greatness." He would have celebrated the Canadian Charter of Rights and Freedoms that came into force in 1982, which addresses exactly that concern. In 2005, I continue to worry for the unity and greatness of a country that trusts more and more to those petty provincial legislatures – natural resources, health care and labour legislation, to name a few. These areas may be defined as provincial, but the federal government used to keep a certain unity in place by its control of the purse strings. That control is now becoming more and more lax, to the detriment of Canadians. A strong central government is essential to a country that is becoming ever more diverse.

My father could not have anticipated the current terrorism that affects the entire world, but he would be as concerned as I am at the overreaction that so many countries, including Canada, have shown as a result. Our civil liberties, no matter how flawed, have certainly been a defining characteristic of Canada and Canadians. But we have set to spying on ourselves to a much greater extent than I would have thought possible fifty-five years ago. This has come partly from external pressure, but that is no excuse. No amount of surveillance is going to stop a determined terrorist, but we are slowly allowing our privacy to be eroded in the name of protection from some unknown.

Canada was not even one hundred years old when my father wrote, "Whenever I have come to grips with life in Canada, I have found it strong and solid and real, the true, fresh growth of a vigorous civilization, neither contemptuous of its roots nor limited by them ... there is nothing feeble or second-rate about the contributions of Canadians to medicine and biology and physics; and when it was necessary to fight a war Canada found men and equipment to fight it in a way that to be part of her was a privilege." (My father came from a British army tradition and served in the Canadian forces in the Second World War.) He objected to those who said there was no Canadian literature. "Perhaps those of us who are writing today are as the pioneer to the dairy farmer, the fur trader to the industrialist ... It is good to be writing at the start of a country's history ..." Today we have no trouble at all running a list of Canadian writers who have made international names for themselves, to say nothing of the many more who write well and help to define our country and ourselves – even if they are not known outside our borders. We certainly have a Canadian literature now.

Canada is still a young country – "not all used up" – though we now realize that we are moving very fast at using up some of our resources. This country is still a place where scientists and writers and people who consider the future have the luxury of time and space in which to search for a way forward that may give my tiny great-grandson a life every bit as good as my own. His will certainly be different, but I would hope that it will be as interesting if he chooses to live it in this country that still has room both to grow and to grow in – to live as a Canadian.

Waterton Park, Alberta
Copyright © 2006 by Valerie Haig-Brown

Valerie Haig-Brown

Valerie Haig-Brown is a writer and editor who lives on a ranch near Waterton Lakes National Park in the Rocky Mountains. She grew up on a small farm on Vancouver Island, attended the University of British Columbia, is married and has two daughters. After some fifteen years working in various writing and editing jobs in Toronto during the 1960s and 1970s, Haig-Brown returned to the West. In the early 1980s, she moved to a ranch on the edge of the Rockies, where she and a friend built the house in which she now lives. She hikes and snowshoes in the nearby mountains most of the year, and often travels to the Atlas Mountains in Morocco. In addition to editing several anthologies of her father's work, she is the author of Deep Currents, *a biography of her parents, Roderick and Anna Haig-Brown.*

GUY SAINT-PIERRE

UN CANADIEN EST . . . un être qui, trop souvent, ignore les nombreux avantages que lui procure son pays. Le Canadien a tendance à envier des pays plus importants ou puissants sur le plan politique, économique ou militaire. Il tend à comparer son pays à ceux qui baignent dans l'histoire contemporaine ou qui ont vécu, dans les rues de leurs capitales, des pages entières de l'histoire humaine. Il est au fait des pays qui semblent avoir des politiques sociales et culturelles plus avancées. Et, bien sûr, il n'a pas de difficulté à nommer les nombreux pays qui ont un climat plus doux, plus agréable que les longs hivers canadiens, ou les courtes semaines d'été qui disparaissent toujours trop vite une fois passés ces quelques longs week-ends tant attendus entre la mi-mai et la mi-septembre.

Ailleurs pourtant, le Canada évoque plutôt un vaste pays, avec ses chaînes de montagnes, ses nombreux lacs et rivières et ses grands espaces à peine habités, sauf sur une bande étroite à sa frontière près du 49e parallèle. On évoque également ses richesses naturelles importantes qui ont assuré sa prospérité dès le départ.

Je ne peux m'empêcher d'évoquer le souvenir d'une visite dans un petit musée près de St Rémi de Provence. C'était en 1958 et j'en étais, avec mon épouse, à ma première visite en France. Nous étions émerveillés de tous ces lieux. Voyant que nous étions Canadiens, la curatrice sortit d'un tiroir un calendrier que lui avait transmis Jean Lesage, alors ministre du Gouvernement du Canada. On peut imaginer les douze magnifiques reproductions de Vancouver, les Rocheuses, les chutes du Niagara, les Laurentides en automne, la ville de Québec, la baie de Fundy, etc. La dame nous expliqua que, pour elle, cela était presque . . . le paradis terrestre. Ma femme et moi étions presque gênés devant cette étrangère qui nous faisait réaliser la beauté de notre propre pays, le Canada. Mais les grands espaces et la beauté naturelle des lieux ne suffisent pas à rendre les gens heureux!

Les caractéristiques du Canada d'aujourd'hui sont, dans une large mesure, tributaires des ancêtres qui sont venus explorer cette partie du monde au XVIIe siècle. Déjà sur place, les autochtones ont dû influencer le comportement des premiers colons. À ces premiers habitants venus de France ou d'Angleterre, il faut ajouter toutes les vagues subséquentes d'immigration, incluant les loyalistes américains entre 1775 et 1820, suivis des Irlandais et des Écossais. Après la Deuxième Guerre mondiale, sont venus s'ajouter les Italiens, les Grecs, les gens des pays de l'Europe de l'Est et, plus récemment, les Asiatiques, les Indiens, les Haïtiens, etc. Au fil des ans, tous ces nouveaux Canadiens ont façonné, à leur façon, la personnalité du Canadien moyen d'aujourd'hui. Encore aujourd'hui, des immigrants nous arrivent chaque année de tous les coins du monde et ils laissent leurs traces sur notre paysage sociologique.

En 1760, au moment de la Conquête, les 80 000 habitants de la Nouvelle-France avaient sûrement une certaine anxiété face à l'avenir. Un siècle plus tard, au tout début de la Confédération canadienne, il n'était pas évident comment évoluerait ce pays que l'on cherchait encore à définir. Même un homme éclairé comme Louis-Joseph Papineau a cru, toute sa vie, que l'annexion du Canada aux États-Unis d'Amérique était inévitable. Aux uns et aux autres, si on avait pu faire dérouler devant leurs yeux l'évolution du pays jusqu'à nos jours, plusieurs, sinon la totalité d'entre eux, seraient demeurés incrédules. Et, même si le XXe siècle ne fut pas nécessairement celui du Canada, comme l'avait prédit Sir Wilfrid Laurier, il n'en reste pas moins que le chemin parcouru est impressionnant.

À divers moments au cours des derniers siècles, plusieurs pays européens ont cru que leur pouvoir, leur influence allaient continuer d'augmenter sans cesse. Qu'on pense à l'Espagne, au Portugal, à l'Autriche, la Russie, la France, l'Angleterre, etc. – or, chacun d'entre eux devait connaître son apogée pour ensuite subir un déclin relatif. Le phénomène ne se limite pas qu'aux pays européens. Qu'on pense à tous les pays de l'Amérique Latine dont plusieurs n'ont pas connu l'essor escompté, sans parler, bien sûr, du continent africain qui, bien qu'affranchi du joug colonial, semble reculer constamment peu importe les indices utilisés.

Comment expliquer le progrès constant du Canada depuis plus de quatre siècles?

Un facteur important me semble une approche prudente dans le changement. Chez nous, il n'y a pas eu de révolutions. Inconsciemment, nous avons préféré le mot évolution à celui de révolution. Il n'y a pas eu de bain de sang majeur nécessaire pour faire évoluer les institutions, les gouvernements, les priorités, les comportements.

Se peut-il aussi que les deux peuples fondateurs nous aient légué un héritage porteur d'avenir? Les Français nous ont légué liberté et fraternité; les Anglais, loi et ordre public. Peut-on penser à d'autres ingrédients essentiels au progrès d'un peuple aujourd'hui? Je ne crois pas. À long terme, le progrès et le développement des individus ne peuvent se réaliser à moins d'avoir un cadre stable et la paix sociale. Ceux qui vivent au Canada ont pu compter, à ce jour, sur un contexte social stable pour progresser sur le plan humain. Quand on vit dans une société où chaque jour la violence, la terreur, la mort guettent chaque citoyen, le progrès humain est presque impossible.

Le Canadien, en général, est tolérant. Il préfère l'évolution à la révolution. Il croit fermement que le progrès sur le plan humain requiert un heureux mélange de liberté, de fraternité, de «law and order». On me permettra de citer le journaliste Ron Graham qui écrivait dans son livre *The French Quarter*: «Private happiness, public strife: that was the mood ... Quebeckers, both French- and English-speaking, show a remarkable ability to have a good time in bad times, and the dour headlines rarely represented the general atmosphere.»

Mais dans ce creuset que fut le Canada depuis plus de trois siècles, il y a une autre caractéristique qui mérite d'être soulignée. En jetant un regard rapide sur l'histoire de l'humanité, on est frappé par le fait que les guerres, les invasions, les luttes entre humains semblent avoir été une donnée constante de l'histoire humaine. Tout au long des siècles et, sur les cinq continents, les guerres ont fait des ravages importants. Chaque siècle apportait sa part de violence et la vie de tous les jours était souvent bouleversée par les invasions, les conquêtes. Encore aujourd'hui, on peut visiter trop de sites qui nous rappellent les millions de morts causés par les abus de pouvoir de l'homme. La Première Grande guerre de 1914 devait être la dernière des guerres. Ce ne fut pas le cas et encore aujourd'hui, aux quatre coins du monde, des conflits importants continuent de faire des ravages.

Dans toutes ces guerres depuis le début des temps, on remarque souvent la présence d'un facteur important: une majorité qui ne peut tolérer la présence d'une minorité ethnique, religieuse, etc. en son sein. Outre le Canada, peu de pays ont pu assurer la coexistence pacifique de minorités importantes avec la majorité. Les uns diront que la majorité au Canada fut, de tout temps, trop tolérante. D'autres diront que la minorité, représentée par le Québec, a manqué de courage pour s'affirmer. Je ne partage pas ces deux points de vue. Pour moi, les Canadiens sont aujourd'hui plus heureux, plus prospères parce que nous avons fait la preuve que majorité et minorité peuvent cohabiter, sur un même territoire, tout en évitant des conflits majeurs.

Je ne tente pas de faire la preuve que le Canada est un pays parfait. Loin de là! Nous avons bien des lacunes et, souvent, les solutions aux problèmes que nous vivons sont lentes à venir.

Pour continuer à progresser, les Canadiens devront relever plusieurs défis importants au cours des prochaines années. J'en mentionne trois:

Dans un premier temps, tous les Canadiens de toutes les régions du pays devront convenir des priorités que le pays doit retenir. On ne peut reporter indéfiniment les décisions nécessaires pour régler certains problèmes. Ainsi, pour corriger les lacunes de notre système de santé, on ne peut plonger le pays dans les déficits importants ou délaisser d'autres priorités comme l'éducation, le renouvellement de nos infrastructures, etc. Le statu quo ne peut que nous faire reculer comme société.

Deuxièmement, les Canadiens doivent s'adapter à l'impact majeur qu'auront sur nos vies l'essor de pays comme la Chine et l'Inde. Déjà, plusieurs secteurs industriels ont vu leurs perspectives d'avenir s'assombrir face à cette nouvelle source de concurrence. Ainsi, aux États-Unis, les meubles qu'on achète ne viennent plus de la Caroline du Nord mais de la Chine! Même chose dans le secteur de la machinerie. Tous les pays industrialisés devront s'adapter au choc que produira la Chine sur l'échiquier mondial.

Un troisième enjeu touche l'immigration. La preuve a été faite à plusieurs reprises que les immigrants aident un pays, une entreprise, une institution à progresser. Le Canada a toujours été une terre d'accueil pour les immigrants. Dans la décennie de 1991 à 2000, le Canada a accueilli 2,2 millions d'immigrants, ce qui représentait 80,9% de l'augmentation de la population. Des rapports récents indiquaient que Toronto était au deuxième rang mondial – après Miami – en ce qui touche le taux de la population qui était née à l'extérieur du pays. En l'an 2000, 18,4% de la population canadienne était née à l'extérieur du Canada, presque deux fois plus qu'aux États-Unis. Durant le XXe siècle, la provenance des immigrants a changé profondément. Ainsi, durant la dernière décennie du XXe siècle, les immigrants venant d'Europe ne représentaient plus que 19% des immigrants alors qu'ils avaient représenté 67,8% dans la décennie des années 60. Par contre, l'immigration des pays asiatiques qui représentait 9,3% des immigrants dans la décennie des années 60s en représentait 59,5% dans la dernière décennie du XXe siècle. Le défi consistera donc à définir une politique qui accueille les immigrants mais qui préserve l'esprit même du Canada.

De plus en plus, les gens de diverses cultures et provenant des quatre coins du monde sont attirés par le Canada et veulent venir s'établir ici. S'il faut être ouvert aux immigrants, encore faut-il que ces derniers respectent l'essence même de l'identité canadienne. Si la majorité des Canadiens doivent faire preuve de tolérance vis-à-vis des habitudes de vie qui peuvent surprendre, les nouveaux Canadiens, de leur côté, doivent s'adapter à notre culture, nos mœurs. Ainsi, je crois qu'une seule Charte des droits et libertés doit avoir force de loi dans nos institutions. Dans les dernières années, on a l'impression que certains individus importent des problèmes d'ailleurs au Canada. Des graffitis et des gestes criminels semblent reliés à des conflits lointains, mais on semble vouloir faire du Canada un nouveau champ de bataille. Je ne crois pas que ce soit sain.

Les Canadiens aiment leur pays. Ce n'est pas un pays parfait et chacun en est conscient. Mais, si on le compare à d'autres pays, on a vite pris la décision d'y rester. C'est un pays légué par nos ancêtres et auquel des générations d'immigrants ont contribué. C'est un riche héritage qui mérite d'être conservé.

Montréal, Québec
Copyright © 2006 by Guy Saint-Pierre

GUY SAINT-PIERRE

A CANADIAN IS . . . someone who too often is unaware of the many advantages provided by his country. Canadians tend to be envious of countries that are more important or more powerful by political, economic or military standards. They have a tendency to compare their own country with those currently in the limelight or those where the streets of the capital city have witnessed whole chapters of the world's history. They are aware of other countries that seem to be more advanced socially and culturally. And, for sure, they have no trouble naming the many countries that enjoy a gentler climate, much better than the long Canadian winters, or stressing the all too short weeks of summer that always vanish too soon after the few long-awaited weekends between the middle of May and mid-September.

Elsewhere, however, Canada conjures up the image of a huge territory, with its mountain ranges, its countless lakes and rivers and its wide open spaces, barely inhabited apart from the narrow band along the border near the forty-ninth parallel. It also brings to mind the country's important natural resources, which have assured its prosperity from the start.

I can't help recalling a visit to a little museum near St. Rémi de Provence. This was in 1958 and, with my wife, I was visiting France for the first time. We were thrilled by what we saw, wherever we went. Learning that we were Canadians, the woman who ran the museum pulled out of a drawer a calendar that had been sent to her by Jean Lesage, at the time a minister of the Canadian government. You can imagine the twelve magnificent full-colour reproductions showing Vancouver, the Rockies, Niagara Falls, the Laurentians in fall, Quebec City, the Bay of Fundy, and so on. The lady explained to us that, for her, all this came close to . . .

paradise on earth. My wife and I were almost embarrassed in front of this foreigner who was making us aware of the beauty of our own country, Canada. But wide open spaces and places of great natural beauty are not enough to make people happy!

The characteristics of modern Canada were set to a large degree by those ancestors of ours who came to explore this part of the world in the seventeenth century. Already established here, the Native peoples inevitably had an influence on the way our first settlers lived. To those first settlers, from France or from England, we must add all the subsequent waves of immigrants, including the Loyalists who came from the United States between 1775 and 1820, followed by the Irish and the Scots. After the Second World War, the new groups who came included Italians, Greeks, Eastern Europeans, and, more recently, people from Asia, India, Haiti, and so on. As the years passed, all of these new Canadians shaped, in their own way, the character of today's average Canadian. Today, immigrants continue to come to join us from every corner of the world, and they are making their mark on our country's sociology.

In 1760, at the time of the Conquest, the eighty thousand people in New France were certainly very worried about the future. A century later, at the very start of Confederation, it was far from clear just how this country that was still in the process of being defined would develop. Even an enlightened man like Louis-Joseph Papineau believed, all his life, that Canada was bound to join the United States some day. In fact, if it had been possible to unwind before the eyes of earlier Canadians the true story of the way our country has developed up to our day, many, if not all of them, would have still refused to believe it. And even if the twentieth century did not necessarily "belong to Canada," as Sir Wilfrid Laurier predicted, there is no doubt that what we achieved was impressive.

At various stages during the past few centuries, some European countries believed that their power and influence would continue to rise, endlessly. Spain, Portugal, Austria, Russia, France, Britain – each one of them experienced its moment in the sun only to later undergo a relative decline. The phenomenon of hopes dashed is not restricted to European countries alone. We only have to think of all of the countries of Latin America, some of which have never achieved the success expected of them. And that is leaving aside the African continent, which, despite being free from the colonial yoke, seems to be constantly regressing, no matter what type of measurement is used.

So how are we to explain the constant progress of Canada over more than four centuries?

One factor that strikes me as important is our cautious approach to change. Here, we have had no revolutions. Unconsciously, we have preferred the word *evolution* to *revolution*. No major bloodbaths have been necessary to effect changes in our institutions, our governments, and their priorities and procedures.

Is it also the case that the two founding peoples have left us a heritage that fits us for the future? The French left us liberty and fraternity; the English left us law and order. Can you come up with any other ingredients that are more essential to the progress of a people today? I don't think so. In the long-term, progress and individual advancement can only happen inside a stable society enjoying social peace. Those who live in Canada have been able, up to now, to rely on such a stable social context in which they can lead good, productive lives.

By contrast, when you live in a society where every day violence, terrorism, and death threaten every citizen, human progress is almost impossible.

In general, Canadians are tolerant. They prefer evolution to revolution. They fervently believe that human progress requires a happy mixture of liberty, fraternity, and "law and order." I would like to quote the journalist Ron Graham, who wrote in his book *The French Quarter*, "Private happiness, public strife: that was the mood . . . Quebeckers, both French- and English-speaking, show a remarkable ability to have a good time in bad times, and the dour headlines rarely represented the general atmosphere."

But in this crucible that Canada has been for more than three centuries, there is another characteristic that deserves to be underlined. Taking a quick glance at human history, an observer is struck by the fact that wars, invasions and battles between people seem to have been a constant of our human past. Down through the centuries and on every continent, wars have inflicted terrible damage. Every century has seen its share of this violence, and everyday life was often thrown into total confusion by invasions and conquests. Even today, it is possible to visit far too many places that remind us of the millions of deaths caused by the abuse of power among men. The First World War of 1914 was supposed to be the very last war. That was not the case, and even today, all over the world, serious conflicts continue to cause appalling devastation.

In every war since the beginning of time, we can often detect an important common factor: a majority that could not tolerate the presence of a minority – whether ethnic, or religious, or something else – in the same community. Apart from Canada, few countries have been able to ensure the peaceful existence of significant minorities living alongside the majority. Some will tell you that the majority in Canada has been, at all times, too tolerant. Others will say that the minority, represented by Quebec, has lacked the courage to stand up for itself. I don't share either of these opinions. To me, Canadians are happier and more prosperous today because we have demonstrated that the majority and the minority can live together, in the same place, without any major conflicts.

I am not trying to prove that Canada is a country that is perfect. Far from it! We have plenty of imperfections, and all too often the solutions to our problems are slow to take effect.

If we are to continue to make progress, Canadians are going to have to find answers to several serious challenges over the next few years. Let me mention just three of them.

For once, all Canadians from every part of the country are going to have to agree on what our national priorities must be. We cannot go on postponing indefinitely decisions that are going to be necessary to come to terms with certain problems. For instance, to fill the gaps in our health system we cannot plunge the country back into deficits or downplay other priorities like education, the renewal of our infrastructure, and so on. Simply preserving the status quo will only cause us to regress as a society.

Secondly, Canadians are going to have to adapt to the major impact that the rise of countries like China and India will have on our lives. Already, several industrial sectors have seen their future prospects darken in the shadow of this new competition. For example, in the United States, the furniture on sale in the stores no longer comes from North Carolina, but from China. The same is true with the manufacturing sector in general. Every industrialized country will have to change to meet the impact that China is going to have on the world scene.

A third area of concern is immigration. Studies have consistently shown that immigrants help a country – or a business, or an institution – to make progress. Canada has always been a place that welcomes immigrants. Between 1991 and 2000, Canada received 2.2 million immigrants, representing 80.9% of the population growth of the country. Recent reports show that Toronto ranked second in the world – after Miami – when it comes to the percentage of the population that was born outside the country. In 2000, 18.4% of the Canadian population was born outside the country, almost twice the American rate. In the course of the twentieth century, the countries from which these immigrants came have changed significantly. For instance, during the 1990s, European immigrants made up only 19% of the total, while in the 1960s they made up 67.8%. By way of contrast, immigration from Asian countries (while only 9.3% of the total in the 1960s) represented 59.5% in the 1990s. The challenge, then, is to find a system that welcomes immigrants but at the same time preserves Canada's character.

More and more, people from a wide range of cultures and coming from all parts of the world have been attracted by Canada, and want to come and live here. If it is important for us to be open to immigrants, in the same way it is just as important for immigrants to respect those things that make up Canada's identity. If it is true that the majority of Canadians must show tolerance toward lifestyles that may be new and surprising to them, the new Canadians, for their part, must adapt to our culture, our customs. For that reason, it is my belief that a single Charter of Rights and Freedoms must have the force of law in our institutions. In recent years, one gets the impression that certain individuals have brought the problems of their home countries with them to Canada. Instances of graffiti and criminal gestures have seemed to be tied to distant conflicts and, despite that distance, some people have appeared eager to make Canada a new battlefield. This can never be healthy.

Canadians love their country. It is not perfect, and everyone knows that. But compare it with other countries and you quickly decide to stay. It is a country bequeathed to us by our ancestors, a country to which generations of immigrants have contributed – a rich heritage that deserves to be preserved.

Montreal, Quebec
Translation copyright © 2006 by Douglas M. Gibson

Guy Saint-Pierre

Guy Saint-Pierre was a director and chairman of the board of the Royal Bank of Canada, and president and chief executive officer and chairman of the board of SNC-Lavalin. He has been a director of many other corporations, including Alcan, Bell Canada Enterprises, General Motors of Canada and Suncor. He was also president of the Canadian Manufacturers Association, the Conference Board of Canada and the Canadian Council of Chief Executives. Guy Saint-Pierre was elected to the National Assembly of Quebec in April 1970, and he held two cabinet positions. He holds a number of honorary doctorates and is a Companion of the Order of Canada. He and his wife live in Montreal.

WILLIAM WATSON

A CANADIAN IS . . . as a rule too fond by half of contemplating what a Canadian is.

Actually, that's only partly true. I suspect ordinary Canadians spend very little time worrying about being Canadian. They do seem to have a rock-solid conviction that it means not being American, which in turn means not sharing the traits that common Canadian prejudice – the only word for it – ascribes to Americans. In brief, not being American means not being loud, jingoistic, obese, self-confident, undiplomatic, self-centred, almost entirely ignorant of Canada and (an apparent contradiction here) dedicated to making this Canada more American, the fifty-first state in fact. These collected "nots" can be completely inconsistent, of course. Thus our supposed lack of self-confidence coexists with a smug superiority regarding American society and culture, and our disgust with jingoism does not stop us from telling all who will listen, and even some who won't, that we are the best country in the world to live in, while our disapproval of American self-centredness exists in spite of our own neurotic obsession with our identity and image. Fortunately, such prejudices are seldom foremost in ordinary Canadians' minds. They do surface at well-defined moments: on Canada Day, for instance. Or in the run-up to any Canada–US hockey final. Or when a tour bus disgorges visiting Americans. Or when we ourselves visit the United States or watch one of Rick Mercer's one-joke comedy specials on "Talking to Americans." Or, finally, when the United States embarks on an especially unilateralist military or diplomatic adventure. But, except on such occasions, most ordinary Canadians seem to get on with their lives and let their Canadianness take care of itself.

"We should all be so ordinary" is my theme here. Alas, non-ordinary Canadians, by which I mean those in the talking, writing and governing classes, are obsessed – truly, madly, deeply – with the idea of what it is to be Canadian. And they judge their own actions and the actions they would have us all take collectively by two standards: 1) is it right? and 2) is it sufficiently Canadian?[1]

I believe we should ditch the second test and simply judge things by the first. Whether an action is right, not how it will look or what people will say, is what we want to focus on. John Updike called his 1989 memoir of his youth *Self-consciousness*. Self-consciousness is a key part of what makes us human (so far as we know, at least, no one yet having success-fully interviewed a dog). A certain degree of self-consciousness is desir-able. Despite what Socrates said, the unexamined life probably is worth living – almost all life is worth living – but it surely cannot be as deep or rich as the examined one. We should always be self-aware and critical of what we do. But acute self-consciousness is an adolescent trait and, as in adolescents, leads to awkwardness, posing, hesitation, uncertainty, irresolution, paralysis. Canadian intellectuals' paranoid tendency to be always looking over their shoulders, measuring themselves by whether they are being sufficiently Canadian or (to call it by its real name) non-American sets up our national life for the distemper that is also charac-teristic of adolescence.

Take our position on the Kyoto Protocol on global warming. How should we have gone about deciding what to do? We should have esti-mated the cost in economic slowdown and restructuring, and then weighed that against our sense of the benefit to the world at large and our willingness to sacrifice in the global interest. Would that have left us with a truly distinctive (i.e., non-American) policy position? Maybe, maybe not. We wrote a proud record of selflessness in 1939-45, but in recent decades, by most objective measures (official foreign aid, for instance), we have not been especially altruistic. And, in fact, our economy tilts slightly more toward energy production than the American, while, given the weather here, energy consumption is obviously crucial to us. So it would have been surprising had our position on how large a Kyoto com-mitment to make been that different from the Americans'. But, of course, to conform with our self-image, it simply had to be. Lucky for us, then, that the US Senate unanimously rejected the deal Vice President Al Gore had brought back from Kyoto. As a result, we have had the best of both worlds. We have established our distinctiveness from, and moral superiority to, the Americans without having to sacrifice too much in terms of energy consumption or production. And, as we all know, a Canadian is . . . never happier than when demonstrating his moral superiority to Americans.

Excessive concern for how things look and for what others will say is unworthy of a mature, successful country. If we truly are different from the Americans, that difference will out. That we protest our differentness so much suggests we are not ourselves convinced of it. Do truly distinctive Canadian values really exist? As an English Canadian, I was raised to think that part of our uniqueness is pathological deference. As the story goes, a Canadian is . . . someone who, if you step on his toe, says "Sorry!" (assuming, of course, the Canadian in question is not Don Cherry). But in *An Elegy for England*, the philosopher Roger Scruton writes that "if an Englishman found himself knocked over by a stranger in the street, or short-changed by a shop assistant, or humiliated by an official, he would at once apologise." This supposedly fundamental Canadian trait is in fact English! Or *was* English: Scruton uses the past tense because he thinks England, civilized England, is gone now, hounded to death by a deliberate campaign of official brainwashing.[2]

We have experience of such brainwashing. In our long, arduous search for identity, the British traditions in law, politics and even apology have now been replaced by so-called Charter values. The obvious problem with the substitution is that a constitutional charter of rights is a very American thing.[3] Indeed, few things are more American. Because it is ultimately inconvenient for a country that above all else prizes its distinctiveness from the United States to adopt as its defining ethical core an American institutional innovation, we have de-emphasized our Charter's focus on individualism and stressed those parts of it that support collective rights.[4] They supposedly are the embodiment of truly distinctive Canadian values, such as a love of diversity. But that, too, is a thin reed for uniqueness. Who these days opposes diversity? Even the Americans are acquainted with the idea of collective rights. Were we as knowledgeable of the world as we suppose ourselves to be, we would know that most of our affirmative action laws, like our methods of railway finance 150 years ago, we have learned from them.

The "Canadian values" that we now supposedly cherish are in fact standard Western values. They were born during the Enlightenment in a handful of European countries and – even anti-imperialists should rejoice – have in the last two centuries conquered large parts of the globe. They are not yet hegemonic. They are resisted, sometimes violently, by various strains of fundamentalism. Since the fall of the Soviet Union, however, these ideas have been in the ascendant. They are variously defined and described – democracy, tolerance, pluralism, diversity, forbearance, rule of law. The one name not given them anywhere else but here is "Canadian."

Another trait that supposedly distinguishes us from the Americans is our reluctance to decide things unilaterally. But what is it exactly that we would decide unilaterally? And would the world care or even notice if we did? Superpowers can decide things unilaterally. If we were a superpower, our reluctance to be unilateral would be admirable. Of course, if we were a superpower, we might not be quite so reluctant to be unilateral. A superpower run by people as convinced as we are of our virtue almost certainly would have messianic tendencies.

Quite apart from its ugliness and hypocrisy, our narcissism is debilitating. It puts us in moral jeopardy when, as occasionally happens, the United States does the right thing. Some Canadians took great pride in our decision to allow Saddam Hussein to stay in power. Given what turned out to be the high cost of removing him, maybe they were right. But mistrust of the Americans, and reluctance to be seen to be their ally, caused some prominent Canadians, even some in positions of political responsibility, to oppose the *first* Gulf War, which was a slam-dunk ethically: the community of civilized nations must resist unprovoked aggression. In my own field of economic policy, fear of being too like the Americans has engendered deep mistrust of market processes, and therefore condemned

Canadians to a lower standard of living than should have been possible. The cost of such underperformance is not purely private. At the turn of the millennium, governments in the United States spent substantially more per capita on their citizens' health care than Canadian governments did. In 1961, the Canadian economist Harry Johnson wrote of

> . . . a certain immaturity in the Canadian national character, expressed in the unwillingness to accept the fact that Canada is, except from the geographical point of view, a small country. Unlike the citizens of other small countries bordering on large countries, Canadians are not prepared to content themselves with the advantages that can be derived from small size, but set themselves the impossible aspiration of equalling the United States, and still more impossible, of getting the United States to treat them as equals. In the nature of things, such aspirations are doomed to disappointment; and their disappointment almost inevitably curdles into resentment against the United States for its effortless imperviousness to the Canadian challenge.

There was progress in the Mulroney years toward being less self-conscious. The free trade agreement with the United States was a huge step toward psychological adulthood. But in the last few federal elections, the Liberal Party of Canada, which, as of this writing, is in the twelfth year of its current dynasty, has come to rely for its perpetuation in power on the need for government to project and defend "Canadian values." That program seems to have found political customers. Maybe the country with its nose pressed up most closely against the window of the world's least self-conscious country cannot help being its most self-conscious. Perhaps, in the end, a Canadian is . . . a person who must be resigned to all this. But I hope not.

Understand, finally, that a Canadian, this Canadian in particular, is . . . not self-loathing. Canada is, in many, many ways, a fine place. If our share of exemplary people is not as great as our self-praise implies, it is probably not less than our share of the species' population. But Canada would be such a better place – we would be such a finer people – if we finally outgrew our self-consciousness. In the end, a Canadian is . . . the citizen of a country still badly in need of growing up.

Montreal, Quebec
Copyright © 2006 by William Watson

Notes

[1] As an economist, I'm bound to think that there is also a third standard: What's in it for me? Granted, the question is seldom posed explicitly, certainly not in public, and not even, I suspect, in the internal monologue that each of us (I extrapolate from my own habits) perpetually conducts.

[2] After the ban on fox-hunting that is part of the campaign, will the phrase "hounded to death" fall into desuetude?

[3] France's Déclaration des droits de l'homme may be a month older than the US Bill of Rights, but, unlike the Déclaration, the Bill of Rights has actually been in effect for over two hundred years.

[4] As Brian Lee Crowley put it in his 1994 collection, *The Road to Equity*, "Canadians are very individualistic, but to say so is to commit a kind of social solecism; to celebrate that individualism and draw from it guiding principles about how we ought to be governed is to make oneself unfit for polite company."

William Watson

Born and raised in Montreal, William Watson is a professor of economics at McGill University. He is best known for his regular columns in the National Post, *the Montreal* Gazette, *and the* Ottawa Citizen *(where he has also served as editorial pages editor), and for his appearances on radio and television. He is a senior research fellow at Montreal's Institute for Research on Public Policy, and a research fellow at the C.D. Howe Institute in Toronto. He is a winner of the National Magazine Awards gold medal for humour and his book,* Globalization and the Meaning of Canadian Life, *was runner-up for the Donner Prize for the best book on Canadian public policy.*

DOREEN BARRIE

A CANADIAN IS . . . a work in progress, and is therefore well equipped to meet the challenges of the twenty-first century.

The Canadian identity is so fluid that some question its very existence or at least the existence of a pan-Canadian identity. Those who deal with the question often apologize for reworking over-tilled soil; others dismiss the exercise as self-indulgent, self-defeating navel-gazing.

How important is an identity? Should we focus on more important priorities like national unity or strengthening the economy? Will a country fall apart without an identity? I believe identity is more important than it has ever been, because developments in the last two decades are challenging assumptions that underpin it. The magnitude of change resulting from globalization and advances in communications is unprecedented. The result has been a dramatic altering of our traditional understandings of belonging and social cohesion.

Technology allows us to become part of a virtual community, as well as a geographic community – i.e., a community in space and a community in place. As geographic location is much less important than in the past, attachment to a specific place and, by extension, to a specific community may be much more tenuous. This is at once exciting and unnerving. Borders have become porous and people are on the move. (Some of this mobility is involuntary, as people are caught up in conflicts from Afghanistan to the Sudan. A number of those displaced find their way to Europe and North America as refugees.) Attempts after September 11 to reduce cross-border mobility by introducing more stringent controls have not been entirely successful, as some changes are irreversible. Since that fateful day, we have also had to grapple with questions about loyalty and citizenship, raising the question: who is a Canadian?

Before dealing with the Canadian case, it would be useful to look at the wider context, as other countries are also preoccupied with issues of identity and self-image. Territorial reorganization following the collapse of the Soviet Union has given birth to states that must define themselves, must fashion a new "narrative" for themselves. Narratives are simply stories we tell about ourselves, and some scholars believe that identity is "unthinkable without narrative" (Friedman 1998, 8). Identity, then, is not immutable; it is a social construct designed to promote social solidarity. It therefore needs be flexible enough to adapt to new situations. As identities dissolved in Eastern and Central Europe, new narratives had to be created, drawing selectively from the past and projecting into the future.

Even "established" countries are feeling the need redefine themselves to address strains in the social fabric: in 2000, a government-sponsored commission examined the implications of a multiethnic Britain. Among its recommendations were that Britain be formally recognized as a multi-ethnic society, and that British history "be revised, rethought or jetti-soned" (quoted in *New Criterion* 2000). Australia and New Zealand are redefining themselves as part of the Asia Pacific region to cope with changing trade patterns and partners. Countries like France and Holland are having to come to terms with a population that is being swelled by newcomers, many of them visible minorities. Lacking the Canadian "we're all immigrants" element in their narratives, and possessed of much longer histories, their experiences are very different from ours. Although the prospect of dumping centuries of history alarms many, the British example underscores the point that history can and is revised to adapt to changing circumstances. Being a much younger country, Canada does not have as much history – in fact, in Mackenzie King's opinion, our problem is that we have too much geography and too little history.

Canada is better placed to deal with a multiethnic identity because it has had a lot of practice! Canada's population has always been diverse: the term *First Nations* reflects the fact that Native people belong to several different groups. Thus, even before the English and French "immigrants" reached these shores, the population was far from monoethnic. While the French and the English are founding European members of the country, their dominance was diluted first by waves of (albeit monochromatic) immigrants to the Prairies prior to the Second World War. Since then, people from over a hundred countries call Canada home. Given the extent of cultural pluralism that already existed in 1971, the multicultural policy adopted by the Trudeau government merely formalized an existing reality.

As mentioned above, the Prairies drew settlers from all over Europe decades before Ontario and Quebec became multicultural; the soil was therefore fertile when immigrants from Asia, Africa and Latin America began arriving here approximately four decades ago. The relative ease with which these non-Europeans were slotted into the Canadian mosaic can be attributed to the "we're all immigrants" element in the Canadian narrative referred to above. This fact has a profound influence on the way Canadians see themselves, and it distinguishes them from people in European countries where immigration has not been a major source of population growth.

I do not wish to exaggerate the ease with which Canada has dealt with diversity. Although the French and English coexisted, there was, at times, a great deal of friction. Native people continue to experience more discrimination than most other citizens, and many immigrants who belong to visible minorities encounter problems. I am simply pointing out that Canada is far ahead of other countries. What is telling is public reaction to reports of discriminatory treatment. The case of Maher Arar, a Canadian citizen whose heritage is Syrian, is an example. Arar was detained in New York as a suspected terrorist and subsequently deported to Syria, where he was tortured. His wife was overwhelmed by expressions of outrage from Canadians at the way he was treated, and by the numerous offers of support. Such spontaneous actions reveal that we genuinely feel that citizenship, regardless of ethnicity, confers the right to equal treatment.

We can at least say that Canada is far more hospitable to its diverse population than other countries. And it will probably get better. A *Globe and Mail* study found that young Canadians are extremely open-minded, welcoming diversity and incorporating it into their lives (Anderssen,

Valpy, et al. 2004). For a class presentation a few years ago, I asked my students to talk about their sense of place – i.e., the geographic space with
which they identified and where they felt they belonged. Practically every
one of them identified with Canada as a whole and mentioned multiculturalism approvingly. A Canadian-born student whose background was
Indonesian remarked that, after his first visit to Indonesia the previous
year, he concluded that he had inherited only his physical traits from that
country. He felt that his value system was so different that he would never
fit in there.

The Canadian narrative has gently shifted to incorporate not just an
acceptance, but also a celebration of cultural pluralism. I would even
venture to argue that newcomers putting out the first hesitant tendril into
Canadian society would feel, by and large, much more secure than their
compatriots who chose some other country as their adopted home.

When Canada adopted a multicultural policy in 1971, some regarded
it as a cynical ploy to downgrade the status of French Canadians. However,
it has taken on a life of its own. It has proven a natural extension of the
Canadian mosaic, which has allowed immigrants to retain their customs
and traditions rather than requiring them to shuck them the moment they
got off the boat. Here again, there isn't unanimity on the merits of the
multicultural policy.

Political scientist Philip Resnick (2005, 59-60) warns against the
"mawkish sentimentality" surrounding multiculturalism. He takes issue
with philosopher Will Kymlicka's phrase the "Canadianization of the
world" to refer to the export of the Canadian model to other countries.
Resnick is also critical of remarks by Supreme Court Chief Justice Beverly
McLachlin, who spoke approvingly about Canadians "encouraging and
nourishing the identity of the other and celebrating the gifts of difference." Resnick rightly points out that the Canadian experiment cannot
be replicated in countries with ancient enmities and very different histories. It would take more than a dose of multiculturalism to cure their
problems. Nevertheless, heterogeneous populations are a reality in Europe
and, as it would not be feasible to deport them en masse, what is the alternative? A first step must surely be to stop regarding them as the "other,"

as a group to be shunned, feared or disdained. Such treatment can only breed resentment and hostility, ultimately threatening the stability of the country in question.

Ethnic nationalism was a non-starter in Canada, given the large percentage of French-speaking citizens. It is not surprising then that we opted for civic nationalism. As the title of Richard Gwyn's book describes it, we have a "nationalism without walls." Civic nationalism implies that the bonds are supplied by a shared set of values and political practices, a community of equal, rights-bearing citizens (Ignatieff 1995). Ethnic nationalism is based on shared ancestry, culture and history. Canadians belong to a political, rather than a sociological, community. Even in Quebec, cultural pluralism is taking root, and one can detect a shift from ethnic nationalism to nationalism based on linguistic ties. The phenomenon of the "ethnic separatist" (something Jacques Parizeau probably considers an oxymoron!) demonstrates that even relatively recent immigrants consider themselves part of the Québécois community.

Multiculturalism received a shot in the arm with constitutional entrenchment of the Charter of Rights and Freedoms in 1982. As the Charter prohibits discrimination on the basis of race and other characteristics, it was enthusiastically supported by ethnic and other minorities. The Charter has become an important unifying symbol, but its instrumental effect, as a tool to secure minority rights, enhances its popularity.

Thus far I have focused primarily on multiculturalism and the Charter, which has permitted it to flourish. One may well ask, however, what it is that defines the Canadian community. To what do the millions who have flocked here want to attach themselves?

Lacking ties of blood and common histories, Canadians wrap themselves around a cluster of ideas and aspirations that are bound up with the awe-inspiring landscape. They have a very strong emotional attachment to the land, the very geography that Mackenzie King derided. The vast empty spaces are beautiful, but also terrifying and humbling. They have inspired generations of writers and artists, as well as the general population. In a speech in Colorado, novelist Wallace Stegner once challenged his audience to create a society that matched the scenery – in Canada, we have done that.

Canadians are committed to equality and to the redistribution of wealth through the tax system. Despite acceptance of the need for deficit-reduction measures, they retain their belief that there is a legitimate role for the state to play. In addition to securing the welfare of society's most vulnerable members, there is a widely shared sentiment that the building blocks of a just society are such things as good, publicly funded education and health care. The tenacious support for health care drives many critics to distraction, as they fail to appreciate that it crystallizes in one program the fundamental values that Canadians hold dear.

While many would argue that each region contains different sorts of people, the core values I have mentioned bind citizens from St. John's to Victoria. The texture and rhythm of people's lives differ from one region to another, and many issues that animate politics inflame regional sentiments. However, we should not confuse regional interest with regional identity. The observation of historian Gerald Friesen (2001, 14) that "our inherited folk tales have grown stale" was a reference to the Prairies, but it could just as easily be applied to the West as a whole or even to other regions. Constantly harping on political squabbles obscures the existence of a national community in this country. Even Quebeckers who might not wish to remain in Canada are bound to us by shared values.

As this new century progresses, we will find that older maps will not be very helpful in finding our way around. There was a time when a tribe could be distinguished visually, by a sort of team uniform. Those visual clues will no longer prove useful. Thousands of people will cross literal and metaphorical boundaries in the coming decades, making it vital to reconceive national narratives.

Although predictions of transnational and global citizenship may be premature, within Canada's borders we see a glimmer of the future: a country where people from many lands are, for the most part, treated with dignity and respect; a place where they feel at home. A Canadian is not a canary in the mine of national identity, but rather a symbol of hope to those who fear an uncertain future.

Calgary, Alberta
Copyright © 2006 by Doreen Barrie

References

Anderssen, Erin, Michael Valpy, et al. *The New Canada: A Globe and Mail Report on the Next Generation*. Toronto: Globe and Mail/McClelland & Stewart, 2004.

Friedman, Susan. *Mappings: Feminism and the Cultural Geography of Encounter*. Princeton: Princeton University Press, 1998.

Friesen, Gerald. "Defining the Prairies: Or, Why the Prairies Don't Exist," in *Toward Defining the Prairies: Region, Culture, and History*. Ed. Robert Wardhaugh. Winnipeg: University of Manitoba Press, 2001, 13-28.

Gwyn, Richard. *Nationalism Without Walls: The Unbearable Lightness of Being Canadian*. Toronto: McClelland & Stewart, 1996.

New Criterion Online. "Will There Always Be an England?" November 2000. <newcriterion.com/archive/19/nov00/notes.htm>.

Resnick, Philip. *The European Roots of Canadian Identity*. Peterborough, ON: Broadview Press, 2005.

Ignatieff, Michael. *Blood and Belonging: Journey Into the New Nationalism*. New York: Noonday Press, 1995.

Doreen Barrie

Doreen Barrie is an adjunct assistant professor at the University of Calgary, specializing in Canadian and Alberta politics. She has written a political biography of Premier Ralph Klein in a book on Alberta premiers, and has also written on environmental protection in federal states. In 2004, she wrote a Citizen's Guide to Canadian Health Care, *which was distributed electronically. She is currently serving as president of the Western Social Science Association and is on the board of directors of the Alberta Civil Liberties Research Centre.*

JENNIFER WELSH

A CANADIAN IS . . . adaptable. To illustrate, consider the depth and breadth of the Canadian woman's wardrobe.

We begin with summer and the swimsuit, for refreshing dips in one of Canada's fresh lakes or calm bays on the Atlantic and Pacific oceans. The Canadian woman's swimsuit is never too daring – pleasant but functional. She also has an all-purpose sundress and sandals for pre-football game barbecues or Stampede pancake breakfasts. But Canada being Canada, the summer wardrobe requires a heavy fleece (or Roots sweatshirt?) to beat back the prairie mosquitoes or the blackflies of Muskoka. Moving into fall, the Canadian woman dons her wool blazer and scarf, and forks out for new back-to-whatever blue jeans. There is the all-purpose turtleneck (usually black) for chillier days, some thick tights, and a nice pair of coloured leather gloves from The Bay.

But it is the winter wardrobe that really defines the adaptable Canadian woman. There is the long wool dress-coat for evenings out, the short car coat for trips to work or to the grocery store, and the heavy ski jacket for multiple purposes – including jaunts outside to plug in the car, shifts at the unheated hockey rink to watch sons and daughters play peewee hockey, downhill skiing at Mont Tremblant or Lake Louise, or walks around Regina's Wascana Lake. (My own version of the ski jacket is a Hudson's Bay parka, made from the old fur trade company wool, with a fur-trimmed hood and embroidered igloos across the bottom. I've worn it for almost twenty years and nothing quite compares.) She has cardigan sweaters, thick crew neck sweaters, and more turtlenecks. And then there is the Canadian woman's nightmare: winter footwear. High dress boots, low fur-lined boots, boots with heavy rubber soles and treads to avoid slipping on black ice, ski boots, skates, or even mukluks. Unfortunately, in some parts of the country, the winter clothes and accessories carry over into spring. But the Canadian woman usually adds some brightly coloured blouses and a spring raincoat to the wardrobe, trying to convince herself that the snow will eventually melt.

In sum, the Canadian woman has clothing to adapt to every possible weather pattern. It is why Canadians build their houses with so much closet space.

Canadian adaptability is a more foundational part of our national character than my superficial fashion analysis reveals. Indeed, adaptability is the word that sums up our country's early history. Every Canadian family has its own version of how previous generations settled the land, and adapted their skills and knowledge to a developing Canadian economy. The Welsh family story begins with a man named George Taylor, who lived in Berwick-upon-Tweed, on the English–Scottish border.

George travelled to Canada in the late eighteenth century on a Hudson's Bay Company ship, hoping to make his fame and fortune as part of the fur trade. And like many of the European men who arrived at fur trade settlements, he adapted to the climate, geography, and practices of the New World. A prime example was his early decision to take a Native woman as his "country wife." Intermarriage between European men and Native women – known as marriage à la façon du pays – became one of the key social features of the fur trade's progress across Canada. The invaluable skills of the women allowed European traders to survive in the wilderness, but also greatly contributed to the productivity of the fur trade itself.

George and his Native wife Jane had eight children together – one of whom, Margaret, became the country wife of the fur trade magnate George Simpson, governor of Rupert's Land. It was Margaret (my great-great-great-grandmother) who accompanied Simpson on his historic cross-continental journey, via canoe and snowshoe, from Hudson Bay to the Pacific in 1828. But as the fur trade progressed, and Europeans no longer needed help acclimatizing themselves to the land, the role of country wife began to diminish in stature. The traders arranged for their European wives to settle in Canada and severed their ties with Native women.

Margaret adapted to these new circumstances by marrying one of Simpson's canoe paddlers, Amable Hogue, a Métis like herself. The couple made their way from York Factory on Hudson Bay to the Assiniboine River in what is today Manitoba. It was there that she died in 1885, the year of Louis Riel's hanging in Regina. At the same time, my great-grandfather, Norbert Welsh, was adapting to another important change in the story of our country's development: the disappearance of the buffalo from the Canadian West.

Norbert's life embodies the Canadian skill of adaptation. Though he had no formal education, he spoke seven languages (English, French, Cree, Sioux, Blackfoot, Assiniboine, and Stoney) and practised almost as many professions during his lifetime. At the age of eighteen, Norbert joined a fur trade party and headed west from Manitoba to hunt buffalo. He followed the herds westward as they began to dwindle, and eventually landed in the Métis community of Lebret (near Fort Qu'Appelle), where he built a log house for his family. When, in his words, the North West turned into "white man's country" and Indians began to move onto reserves, he bought his own harvester and turned his hand to farming. But Norbert soon tired of the brutal prairie weather and its destructive impact on his crops, and so took to freighting flour between Shoal Lake and Fort Qu'Appelle. During the 1885 Métis Rebellion, he found himself on the wrong side of Riel and lost his livelihood, but managed to reinvent himself as a rancher near the southern branch of the Saskatchewan River. He lived out his last days as a butcher and shopkeeper back in Lebret, and is buried in a small cemetery next to the lake.

While the adaptability of Canadians has been focused largely on the experiment of building a just and prosperous society north of the forty-ninth parallel, we have also built and adapted a global persona. In historical terms, Canada's track record as an international actor is relatively short. Until the passing of the Statute of Westminster in 1931, the Dominion of Canada deferred to the principle of British primacy in imperial foreign and defence policy, sacrificing thousands of its young men to the cause of European peace during the First World War. Nonetheless, the tale of seventy-odd years of Canadian-made foreign policy makes for riveting reading. We entered the Second World War as part of a loyal British Commonwealth, and emerged as the closest neighbour of the most powerful country in the world. Canada quickly adapted to this new Pax Americana by lending its resources and ideas to the founding of the United Nations, the Bretton Woods System, and the North Atlantic Treaty Organization. As the Cold War enveloped the globe, threatening to extinguish the postwar multilateralist flame, it was Canadian inventiveness that helped to breathe new life into the UN, in the form of peacekeeping. Near the end of the twentieth century, Canada adapted its skills as broker and peacemaker by playing a pivotal role in the campaign to rid the world of landmines and the establishment of the International Criminal Court.

Throughout this post-1945 period, the label "middle power" has been used as a shorthand to describe Canada's role in the world. Canada has adapted to its relative lack of economic and military capability by carving out a special niche in the international hierarchy, and leveraging it to great effect. The language and practice of middle-power diplomacy has given Canada a disproportionate influence in international affairs, and furnished us with a distinctive global persona.

Can middle-powership sustain us in this new century? During the frosty decades of the Cold War, the notion of a middle power seeking to find a platform between the United States on the one hand and the Soviet Union on the other made a lot of sense for Canada. It even had a measure of utility in the early years of the 1990s, as the world was adjusting to the breakup of the communist bloc, focusing on the global economy, and building new forms of international collaboration. But the recent transformation of the international context, combined with significant changes within the North American region and the Canadian federation, has made the middle-power vocation outdated.

The first problem with the middle power persona is a conceptual one. What does it mean today to be in the middle? We no longer live in an international system where great powers are pitted against one another, and smaller powers like Canada work skilfully to find a path through the middle. Instead, we live in a world with a single superpower that far outstrips its rivals in military might and political influence. Moreover, it is less clear what power means in the twenty-first century. If power is associated with the possession of certain resources (population, territory, military strength, economic size), then it is clear that the United States is the world's unrivalled hegemonist. But how should we categorize other states? While some might be considered great in economic terms (e.g., Germany) or in population (e.g., India), they may not necessarily be granted that label in military terms. Similarly, while certain components of "hard power" remain essential to superpower status (such as nuclear weapons), other features of what Joseph Nye calls "soft power" are becoming more decisive as states seek to convert their power resources into effective influence. Sometimes the most effective power is often not commanding but co-optive: getting others to want what you want. The track record of the US-led coalition in reconstructing Iraq is an obvious example: to "win the peace," the United States needs to show as much skill in using soft power as it did in using hard power to win the war.

Aside from these analytical problems, the middle-power persona faces a normative challenge. It is mostly about process and tactics: compromising, building coalitions, participating in international organizations and forging consensus. But what are we trying to achieve through middle-power means? For Canada, middle-powership is largely about a *way* of conducting foreign policy. Yet, values and purposes have become all important in our post-9/11 world. In the new context of global terrorism, failed states, infectious disease and environmental degradation, Canada's friends care less about how many international organizations it has joined, and more about what it stands for, and what it is willing to bring to the table.

Finally, the middle-power persona no longer inspires Canadians from a new generation. The formative experiences of young Canadians – particularly their exposure to global media and the borderless worldwide web – have made them inherently internationalist. Now they passionately believe that they will do great things in the world. To be a middle power is to settle for mediocrity.

The longer we fiddle, the harder the process of adapting will be. The signs of crisis are real and mounting. Canada's military capability has deteriorated rapidly (it ranks near the bottom of the NATO roster in terms of percentage of GDP devoted to defence), its policy leadership on key issues like the environment has evaporated, and its international aid budget has dwindled from a high of 0.53% of GDP in 1975 to 0.28% in 2004. Even Canada's much-heralded reputation as the world's peace-keeper has been damaged by its traumatic experience in Somalia and prolonged underinvestment in the armed forces. Once Canadians were part of every UN peacekeeping mission; at this time of writing, we rank thirty-fourth on the list of contributor countries, and have had to turn down a series of requests to send our forces to war-torn countries. In short, Canada has less meat to put on the international table, and is increasingly relying on its past record of good international citizenship.

The magic of Canada lies in its capacity for change. It is a country continually in the process of becoming. Today, we must practise that magic beyond our borders as well as within them. It is time for Canadians to draw on their talents of adaptation yet again, and forge a new global persona for the twenty-first century.

Oxford, United Kingdom
Copyright © 2006 by Jennifer Welsh

Jennifer Welsh

Jennifer Welsh was born in Regina, Saskatchewan. She holds a BA in political science from the University of Saskatchewan (where she won the Governor General's Medal) and a master's degree and doctorate in international relations from the University of Oxford (where she studied as a Rhodes Scholar). She is a former Jean Monnet Fellow of the European University Institute in Florence, and was a Cadieux Research Fellow in the policy planning staff of the Canadian Department of Foreign Affairs.

Welsh has taught international relations at the University of Toronto, McGill University, and the Central European University, and she is currently university lecturer in international relations at Oxford, and a fellow of Somerville College. She is the author and co-author of five books and a series of articles on international relations. Her most recent publications include Humanitarian Intervention and International Relations *and* At Home in the World. *She spends her summers at Lumsden Beach, Saskatchewan.*

BOB RAE

A CANADIAN IS . . . a wonderful thing to be.

I write these words at thirty thousand feet, on my way to a conference in India on ethnic conflict and nation-building. This is one of my keen interests, exploring how countries and regions can explode with violence, and in turn find ways to put themselves back together.

We like to think of ourselves as a peaceable kingdom, whose history is as dull as ditchwater, and whose politicians are full of it. Yet conflict and its resolution have been an indelible part of our story.

The meeting between priests, soldiers, explorers and Aboriginal people was hardly a friendly event – it was a shattering encounter whose effects we feel to this day. It is traumatic because, while the official versions of Canada – its Constitution, the speeches of its politicians – talk about embracing the Aboriginal roots of the country, this has yet to really happen. Here the contrast with our NAFTA partner Mexico is fascinating: it is impossible to "see" Mexico without feeling the Aztec and Mayan reality every day – in the faces of its people, its art, its culture. Of course, Mexico has its own issues, but ironically the extent of integration has perhaps more successfully forged a new identity.

Just as Britain's overseas empire came home in the middle of the twentieth century, so too we now must recognize that the era of the "away-ness" of Aboriginal Canada is over. The population explosion and the movement off remote and northern reserves to urban centres is well underway. The great Canadian challenge of the twenty-first century will be to embrace this change, and to make it work. Jobs and education are part of an even bigger cultural shift – a country whose majority has for centuries defined itself as an offshoot of Europe must now see itself for what it is, not what it was. This is never easy, because, as Marshall McLuhan told us, we see life through a rear-view mirror.

The multi-decade conflict between English and French was not resolved in 1759. The two foreign empires fought battles. But it was up to the settlers to figure out how to share the land. It took over a hundred more years to build a new way of living together. This conflict is an issue that we continue to work through every day.

The morality of federalism triumphed over other visions, because it alone allowed different people and groups to live together without submerging their respective identities. The Supreme Court of Canada put it this way in their landmark unanimous opinion on secession: "A thousand strands of accommodation make a nation."

These acts of accommodation are not signs of weakness. The active celebration of diversity, the recognition of difference, the acknowledgment of the integrity of "the other" – all of these imply a rejection of something else: a view that my beliefs, my "one Canadianness" might make a better bumper sticker, but they are a lousy way to build a country.

This question of identity is never easy. Generations of Canadian nationalists felt the powerful need to define the country as not British, then not American. The dramatic change in our immigration policy in the 1960s – far more revolutionary than we ever knew at the time – allowed us to fall into allowing "multiculturalism" to then define who we are.

But this isn't good enough either. If we see Canada as simply a geographical space that is shared by millions of people from around the world, who go about their business but don't really know or care about each other, then we are not building a country. We need a greater sense of common purpose than that. This tension is drawn very tightly by the globalization of conflicts that were at one time confined to other places that seemed far away.

The celebration of difference does not mean that we should tolerate our neighbours building bombs in their basement or fomenting hatred. Yet we now realize that these things can and do happen. We stop them not by closing our doors, which is impossible, but by being less naive about the world we are now in, and by being clearer about the common terms of citizenship.

Former Quebec premier Lucien Bouchard sparked outrage when he said that "Canada is not a real country." Having fought in two world wars and Korea, and having been peacekeepers for half a century, Canadians might be forgiven for reacting harshly. Yet the statement poses a challenge: what does it mean to be a real country? If Bouchard was referring to the old canard that a country has to possess a common language, a common culture, a common ethnicity, it is easy enough to refute. And yet it must be said that a real country stands for certain values, and does what it can to make sure its citizens understand and uphold them. A real country will work determinedly for its unity – not by enforcing a rigid conformity, but by being clear (the *Clarity Act* comes to mind) on the conditions for trying to leave. A real country is not about passive indifference or benign neglect.

We define ourselves by what we are, as well as by what we are not. Our self-definition includes that we are North Americans, that we share a continent with others who are at once more populous and powerful than we are. Anti-Americanism, with its roots going back to the very formation of our country, is too limiting, too narrow, too carping, to really reflect who we are today. We are like the Americans and we are different. We shouldn't be preoccupied with proving either.

The comedian John Ling defines Canadians as "Americans with health care and without guns." He might now add "with gay marriage," and "who didn't invade Iraq." Like all jokes, there is more than a grain of truth in the irony. We are constantly comparing ourselves, because we live next door, we are smaller, and we spend many hours watching their television and movies.

But perhaps without fully realizing how it happened, we have in fact created a different culture. Comparing bestseller lists a few years ago, I found that there were more Canadian books on the Canadian fiction list than German books on the German list. It might have been a fluke, but no one sits anymore around wondering who will write the great Canadian novel. There are dozens of them. NAFTA, contrary to the widely shared mythology, did not swamp our culture, or make us just like the United States. We are more resilient than we know.

What will be the great Canadian debates of the future? There is a realistic chance that we shall face yet another referendum in Quebec. We have been sleepwalking a bit on this, and will have to wake up. Is a break unimaginable? Unfortunately, it is not. But it would be a tragedy painful and harmful to all. We have to do everything we can to make sure it does not happen.

A more mundane, but in fact vitally important, debate will be driven by the inexorable drive of demographics. The key social policy of the present and future is education. This viewpoint runs against the grain of a generation of Canadians who value security above all else. Health care has been seen as the "top of mind" issue, and health spending crowds the fiscal agenda. But it will have to share the limelight.

And then there is the land. We love Canada for its people and for the communities we have built – just as we should lament the urban sprawl, global warming and degradation of our water and air that have accompanied our prosperity. Yet Murray McLauchlan is right when he sings that the soul of the country is north of the timberline. That is the Canada of our imagination. We know from myth and legend what the Aboriginal people who made the remarkable trek across the Bering Strait believed. The accounts of the early missionaries speak of the beauty and bounty of the place, as well as its harshness. The Group of Seven and Emily Carr showed us that ours is not the pampered landscape of the Old World. That land will never die.

A Canadian is anyone who loves this land and its people and has chosen to make it home. Period.

Aboard a flight to New Delhi, India
Copyright © 2006 by Bob Rae

Bob Rae

Bob Rae served as Ontario's twenty-first premier and was elected eight times to federal and provincial parliaments before his retirement from politics in 1996. He is a partner at the international law firm Goodmans, as well as the chair or director of several boards and the national spokesperson of the Leukemia & Lymphoma Society of Canada. In 2005, he was appointed chair of the Air India Inquiry and review.

Bob Rae is the author of two books, From Protest to Power *and* The Three Questions, *and is an adjunct professor at the University of Toronto and senior fellow of Massey College. He has received numerous honorary degrees and awards.*

In 2006 he began his campaign for the leadership of the Liberal Party.

AFTERWORD BY IRVIN STUDIN

A CANADIAN IS ... a fox, and therefore no more and no less than a citizen of the state called Canada.

Let me explain ...

If it is true, as Bernard Crick once wrote, that "boredom with established truths is the great enemy of free men,"[1] then it is also true that free men do not often ask themselves questions that may occasion answers that risk undermining their very self-conception. What is a Canadian? In other words, who is a Canadian? The line of inquiry may well be too direct for the Canadian consciousness ...

As editor of this book, I have the distinct "last-mover" advantage of offering a response after having read and reflected on the considered responses of forty-two distinguished Canadian thinkers. Admittedly, the answers offered by these thinkers often go beyond the "what is" to offer glimpses of what *the Canadian* could or should be. The book is more interesting for this deviation. Still, the fact that there is far greater variety in the responses in this book than in those in Ben-Gurion's collection on who is a Jew reveals the very complexity of the task of settling on an agreeable and meaningful understanding of *the Canadian*. It shows that Canadians are very much foxes, to borrow from Isaiah Berlin: they stand for many things, but unlike the hedgehog, are not animated by a single, or coherent, force, motif or logic.[2] In short, the Canadian, at this time of writing, has no essence. Indeed, *the Canadian* is, in the only meaningful sense, a citizen of Canada.

We might reach such a conclusion by briefly analyzing the several distinct schools of thought that can arguably be traced in the responses provided by the sages in this book.[3] The first of these schools, exemplified chiefly by Peter Hogg, Denis Stairs, Charlotte Gray, Jennifer Welsh, Silver Donald Cameron, Yves Fortier and Kent Stetson, among others, is what I would call the *idiosyncratic school,* conceiving *the Canadian* as defined by certain distinctive, often primordial, character traits, a particular personality-type or specific values. According to this line of thinking, *the Canadian* is variously law-abiding, liberal and enlightened. *The Canadian* is also famously tolerant, polite and generous; also diplomatic. In the late Pierre Berton's view, *the Canadian* is apparently famous for being able to make love in a canoe without tipping it. He or she is, to take the less auspicious view, a historical amnesiac (or historically ignorant), parochial, pathologically deferential, complacent, too comfortable with mediocrity, all too easily racist (despite apparent good intentions) and, as Thomas Homer-Dixon suggests, prone to *Schadenfreude.* Apparent or claimed value differences with the American, as William Watson, George Elliott Clarke and Paul Heinbecker note, are often central to this line of argument.[4] It goes without saying, I might counter, that none of these traits, good or bad, exists invariably in each and every person we may wish to call Canadian. Indeed, such traits may not even necessarily be more true for *the Canadian* than for, say, the Italian, Greek or any other Westerner, for that matter; although the chances are quite good that, between the Italian and the Canadian, the Italian would sooner tip a canoe when lovemaking if the Canadian lover in question hailed from the Yukon.

Definitions of *the Canadian* from the *circumstantial* viewpoint – e.g., the Canadian is "lucky" – as variously suggested by Hugh Segal, John C. Crosbie, Wade MacLaughlan and Guy Saint-Pierre – or a creature of nature and cold weather (see Roch Carrier and, from the Cree perspective, Mary Ellen Turpel-Lafond) seem also to belong to this same idiosyncratic school of thought. Again, I might argue, some Canadians are lucky and some are not, for various reasons; reasons that, as Wade MacLaughlan and Maria Tippett indicate, are often a function of time and place. And while the peculiar nature and weather that mark the territory of the Canadian polity may well appear to have a connection to a presumed Canadian consciousness, the country is geographically massive,

and experience of weather and nature is highly variable across the land
– there being no common ground between the Victoria native playing
soccer in January and this Ottawa-based Canadian freezing his tail off at
the same time of the year, three time zones away, in one of the world's
coldest capital cities.

A second school of thought may be what I would call the *sociopolitical
school* – i.e., *the Canadian* is a "work in progress," is "under construction,"
or is humanity's best answer (to date) for dealing with ethnocultural diversity. George Bowering, Thomas Franck, Doreen Barrie, Catherine Ford,
Audrey McLaughlin, Valerie Haig-Brown, Saeed Rahnema and perhaps
even Margaret MacMillan and Mark Kingwell appear to varying degrees
to share this view. *The Canadian* is, they argue, identified with certain key
public policies, societal principles or values – such as multiculturalism,
universal health care, and the Charter – which are thought to underpin
his or her civic essence. Indeed, medicare and the Charter have been
described as "the tectonic plates of the modern idea of Canada."[5]

I would again counter that public policies and principles are made to
be amended, rescinded or even ignored, depending on the political imper-
atives of the day, and it is therefore difficult to proclaim that *the Canadian*
is categorically a creature of certain policies – particularly when such policies clash, as with the June 2005 Supreme Court decision in respect of
private health insurance.[6] And given that the said "tectonic plates" of
Canadianism do not predate the 1960s, *the Canadian* of the sociopolitical school must be seen as transitory or evolutionary in nature.

The *constitutionalist school* is close to the sociopolitical school, but
refers to the actual Canadian Constitution as the key descriptor by which
the Canadian may be defined. This school sees the policies and policy-
consequences discussed by the sociopolitical school as necessarily flowing
from the Constitution. Sujit Choudhry and Douglas Glover have this
take, suggesting that *the Canadian* is contingent on the constitutional
makeup – the first principles, if you will – of the Canadian state.

I would note that, to various extents, we can also detect a *sceptical
school* of thought in the answers of such thinkers as Mark Kingwell,
Thomas Homer-Dixon, Roy MacGregor and even Jake MacDonald –
indeed, among many thinkers in the sociopolitical school (although not

only in this school). The sceptic would hold that *the Canadian* is "imaginary" or "invented,"[7] or at least so contingent in nature as to have his or her essence constantly overstated by overly keen commentators.

A final school would appear to be the *dissenting school* or, in some cases, the *rejectionist school*, whose exponents speak to varying degrees of alienation from what they may perceive as a majoritarian conception (or indeed, the state's conception) of *the Canadian*. In short, they do not see themselves in *the Canadian*, as currently defined. Guy Laforest and Christian Dufour certainly write in this vein, calling themselves "exiles" within Canada, and thus outside of the Canadian "mainstream," as they see it. The grievances of these particular Québécois – more *Canadien* than *Canadian*, if you will – appear first and foremost to be political or constitutional in nature, with particular emphasis placed on the absence of Quebec's signature on the Constitution Act of 1982, and on the failures of the Meech Lake Accord in 1987 and the Charlottetown Accord in 1992. Louis Balthazar offers, however, that these grievances predate Meech and Charlottetown, and have roots in an alleged violation of the original political bargain that shaped Canada: to wit, the idea of a recognized and distinct French-majority Quebec, sovereign within its spheres of responsibilities under the federal model. In fact, in each of the arguments of members of this school, one may find strands of alienation that are variously political, linguistic, cultural, regional and, yes, tribal. (I note in this context my surprise that neither Western regionalism-cum-nationalism nor Newfoundland nationalism were really taken up as major drivers of dissent among writers in this book. A different sample of Canadian sages may well have yielded such themes.)

Given the great diversity of responses to the question at play, I am inclined to conclude that the only coherent way to answer the question may be to suggest, as I have above, that *the Canadian* is nothing more (and nothing less) than a citizen of the state called Canada. As Patrick Weil concluded in his famous essay on the French, «est français celui que l'État considère comme tel» (He is French whom the State so deems).[8] That is, *the Canadian* is certain to be a citizen of the physically colossal federation occupying the northern half of North America, consisting, at this time of writing, of ten provinces and three territories, and operating under the democratic laws and institutions established in the Constitutions of 1867 and 1982. This determination of citizenship lies within the jurisdiction of the Canadian federal government, and is determined by a legal framework built primarily around the *Citizenship Act*. The Canadian, as a citizen of the Canadian state, is susceptible to all of the obligations, formal and informal, attendant to this citizenship, and is the beneficiary of the vast complement of rights and freedoms secured by this citizenship. And yes, as Guy Laforest stresses in his response, many, if not most, of these rights and freedoms predate the 1982 Charter of Rights and Freedoms.

The Canadian, on this understanding, must not only be differentiated from, but must subsume *le Canayen* or *le Canadien*[9] who was the ancestor of the modern French Canadian (specifically, today's Québécois), as well as the Canadian who was the citizen of all precursors to the modern Canadian state – for example, the Canadian of Upper Canada or Lower Canada. In short, today's Canadian exists only on the strength of the existence of today's Canadian state. Conversely, he or she *cannot* exist (as a Canadian properly called!) outside of the organizing framework called Canada or the Canadian state.

One might well object that such a conception of *the Canadian* is too legalistic, minimalist, reductionist or just plain boring, but I think that it begins to tell a more honest story about our protagonist. Indeed, as Douglas Glover observes in his response, no other definition of *the Canadian* can hold for most, if not all, Canadians. At best, without the Canadian state, *the Canadian* is likely to be a non-American North American or, more generally, a Westerner (or "liberal," to use Denis Stairs' terminology) – animated by, and loyal to, the complement of values and ethics particular to Western civilization.[10] Anything beyond this baseline definition of *the Canadian* as citizen of the state, I would argue, either applies with too many exceptions to most of those we would call Canadians or takes us too far away from reality, toward the normative – i.e., the "what should be" of *the Canadian*.

Anything beyond this baseline definition would also likely suggest a fundamental and universal Canadian *essence* or even *soul*, which, as I've argued, is not yet there. If it were there, this essence would consist in a value or belief system, behavioural or physical traits, reference points and language that are peculiar to most, if not all, Canadian citizens. For "hedgehogs" like the Pole, Turk, Persian, Japanese, Russian, German and Jew – all members of very old nations – such an essence, while doubtless variable at the edges, is arguably there, the product of centuries of painful fermentation. For the American, my guess is that this essence is advanced, but not yet complete, and therefore still highly malleable.[11] And for *the Canadian*, the "fox" – as all too unscientifically suggested by the responses in this book – this essence is still contested and contingent.

Of course, the fact that *the Canadian* lives in one of the most peaceable, just and civilized countries in the world is no trivial matter. Indeed, it is precisely what makes the Canadian and his or her Canada so worthy of defence! The intent here, however, is to attempt to paint *the Canadian* as he or she *is* – the product of a state less than a century and a half old; indeed, one of the oldest democracies and federations in the world, but not at all old in the historical scheme of things.

So *the Canadian* exists only as a function of the Canadian state. And without the Canadian state, whoever we call a Canadian may not be anyone peculiar at all. The insight is not banal. It means that *the Canadian* is a political creature; he or she exists only because the Canadian political project exists, and will continue to exist only if the political project moves forward. In other words, politics – the means by which the business of the Canadian state is conducted – matters *existentially* to the Canadian. *The Canadian* may therefore very well be a "work in progress," as some of the writers here have argued, but this work in progress can only be advanced in the political context – in the bosom of the state called Canada.

To paraphrase Pericles: while *the Canadian* may not be interested in politics, politics is necessarily interested in *the Canadian*! I understand this politics to be the complex process by which the Canadian state and its affiliated institutions are able to assimilate, reconcile and broker among the multiple and often competing and contradictory claims, opinions and visions of over 32 million Canadian citizens (not to mention the multiple schools of thought that seek to define these Canadians). Mine is therefore not a platitudinous plea for increased civic engagement. Rather, it is an argument for recognition and protection of a basic, existential fact: *the Canadian* as a political fact, and *the Canadian* as fact only in virtue of the political. The rest is commentary.

The political, as distinct from the ethnic, commercial or strategic conception of *the Canadian* was very much alive at Confederation in 1867 and at the constitutional conferences preceding the founding of the country. That the Fathers of Confederation could have created a functional political whole – a country or state – of disparate and often dissimilar parts and interests speaks to the wholly *practical* nature of Canadian identity; one can think of no other way to describe the fact that individuals apparently connected at their core by only their common citizenship of the Canadian state should live, although imperfectly, in relative security and prosperity, while other non-Canadian individuals from all over the world joined by much thicker bonds of nationhood and blood should be without a state or, even with a state, bereft of the quality of life of the average Canadian.

It is this very practical, political character of Canadian identity that allows the Canadian project to survive in spite of the apparent lack of a natural Canadian essence. It follows, quite plainly, that failure to appreciate the fundamentally political nature of *the Canadian* is the very danger which, over the long run, may compromise the Canadian state and, by definition, lead to the extinction of *the Canadian*. The point can be made with reference to the Constitution and the Quebec question: The modern Canadian state is the product of intense constitutional (yes, political!) debate, bargaining and accommodation. This constitutional "discourse," as Sujit Choudhry describes it in his response, is the lifeblood of the state. Yet a long-standing *fiction* appears to persist in much of English Canada that Trudeau's 1982 Constitution was necessarily the final volley in Canadian constitution-making – something arguably proved by the failures of both Meech Lake and Charlottetown. This analysis has obscured from Canadians the continuing threat of Quebec separatism, and the nagging but critical need to deal with the place of Quebec in the Canadian federation.[12] By this I do not mean dealing with the question of Quebec "once and for all," but once and then again, and then again, if necessary. The constitutional discourse that underlies the state and underpins its politics does not end after a single transaction, even if that transaction is major.

An equally frustrating and irresponsible myth pervades in much of Quebec: that is, that a meaningful Canadian essence or identity would survive the secession of the province and the breakup of the Canadian state. But if *the Canadian* is but the citizen of the Canadian state, then this line of argument cannot stand. Let me be blunt, for the issue presses: no Quebec, no Canada. No Canada, no Canadian. This would not be so painful a conclusion for me to draw from the above analysis if the possible loss of the Canadian state and the consequent demise of *the Canadian* would not come with a multitude of *practical* costs – most evidently, a significant hit to the quality of life enjoyed by the erstwhile Canadian (Québécois and non-Québécois alike), but also an indictment of a politics – a political system and culture – that is still the envy of the civilized world.

Many of my fellow Canadians will doubtless plead fatigue with the Constitution! We are tired of the debates, the confrontation, the gamesmanship, they cry. What is less evident, however, is that Canadians who plead fatigue or exhaustion with this discourse, to the point of inaction, plead fatigue or exhaustion with the very process that allows them to be Canadians.[13] In short, negation of the discourse may, over time, negate *the Canadian*.

There are, of course, other important issues that animate the Canadian political project. Nonetheless, unlike the Quebec issue, none of these is likely to threaten the very existence of the Canadian state (and therefore *the Canadian*) in the foreseeable future. Among these issues, I might again mention the other powerful centrifugal forces that pull at the chords of the Canadian federation – notably, Newfoundland and the fast-rising West – driven by an ever-confident and assertive Alberta. I might also mention Canada's growing strategic irrelevance and its diffidence in defending an ambitious set of national interests in the wider world – problems that have been allowed to fester on the strength of the long-held fiction that Canadians are so well-liked by the rest of the world that they rarely attract enemies. Finally, I might mention the constant need to redress the stubbornly tragic lot of our First Peoples, as well as the ongoing and ever-delicate balancing act that must occur in order that Canadian society may effectively integrate our Latest Peoples – the world's immigrants.

About all of these important issues our sages have written with verve. Still, we cannot allow treatment of these issues to overstate the existence of a Canadian essence (or of a *unique* and *special* Canadianness in the world) and, at the same time, undersell the centrality to *the Canadian* of the existence of the Canadian state and the political process that supports it. In the long run, such a mistake would surely sound the death knell of *the Canadian*. A much more favourable future, by contrast, is one in which we can muster the political courage and ingenuity to strengthen and renew the state again and again to defend against persistent threats and to reflect realities, old and new. It would seem that any serious talk of a "Canadian soul" will only ensue after this process has been repeated many, many times over.

Ottawa, Ontario, and Canberra, Australia

Notes

[1] Bernard Crick, *In Defence of Politics* (Middlesex: Penguin Books, 1964).

[2] Isaiah Berlin, *Russian Thinkers* (London: Penguin Books, 1978).

[3] I would emphasize that these "schools of thought" are in no sense comprehensive or even mutually exclusive. Indeed, many of the responses in the book, nuanced as they are, fall into more than one school.

[4] Most recently and famously in Michael Adams' *Fire and Ice* (Toronto: Penguin Canada, 2003).

[5] Rex Murphy, "Clash of the Canuck Titans," *Globe and Mail*, January 11, 2005, p. A17.

[6] *Chaoulli et al. v. Québec (A.G.) et al.* (2005), SCC 35.

[7] For a discussion of the role of invention in nationalism, read Eric Hobsbawm and Terence Ranger (eds.), *The Invention of Tradition* (Cambridge: Cambridge University Press, 1983).

[8] Patrick Weil, *Qu'est-ce qu'un Français?* (Paris: Éditions Grasset, 2002).

[9] Note the 1806 poem by Joseph Quesnel, which portrays the dichotomy between *le Canadien* and the Anglo: «Faucille en main, au champ de la Fortune/On voit

courir l'Anglois, le Canadien/Tous deux actifs et d'une ardeur commune/Pour acquérir ce qu'on nomme du bien/Mais en avant l'Anglois ayant sa place/. . .» quoted in Fernand Dumont, *Genèse de la société québécoise* (Québec: Boréal, 1993), pp. 156-57.

[10] Will Kymlicka, "Being Canadian," *Government and Opposition*, 38:3 (July 2003), pp. 357-85.

[11] See, for instance, Samuel P. Huntington's controversial new book, *Who Are We?: The Challenges to America's National Identity* (New York: Simon & Schuster, 2004).

[12] I stress the Quebec issue as primordial to the existence of the federation. Issues such as Senate reform and possible reorientation of federal-provincial powers seem to me, at this time, to be two other key *enjeux* for a future constitutional round, consistent with the need to calibrate the state's organizing framework and institutions with the challenges of the twenty-first century.

[13] Michael Ignatieff eloquently called this "the argument from exhaustion" in "The Coming Constitutional Crisis," *National Post*, April 19, 2005, p. A19.

ACKNOWLEDGEMENTS

Special thanks go, first and foremost, to Alla (Allachka), my love, my life, my best friend, for your constant love and support; to my best man, Sam (Sasan), for consistent big-ups and indefatigable advocacy; to Sheila Fischman de Montréal (may we at last meet), for the many leads, and for your interest; to my family (always): Papa and Mama, of course, as mentioned, but also Rebecca, Sophia, Aunt Genya and Babushka Nina; and now Eugenia and Josif (new family); and to Doug Gibson, for strong encouragement *ab initio* . . .

I would like to extend my sincerest thanks to the forty-two "sages" (thinkers, writers) who took the time out to respond to my query. Many of them generously donated their writer's fees to enable the establishment of university scholarships in Canadian studies.

Finally, I should note the several friends and colleagues who provided me with honest criticism and advice on the project and its several manuscripts: Sam Shoamanesh (mentioned above), Saeed Rahnema, Gowan Tervo, Daniel Friedrich, Glenn Bezalel and Michael Vital.

IRVIN STUDIN

Irvin Studin spent several years as a policy strategist and senior policy analyst for the prime minister at the Privy Council Office in Ottawa. He has also worked as a senior policy advisor in the Department of Prime Minister and Cabinet in Canberra, Australia. He has advised on issues as diverse as the wars in Iraq and Afghanistan, national security, foreign policy, democratic governance and transportation policy. Studin holds degrees from the Schulich School of Business at Toronto's York University, as well as from the London School of Economics and the University of Oxford, where he studied on a Rhodes Scholarship. In 2000, he was listed by *Maclean's* magazine as one of "100 Young Canadians to Watch."

In his past life, Studin was an All-Canadian university athlete and dabbled in professional soccer in several countries. He and his wife, Alla, a schoolteacher, are frequent travellers. They divide most of their time between Toronto and Ottawa.

OTHER TITLES FROM
DOUGLAS GIBSON BOOKS

PUBLISHED BY McCLELLAND & STEWART LTD.

CHARLES THE BOLD *by* Yves Beauchemin; *Translated by* Wayne Grady
An unforgettable coming-of-age story set in 1960s and 1970s east-end Montreal,
from French Canada's most popular novelist. "Truly astonishing . . . one of the
great works of Canadian literature." – Madeleine Thien
Fiction, 6 × 9, 384 pages, hardcover

YOUNG TRUDEAU: 1919–1944 *by* Max and Monique Nemni; *Translated by*
William Johnson
A disturbing intellectual biography of Pierre Trudeau that exposes his
pro-fascist views until 1944, completely reshaping our understanding of him. "I
was extremely shocked." – Lysiane Gagnon, *Globe and Mail*
Biography, 6 × 9, 384 pages, trade paperback

STILL AT THE COTTAGE *by* Charles Gordon
The follow-up to the classic *At the Cottage*, this is an affectionate and hilarious
look at cottage living. "Funny, reflective, and always insightful, this is Charles
Gordon at the top of his game." – Will Ferguson
Humour, 6 × 9, 176 pages, illustrations, trade paperback

SORRY, I DON'T SPEAK FRENCH: Confronting the Canadian Crisis That
Won't Go Away *by* Graham Fraser
The national bestseller that looks at how well official bilingualism is working in
Canada. "It's hard to think of any writer better qualified to write about language
than Mr. Fraser. . . . He is informed, balanced, judicious and experienced, and a
very clear writer." – Jeffrey Simpson, *Globe and Mail*
History, 6 × 9, 352 pages, hardcover

CRAZY ABOUT LILI: A Novel *by* William Weintraub
The author of *City Unique* takes us back to wicked old Montreal in 1948 in this
fine, funny novel, where an innocent young McGill student falls for a stripper.
"Funny, farcical and thoroughly engaging." – *Globe and Mail*
Fiction, 5½ × 8½, 272 pages, hardcover

THE QUOTABLE ROBERTSON DAVIES: The Wit and Wisdom of the Master
selected by James Channing Shaw
More than eight hundred quotable aphorisms, opinions, and general advice for
living selected from all of Davies' works. A hypnotic little book.
Non-fiction, 5¼ × 7, 160 pages, hardcover

ALICE MUNRO: Writing Her Lives. A Biography *by* Robert Thacker
The literary biography about one of the world's great authors, which shows how her life and her stories intertwine.
Non-fiction, 6½ × 9⅜, 616 pages plus photographs, hardcover

MITCHELL: The Life of W.O. Mitchell, The Years of Fame 1948–1998 *by* Barbara and Ormond Mitchell
From *Who Has Seen the Wind* on through *Jake and the Kid* and beyond, this is a fine biography of Canada's wildest – and best-loved – literary figure.
Non-fiction, 6½ × 9⅜, 488 pages plus photographs, hardcover

ROLLERCOASTER: My Hectic Years as Jean Chretien's Diplomatic Adviser 1994–1998 *by* James Bartleman
"Frank and uncensored insider tales of the daily grind at the highest reaches of the Canadian government. . . . It gives the reader a front row seat of the performance of Jean Chrétien and his top officials while representing Canada abroad." – Ottawa *Hill Times*   *Autobiography, 6 × 9, 376 pages, hardcover*

DAMAGE DONE BY THE STORM *by* Jack Hodgins
The author's passion for narrative glows through this wonderful collection of ten new stories that are both "powerful and challenging." – *Quill & Quire*
Fiction, 5⅜ × 8⅜, 224 pages, hardcover

DISTANCE *by* Jack Hodgins
"Without equivocation, *Distance* is the best novel of the year, an intimate tale of fathers and sons with epic scope and mythic resonances. . . . A masterwork from one of Canada's too-little-appreciated literary giants." – *Vancouver Sun*
Fiction, 5⅜ × 8⅜, 392 pages, trade paperback

ON SIX CONTINENTS: A Life in Canada's Foreign Service 1966-2002 *by* James K. Bartleman
A hilarious, revealing look at what our diplomats actually do, by a master storyteller who is a legend in the service. "Delightful and valuable." – *Globe and Mail*
Autobiography, 6 × 9, 272 pages, trade paperback

RUNAWAY *by* Alice Munro
The 2004 Giller Prize-winning collection of short stories by "the best fiction writer now working in North America. . . . *Runaway* is a marvel." – *New York Times Book Review*   *Fiction, 6 × 9, 352 pages, hardcover*

TO EVERY THING THERE IS A SEASON: A Cape Breton Christmas Story *by* Alistair MacLeod, with illustrations *by* Peter Rankin
Almost every page of this beautiful little book is enriched by a perfect illustration, making this touching story of a farm family waiting for Christmas into a classic for every home. A "winsome tale of Yuletide past." – *Toronto Star*
Fiction, illustrations, 4⅝ × 7¼, 48 pages, hardcover

HERE BE DRAGONS: Telling Tales of People, Passion and Power *by* Peter C. Newman
The number one bestseller by the man whose books on politics, business, and history have sold two million copies, *Here Be Dragons* tells the story of his own life, from child fleeing the Nazis to editor of *Maclean's*. The *Globe and Mail* calls this autobiography "a work of genius wit and insight."
Non-fiction, 6 × 9, 744 pages plus photographs, trade paperback

WORTH FIGHTING FOR *by* Sheila Copps
The former Deputy Prime Minister and life-long Liberal tells all in this revealing look at what really goes on behind the scenes in Ottawa. "Copps gives readers a blunt, no-holds-barred glimpse into the seamy backrooms of Canadian politics." – Montreal *Gazette*   *Non-fiction, 6 × 9, 224 pages, hardcover*

RAVEN'S END: A Tale of the Canadian Rockies *by* Ben Gadd
This astonishing book, snapped up by publishers around the world, is like a *Watership Down* set among a flock of ravens managing to survive in the Rockies. "A real classic." – Andy Russell
Fiction, 6 × 9, map, 5 drawings, 360 pages, trade paperback

THREE CHEERS FOR ME: Volume One of the Bandy Papers *by* Donald Jack
The classic comic novel about the First World War where our bumbling hero graduates from the trenches and somehow becomes an air ace. "Funny? Very." – *New York Times*   *Fiction/Humour, 5½ × 8½, 336 pages, trade paperback*

THAT'S ME IN THE MIDDLE: Volume Two of the Bandy Papers *by* Donald Jack
Canadian air ace Bandy fights at the front and behind the lines in the U.K., gallantly enduring the horrors of English plumbing. "A comical tour-de-force." – Montreal *Gazette*   *Fiction/Humour, 5½ × 8½, 364 pages, trade paperback*

ACROSS THE BRIDGE: Stories *by* Mavis Gallant
These eleven stories, set mostly in Montreal or in Paris, were described as "Vintage Gallant – urbane, witty, absorbing." – *Winnipeg Free Press* "We come away from it both thoughtful and enriched." – *Globe and Mail*
Fiction, 5⅞ × 8⅞, 208 pages, trade paperback